KITAHARA HAKUSHŪ

KITAHARA HAKUSHŪ
HIS LIFE AND POETRY

Margaret Benton Fukasawa

with a foreword by
Donald Keene

East Asia Program
Cornell University
Ithaca, New York 14853

The *Cornell East Asia Series* publishes manuscripts on a wide variety of scholarly topics pertaining to East Asia. Manuscripts are published on the basis of camera-ready copy provided by the volume author or editor.

Inquiries should be addressed to Editorial Board, East Asia Series, East Asia Program, Cornell University, 140 Uris Hall, Ithaca, New York 14853.

ISSN 1050-2955
ISBN 0-939657-65-1

CONTENTS

FOREWORD

Most Japanese poets of the Meiji period burnt themselves out as poets early in their careers. Shimazaki Tōson wrote his last poems in 1901, when he was not even thirty, and then became a celebrated novelist. By an odd coincidence, Susukida Kyūkin was also twenty-nine when he published his last collection of poetry, though he lived another forty years. Kambara Ariake's career as a poet lasted somewhat longer, until he was thirty-two; though in the next forty years he occasionally published new poems, they contributed nothing to his fame. Ishikawa Takuboku died at the age of twenty-six, but he was already showing impatience with poetry as a means of expression.

In contrast to these (and other) Meiji-period poets, Kitahara Hakushū (1885-1942) from the time of his precocious debut in the world of poetry at the age of seventeen, continued to write poetry in many forms until virtually the day of his death. He early gained a reputation for his poems filled with seductively exotic words that conjured up Japan in the sixteenth century, when Portuguese and Spanish missionaries came to Hakushū's native Kyushu:

> I believe in the heretical teachings of a degenerate age, the
> witchcraft of the Christian God,
> The captains of the black ships, the marvellous land of the
> Red Hairs,
> The scarlet glass, the sharp-scented carnation,
> The striped calico of the Southern Barbarians, the arak, the
> *vinho tinto*....

Hakushū never abandoned his interest in the exotic, even the exotic represented in the machines of modern industry:

The gods are present, they are in the weird steam engine.
The gods are present, they turn with the motor.

The attraction he felt for whatever was new, in poetry as well as his daily life, had a counterpart in the nostalgia he felt for the past, not only the distant past evoked by mention of scarlet glass and <u>vinho tinto</u>, but the past of his childhood, to which he returned again and again. After achieving fame with highly successful collections of modern poetry, he published several volumes of tanka. The form was old, but the contents were often strikingly modern, as in the following example, translated by the author of this book, Margaret Benton Fukasawa:

usuakaki	The drop of milk,
tsume no urumi ni	which had fallen
hitoshizuku	on the light red polish
ochishi miruku mo	of her nails,
natsukashi to minu	made me yearn for the past.

The red nail polish and the drop of milk are both untraditional, yet seeing them somehow made Hakushū yearn for the past. It is difficult to say why a combination of these two elements of everyday, modern Japanese life should have aroused a sensation of nostalgia, but we can be fairly sure there was some memory of childhood involved, as in so many of his other poems.

Hakushū was known for his children's songs, many of which, like his folk songs, were set to music and sung by people who had no idea who composed them. His last volume of poetry, published in 1943 after his death, consisted of war songs for children. These do not show Hakushū at his best, but it is noteworthy that in the midst of a war, at the end of a long and fruitful career as a poet, he should still have chosen to convey his emotions in simple, heartfelt poems. Some of his poems are so determinedly modernist as to defy explanation, but he probably will be remembered most of all for his love of the music of the Japanese language and for the mood of nostalgia he evokes, linking his poetry with a most pervasive strain in the great poetry of the past.

Margaret was my student when she wrote her doctoral dissertation fifteen years ago, and I remember the dedication with which she approached her research. I am delighted that her thoroughgoing study is now being published in book form and will reach the wider audience it, and Hakushū, deserve.

Donald Keene

EDITOR'S PREFACE

This is the first full-length work in English about Kitahara Hakushū. It was originally a doctoral dissertation for the Department of East Asian Languages and Cultures, Columbia University, 1977. When the Cornell East Asia Series accepted it for publication in 1992, the reviewers knew that the author, who had brain cancer several years ago, would not be able to revise it. They decided, however, that the value of the work was such that simply bringing it into the public domain was important. Accordingly, it is published now as it was then.

In her Preface, Margaret wrote that it was time for a re-evaluation of Hakushū's work. What she was too modest to add was that her own study was just such a re-evaluation. The portrait of Hakushū presented here is much fuller than any available in 1977 or even now, in spite of the fact that the 40-volume Iwanami Shoten *Hakushū Zenshū* (1984-1988) has since brought a much wider range of materials within reach. Most readers still define Hakushū in terms of the works of his youth; only a minority, mostly poets themselves, appreciate the later tanka collections. Margaret's main contention, that Hakushū's later tanka poetry is underrated and unfairly ignored, remains almost as true today as it was in 1977.

This study is also unusual in its emphasis on the interplay and cross-influences between Hakushū's traditional poetry (tanka and *chōka*) and his modern-style poetry (*shi*). We watch a modern Japanese poet as he crosses mined fields, striving to write 'poetry' in the universal sense, while still fulfilling the restrictive and sometimes mutually contradictory demands of different poetic forms, forms which in themselves represent, in Japanese context, not merely technical options but complete world-views, fateful personal and cultural choices. The skill with which Hakushū negotiated these border crossings and re-crossings was epitomized by "Karamatsu" (Chinese Pines), the famous modern-style poem which, Margaret argues convincingly, was originally not conceived as a modern-style poem at all, but actually as a traditional chōka. Winding like a river through all these poetic permutations, now hidden, now exposed to view, is Hakushū's love for his birthplace, Yanagawa, with which the book begins and with which it so movingly ends.

It has been my pleasure and honor to shepherd this manuscript through the publication process. Early on, in accord with Margaret's wishes and my own instincts, the decision was made not to try to bring the manuscript up to date. Hakushū's disciples Kimata Osamu (1906-1983) and Yabuta Yoshio (1902-1984), who were so helpful to Margaret, walk through these pages alive, and the close reader will sense how important they were to Margaret in reaching backward to Hakushū. In going over the manuscript, I made virtually no changes in content and only limited ones in style, those strictly necessary for the sake of consistency or clarity.

Thanks are due to Nancy and Victor Koshmann for submitting the manuscript to Cornell East Asia Series. And for practical advice and concrete help at various critical junctures, to: Louise Shimizu, Amy V. Heinrich, Carol Gluck, Virginia Anami; Karen Smith of the East Asia Series; Yamamoto Takeo and Yamazaki Akira. Most of all, to Margaret and her husband, Shigeyuki Fukasawa, who have blessed me with trust, patience and the warmth of more than twenty years of friendship.

Janine Beichman

AUTHOR'S PREFACE

If a poll were taken to determine the most popular modern Japanese poet—it is surprising in view of the Japanese penchant for making opinion surveys that this has not in fact been done—first place would probably be won by Kitahara Hakushū (1885-1942). His gift for lyricism, rare in his age, has endeared him to his countrymen. Children grow up singing his nursery rhymes, and even people who profess no interest in poetry can recite, if pressed, his most famous verses. His folk songs, the most important modern addition to the repertory, are sung in rural areas as if they had existed for hundreds of years. He is universally acknowledged to rank among the top five modern tanka poets.

His gift for lyricism and preoccupation with the language and imagery of poetry gained for him the hearts of his countrymen, but it has also estranged many contemporary poets and scholars, who pass over his contribution to modern poetry with a few remarks on the lack of intellectual substance in his works. Contemporary tastes in poetry tend to reject the very qualities that have made Hakushū's poetry great, particularly his genius for rhythm and his keen sensitivity to sense perceptions.

In view of contemporary distrust of readily intelligible lyricism, it is not surprising to discover that we owe the most important research on Hakushū not to scholars but to two of his disciples, Kimata Osamu and Yabuta Yoshio. Any new study of Hakushū's poetry cannot help but be indebted to the research of these two men. The appearance of Yabuta's biography *Hyōden Kitahara Hakushū* (A Critical Biography of Kitahara Hakushū)[1] in 1973 immediately prompted numerous calls for a reevaluation of the significance of Hakushū's poetry. One important reason why no one has undertaken this task is probably the lack of a complete edition of Hakushū's works. The *Hakushū Zenshū* (Complete Works of Hakushū), which has never been reprinted, contains none of his writings after 1934.[2] The need for a new complete edition of his works is continually discussed, but disputes over publication rights make its appearance impossible at this date.

No one can deny Hakushū's importance in poetry circles of his day. From the start of his career, he participated in major poetry movements, more often than not as the leading figure. He founded a large number of poetry groups, and ten poetry journals. He exerted a major influence not only on poets of his own time, but also on the next generation of modern poets, many of whom, like Hagiwara Sakutarō and Kimata Osamu, began their careers under his tutelage.

Despite Hakushū's popularity and his influential position in poetry circles, scholarship on Hakushū has stagnated. Histories of modern Japanese literature tend to separate his achievements in the *shi* (modern poetry) from those in the tanka. In Japan, where most poets concentrate on one or the other of these forms, this approach is perhaps inevitable. Hakushū, however, wrote with equal facility in both forms; he also composed folk songs, children's poetry, haiku, *chōka* and colloquial tanka. Because he believed that the experience gained in one verse form should be brought to one's other work, cross-influences constitute an important theme in his poetry. Furthermore, the enormous influence of Hakushū's first three collections tends to overshadow his other contributions. Too little has been said about his later poetry. In this study, a literary biography of Kitahara Hakushū, I have attempted to correct these biases, and I have therefore allotted a perhaps disproportionate space to Hakushū's later poetry, especially his tanka. Hakushū wrote his most important poetic criticism for the tanka; the literary value of the poems alone is enough to justify more attention.[3]

I began this study four years ago. All the research and writing have been done in Tokyo. It could not have been undertaken elsewhere. Even in Tokyo, finding first editions of Hakushū's poetry collections and copies of the magazines he worked on has not been an easy task. I am indebted to Professor Donald Keene for suggesting this topic and for the countless hours he devoted to reviewing my manuscript. His comments made me question my ideas and stimulated me to examine areas I had not planned to treat.

Not the least of the rewards of working on a modern poet has been meeting and talking with his disciples Kimata Osamu and Yabuta Yoshio. Both men have allowed me to peruse sources from their private collections and willingly answered my queries.

Thanks are also due to my family and friends whose encouragement made the completion of this study possible.

Tokyo, 1977   Margaret Benton Fukasawa

1

EARLY YEARS IN YANAGAWA
1885-1904

Kitahara Ryūkichi, who would later gain recognition as the modern Japanese poet Kitahara Hakushū, was born on January 25, 1885.[1] He was the eldest son of a prominent family in Yanagawa, a town on the Tsukushi Plain of northwest Kyushu in present-day Fukuoka Prefecture. All of his five siblings showed interest in the arts,[2] and his two younger brothers, Tetsuo and Yoshio, became important in the world of literature as the presidents of two major publishing firms.[3]

For generations, the Kitahara family had operated a large wholesale business in marine products. During the Tokugawa period it was known throughout Kyushu as "Fuddoiya" or "Ancient Wholesale Firm,"[4] and had served as the exclusive purveyor to the local daimyo.[5] Hakushū's grandfather had begun to produce sake as a sideline, and by Hakushū's father's day the brewery had become one of the largest in Kyushu.[6]

As its name, "Willow River," suggests, Yanagawa is a picturesque town with willow trees lining the numerous canals that crosscross the area where a castle originally stood. During the Tokugawa period, it had been the bustling capital of the Yanagawa *han*, the feudal domain of the Tachibana family, and prospered as an important crossroad of transportation and travel among three important centers of northwest Kyushu: Kumamoto, to the south; Saga, northwest across the Chikugo River; and Fukuoka, northeast by way of Kurume. Furthermore, thanks to its position on the Ariake Sea at the mouth of the Chikugo River, Yanagawa benefited from domestic sea trade and was an important market for fish and other marine products.

In the Meiji period, however, Yanagawa lost its prosperity. Transition from a castle town to a modern city was not easy. Decline began with the abolition of the han and reorganization of Japan into centrally controlled prefectures in August 1871. Once it had lost its special status as a castle

1

town, Yanagawa suffered because it had no local industries to attract capital and was passed by when the main railway lines of northwest Kyushu were built. It is easy to see why the sake brewery, rather than the wholesale business, prospered, supporting the Kitahara family in Hakushū's youth. But even the brewery eventually failed, too.

Hakushū's memories of childhood in Yanagawa provided the subject matter for his second collection of poetry, *Omoide* (Memories),[7] written after he had settled in Tokyo. In the introduction, "Wagaoitachi" (Growing Up),[8] he recalled his birthplace with undisguised nostalgia.

> My birthplace Yanagawa is built on the water. Furthermore, it is one of those quiet cities history has passed by. Nature here is quite tropical. The old white walls left from feudal days, slowly crumbling in the stench of the countless canals criss-crossing Yanagawa, cast shadows more evocative than ever to me now.[9]

In the second section of "Growing Up," perhaps the most skillfully written of the ten parts of this deservedly famous poem in prose, Hakushū traced the outlines of Yanagawa by following the course of the canals as they wound through the town. He pictured a forgotten castle town, where the brothels were empty and the silence of noontime broken only by the strumming of a samisen.

> As the water flows crystal clear into this forgotten city, it winds under the kitchens of abandoned brothels through the white cloths of washerwomen and is finally dammed at a watergate. It wavers in grief beside small restaurants which, like black dahlias, line its way at noontime, when even the sound of a samisen seems languid. It becomes the water for brewing sake, or rinses the lips of a consumptive girl who stands on the stone steps leading down to the water, her skin pale after a bath, or is agitated by the feathers of timid ducks. Then, at night, the water flickers with reflections of lights from paper lanterns strung for a recitation of the Kannon Sutra and flowing past a dike, runs down into the salty river close to the sea at Okinohata. In this fashion the numerous canals quietly cast forlorn reflections on the white walls of times past. Depending on the season, they become the routes for a floating dramatic spectacle; or they provide snakes with a place to glide; or they nurse the secrets of moody adolescents.

Yanagawa and all her canals are like an ash-colored coffin
floating on the water.[10]

Hakushū's description begins in the morning when the water, still fresh and
clear, enters the city. As he traces its course, the day grows later, and the
water picks up the impurities of the people and animals who use it, finally
flowing at night into the ocean at Okinohata, a small fishing village on the
Ariake Sea about a mile south, where Hakushū's home was.

The ties between Okinohata and Yanagawa proper have always been
close; today, in fact, Okinohata is within the city limits. According to legend,
it was founded by six provincial warriors from the Taira clan, who had fled
the capital after the defeat of their troops by the Minamoto in 1185 and
settled here as fishermen. Another name for it was Rokkyu (Six Horse-
men).[11]

Hakushū compared Yanagawa to an "ash-colored coffin floating on
the water." This simile was an exaggeration, but Yanagawa had indeed seen
better days. Okinohata was much livelier. The bay was lined with docks
where local fishermen brought in their catches, and boats from ports along
the Ariake Sea would stop. A wholesale fish market, also managed by the
Kitahara family, stood near the brewery, which in season employed some
150 workers. These activities and the natural layout of the land, open to the
sea and sunny, gave Okinohata a vitality not found in Yanagawa proper.

> Although [Okinohata] is properly considered a part of Yanag-
> awa, its proximity to the sea makes its ways seem somewhat
> more tropical, its people more indolent and irresponsible.
> Furthermore, in contrast to Yanagawa, where lewd secrets lie
> hidden underneath old-fashioned, elaborate silk coverings, here
> everything is open, healthy, and gay.[12]

The bustle of the family sake brewery must have added to the gaiety.
In typical Japanese fashion, business and family affairs were combined under
one roof. Hakushū's home centered around a large entrance hall with a
beaten earth floor, where sake ready for market was stored in lacquered vats.

> Anyone who happened to glance into my house, peering
> through the outdated latticed windows under the decaying old
> sod roof on which thistles and dandelions flourished, would
> probably first notice five vermilion lacquered vats brimful of
> good sake and several liquid measures of the same color.
> There were days when little blue swallow chicks would be
> chirping, their peony-colored cheeks peeking fondly from a

nest on one of the rafters overhead. The spacious earthen
entrance hall was lined with glass cabinets, of the kind found
in an apothecary shop and papered a smoky yellow-green.
Inside one cabinet on a column, an ancient Dutch wall clock
continued to tick away the soft seconds, always precisely,
above the blue-eyed, white-bosomed profile of a girl which
adorned it.[13]

The Dutch wall clock mentioned here was but one of a number of
foreign articles familiar to Hakushū from early youth. He traced his later
attraction to the exotic back to this environment.

In my childhood an interest in things foreign was already
formulating. I flew a diamond-shaped Western kite, had some
seven or eight shirtless men from the brewery help me get up
my orange face-kite (an orange kite in the likeness of a face;
the one Tonka John [i.e., Hakushū] had measured nine feet
across), made tar, operated a magic lantern, and sang ditties in
accents influenced by the Dutch language.[14]

Boats from Nagasaki, the only port open to foreign traders for most of the
Tokugawa period, had periodically visited Okinohata, bringing foreign goods,
spices, and foods to trade. In Hakushū's youth, these articles were still
unusual.[15]

Hakushū stressed the more colorful aspects of Yanagawa in
Memories. Not only were people in this part of Kyushu familiar with foreign
clocks and kites, but according to Hakushū, their dialect incorporated words
of foreign origin.

When the sounds of daytime left this sleeping town, whose
inhabitants were hesitant and somewhat shy, only the evening
murmurings of the Gonshan (dialect: young ladies of good
families) could be heard. Their words were full of feeling,
flowing and soft, and in intonation closer to Kyoto speech than
Kyushu dialect. Yet they incorporated accents clearly of Dutch
origin.[16]

Dialect words attributed to foreign origin are scattered throughout Memories,
often spelled out in roman letters, like "Tonka John" and "Gonshan" in the
quotations above.

The most detailed explanation of "Tonka John" is found in a note to
one of the poems in Memories: "Tonka John. Older son of an important

man, in contrast to the younger. Yanagawa dialect. This was my childhood nickname. People usually call a younger son Tinka John. Dutch origin?"[17] The romanization "John" instead of the expected "Jon" definitely gives an exotic nuance, suggesting also the possibility of an English origin. Other evidence, however, points to a derivation closer to home.[18]

As for "Gonshan," it is definitely of Japanese origin.[19] "Soribatten" (however), another frequently used word, is clearly no more than a dialectic variation of the standard Japanese *sore da keredomo*, despite a note by Hakushū suggesting otherwise.[20] The examples of words of indisputable foreign origin, such as "ball"[21] and "banko,"[22] are few and clearly outnumbered by words of native derivation.

Despite Hakushū's etymological mistakes, however, it is the unusual diction, whatever its source, that gives this piece its enduring charm. If Hakushū made the language of Yanagawa seem more exotic than it in fact was, he had his reasons, perhaps the most important being his separation from Yanagawa in time and distance when writing "Growing Up."[23] In recalling his birthplace, he created an image that reflected his own nostalgia, painting his scenes in colors stronger than those actually found in Yanagawa.

Hakushū's father was a stern man who demanded obedience from both his employees and his sons. He frequently threatened to confine Hakushū and his brothers in one of the warehouses or in the dark storeroom where yeast for brewing sake was kept, in punishment for their boyish pranks.[24] Besides managing the brewery, the fish market, and the marine wholesale business, he cultivated exotic plants and bred various animals as a hobby. His ventures into gardening and animal husbandry, however, invariably failed.

> The objects of my father's hobbies changed yearly. He raised ducks when he tired of chickens. He dug up his roses by the roots and discarded them for morning glories. He even built a pigpen in our garden. His attitude toward all these hobbies was capricious.[25]

An impractical side to his character and perhaps a lack of business acumen no doubt contributed to the eventual bankruptcy of the family business.

Hakushū's mother, who had to manage the affairs of her large household as well as miscellaneous matters connected with the sake brewery, hired nurses to watch over each of her children. As part of her chores, she supervised the meals and affairs of the workers who lived on the premises when sake was being produced. The size of the family's businesses demanded her participation as a fulltime partner to her husband.

Hakushū shared a large room with Tetsuo on the second floor of the house.[26] Besides the family's quarters, there were also two large dining rooms for the workers, and several rooms used as offices. Adjacent to the house was over an acre of land, intersected at several places by canals that provided the water in which the rice used to make sake was washed. White walls enclosed ten warehouses for storing sake. There was also another building where rice was kept. In the area not taken up by these structures were three ponds and several flower and vegetable gardens.[27] Hakushū and his siblings had free run of the gardens and often played cards in one of the warehouses.[28] As the eldest son of this large household, Hakushū led a full and varied childhood, surrounded by adults who showered affection on their young master, Tonka John.

Second only to Yanagawa was Hokame, the small village located deep in the mountains some twelve miles from Yanagawa where his mother's family lived. Hakushū spent his summers here with relatives, and their influence was crucial.

It was his relatives at Hokame who christened him *biidoro bin* (glass bottle), a nickname referring to his delicacy and sickliness as a child. Even ordinary illnesses had severe repercussions on the child. At two he contracted a nearly fatal case of typhoid fever, recovering only to transmit it to his nurse, who died of the illness.

> It was mother
> Who held me.
> In the shade of the flowering shaddock tree,
> I stretched to look through the leaves, crying.
> "Look. There goes nurse's coffin."[29]

A cholera epidemic that occurred in 1890, when Hakushū was five years old, left a lifelong impression. Its image recurred in his poetry later as a vehicle for the fearful, the eerie, and the ominous.[30] Sickness or pain would often be closely associated with sensual perceptivity as well.[31] His own frailness magnified a fear of death, death brought unnaturally close by the cholera epidemic. In the following poem, he evoked this anxiety by imagining that the funeral urn borne in procession past his house carried his father's, his mother's, and then his own remains.

> "A green funeral urn."—The sun pales,
> Everyone remained speechless—incense crept by
> In snake coils, the air grew hot and oppressive.
> They passed by again; I laughed weirdly.

It was mother.—(my mother sat close by)—
Cold wrinkles reflected in the glass door.
Again they go by.—For an instant,
It was me.—In a small green urn,
I saw myself,
Sobbing and spitting black blood.
I knew for a moment. The fear of hell.[32]

The special parental caution necessitated by his physical delicacy no doubt nurtured Hakushū's emotional sensitivity.

Because I was high-strung, my skin and my spirit never failed to quiver, like the thin legs of a grasshopper, with pleasure at a new discovery. All in all, I was very impressionable. My five senses, still as fresh as when I was born, told of a "mystery" within myself and aroused, however faintly, the first germinations of "skepticism."[33]

The mystery he talks of here refers to the awakening of sexual desire; at the same time, it also tells of a growing awareness of the uniqueness of his own sensual impressions, impressions which caused him to be unusually perceptive to his surroundings. By recognizing this, he learned to be on guard, watching himself as he reacted and judging his own impressionability. This "skepticism" toward his own feelings would later allow him to relate these sensual impressions in his poetry.

Hakushū's maternal grandfather had a large library at Hokame. In spite of strict prohibitions on its use, Hakushū's fascination with books drew him to its forbidden shelves. In "Growing Up" he mentions some of the books he secretly read during the summers at Hokame: kibyōshi, *Tales of Moonlight and Rain*, novels and stories of all sorts, mystery adventures, novels on the French Revolution, *Inspiring Instances of Statesmanship*, *Romance of the Three Kingdoms*, and *Journey to the West*.[34] In the same place he notes his early interest in European literature, which he discovered in the Hokame library. "To fulfill the as yet uncertain desires of preadolescence, there was nothing which aroused the young soul of Tonka John more than new books, especially Western books."[35]

The youngest of his four maternal uncles, Ishii Michizane, shared Hakushū's fascination with books. At two critical junctures in Hakushū's life, Michizane directed his attention to a new type of literature. Literature from the West—Hakushū recalled *The Arabian Nights*, fairy tales, and the Christian hymnal—was one area Michizane introduced to him, though in a rather unusual manner: after forcing the reluctant Hakushū into the dark room used for silkworm cultivation and attempting to hypnotize him, he soothed the boy, who was by then sobbing in fright, by telling him stories.[36] Of even more significance, a number of years later in 1900, when Michizane was in Tokyo, he began to send Hakushū, a student in middle school, copies of the literary magazines *Bunko* (Library of Literature)[37] and *Myōjō* (Morning Star).[38] These were the first magazines in which Hakushū published his poetry.

An absorption with literature began to dominate Hakushū's life even during his early school days in Yanagawa. His years at Yadomi Primary School were ordinary enough, but he graduated first in his class. Yanagawa Upper Level Elementary School (the educational system at the time required four years each of lower and higher primary school) was also easy for him; he finished his course in two years instead of four, setting a record at the school never again equalled. In 1897, at the age of twelve, he entered the prefectual middle school Denshūkan in Yanagawa. During his first few years in middle school, he maintained the same high level in his studies. Nevertheless, before long his interest in literary pursuits began to overshadow his schoolwork. He failed an important geometry examination, which made it necessary to repeat his second year in spite of an overall ranking of second in his class; this setback apparently crystallized his dislike for school.

During the next year his uncle Michizane continued to send him copies of poetry magazines and recent collections of poetry from Tokyo. Hakushū avidly read whatever he could get his hands on. He later recalled enjoying in particular Shimazaki Tōson's *Wakanashū* (Seedlings)[39] and *Library of Literature*.

His interest in literature was not confined to reading; by 1900 he was regularly composing tanka with school friends. In 1901 Hakushū and these friends started their own small magazine, *Hōbun* (Random Pieces of Literature), for private circulation. Furthermore, they decided to use pen names which would consist of the character 白 *haku* (white) plus another character to be decided by lots. Hakushū drew the character 秋 *shū* (autumn), producing the name by which he would hereafter be known in journals and literary circles.[40]

Hakushū later recalled that he published his first tanka in the poetry column of the *Fukuoka Nichinichi Shinbun* in 1900.[41] No tanka by Hakushū can be found there from that year, but there is one dated two years later, June 3, 1902.[42] No doubt this was a lapse of memory on Hakushū's part. In September and October the newspaper published four more of his tanka.

Hakushū's relationship with the magazine *Library of Literature*, also begun about the same time, was of much greater importance in his development as a poet. In all, *Library of Literature* published some 181 of

Hakushū's tanka during the period from October 1902, when his first tanka appeared, until January 1904. Such recognition must have encouraged the young poet. However, despite his early success (Hakushū was only seventeen when *Library of Literature* accepted his first tanka), Hakushū's relations with the tanka editor of this magazine, his teachers, and his father were all marked by difficulties.

Hakushū had been fortunate in finding a receptive tanka editor at the *Library of Literature;* Hattori Motoharu (1875-1925) immediately picked one tanka for publication in October 1902 from the first batch submitted by the young poet. In the following month he published another twenty-one at the head of the tanka column, and then another twenty-six in January 1903. In less than two years, however, this relationship, begun so auspiciously, began to deteriorate. Hakushū deeply resented Hattori's criticism of a tanka published in the September 1903 issue of *Library of Literature.* Having come to expect praise from him, he overreacted to a rather pedantic comment on an obscure allusion to the *Man'yōshū*.[43] No doubt Hakushū's extreme youth prevented him from accepting criticism with detachment. In anger, he at once stopped submitting tanka to *Library of Literature.*

His anger was directed at Hattori rather than at the magazine itself, and he now began to submit shi instead, for which there was a different editor. His poetry in this form began to appear in *Library of Literature* three months later, in December 1903. He did not compose tanka again seriously until 1909.

As Hakushū's interest in literature heightened, conflicts with his father and teachers had become severe. Unable to cope with these tensions, he had taken six months off from school in 1902 and spent them at a hot spring resort. Away from his father, who forbad him to pursue his literary interests, he composed tanka for *Library of Literature.* The monotony of classes that had little relation to his poetry must have exasperated the precocious poet, and he was undoubtably also depressed by the obstinacy with which his father refused to recognize that his oldest son's talents were not suited for managing the family businesses. New crises compounded these difficulties.

On the last day of March 1901, a fire had broken out in the nearby boatworks and spread throughout Okinohata. Most of the sake warehouses belonging to the Kitahara family went up in flames; the canals flowed with liquor. "Saturated with sake, many small river fish floated dead on the water. Men drank from the streams of liquor, became inebriated, rolled into the main house, which had been barely left standing, tore off the doors from our large Buddhist altar, and sang and danced,"[44] Hakushū would later recall.

During the fire, he stood in the nearby fish market, guarding the family papers. His copy of Tōson's *Seedlings* lay open in the mud at his feet.[45]

The year 1901 brought other griefs to the family. Hakushū's sister Chika died of typhoid fever. The property of his mother's family at Hokame was unwisely invested or squandered on politics, and the large house fell to ruin. Hakushū's father immediately rebuilt his brewery on an even grander scale, but the family never recovered from the losses sustained in the fire.

TO TOKYO

The anxiety born of these hardships exacerbated the already tense father-son relationship. To his father's dismay, Hakushū had decided in 1901, under the influence of a history teacher at Denshūkan Middle School, to leave Yanagawa for Tokyo, a more suitable place to pursue a career in poetry. Here he hoped to enroll at a preparatory school attached to Waseda University.[46] In spite of Hakushū's determination, his father, no doubt discouraged by the recent calamities, continued to pin his hopes for a recovery of family prosperity on Hakushū. Hakushū's younger brother, Tetsuo, gives this vivid account:

> For some time now, Father had been eyeing Hakushū as successor to the family business, hoping that with Hakushū as his right-hand man he might somehow work a change in family fortunes, which at the time had already begun to decline. Father intended to enroll him in a commercial school when he had finished his course at middle school. His most fervent desire was to get my brother's help in his business as quickly as possible. My brother, however, who rebelled against both Father and his plans, had his heart set on a career as a poet. At first, Father pretended not to notice, but as my brother's determination to study literature grew firm with the publication of his poetry in a large magazine in Tokyo [i.e., *Library of Literature*], Father lost his composure. He tried every way he knew to dissuade my brother, all to no avail. Realizing the futility of his efforts, he became despondent. Needless to say, the friction between the two made the atmosphere at home altogether gloomy.[47]

Frustrated by his father's lack of understanding, Hakushū retaliated by frequently skipping school. Then he failed to appear for the latter half of his graduation examinations. Although he promptly submitted a request to make them up, several teachers opposed granting him permission because of his frequent truancy. After some deliberation, the school finally ordered Hakushū to repeat his final year. Furious at this decision, Hakushū withdrew from middle school.

Hakushū's father immediately requested the school to reconsider its ruling. But Hakushū's determination to leave school was firm and remained so, even after Denshūkan agreed to take a more lenient stand. The antagonism between father and son flared up once again over this issue. Hakushū refused to compromise with either his father or the school and announced that he would leave for Tokyo on the spot. His father's anger at his obstinacy grew fiercer day by day.

Hakushū's mother, who did not feel that it would benefit either Hakushū or the family business to force the young man into a career so obviously unsuited to his abilities, tried to reason with her husband, but met no success. Finally, seeing no way out of the conflict, she and Tetsuo secretly helped Hakushū collect his baggage and saw him off. In April 1904, Hakushū successfully enrolled in the preparatory course of the English Literature Division at Waseda. In many ways he was more than adequately prepared to make a name for himself in the world of poetry.

2

ESTABLISHING A NAME IN TOKYO
1904-1911

In March 1904, one month before Hakushū left Yanagawa, one of his best friends, Nakajima Tetsuo, a young man who had shared his interest in poetry, committed suicide.[1] Hakushū's sorrow over Nakajima's death made it difficult to concentrate on schoolwork, explaining in part his frequent absences from school and the failure to complete his graduation examinations. Before he left Yanagawa, Hakushū wrote a long shi of over 400 lines, "Rinka no Mokusō" (Sylvan Meditations), dedicated to Nakajima, who in his farewell letter to Hakushū had urged his friend to pursue a career in poetry, a dream they had both cherished.[2] This incident no doubt cemented Hakushū's resolve.

The April issue of *Library of Literature* devoted the entire shi section to "Sylvan Meditations." Kawai Suimei (1874-1965), the shi editor, did his utmost to encourage the young poet. As if to compensate for Hattori's blunder, he faithfully published virtually everything Hakushū sent him. In the January 1905 issue another long shi by Hakushū, "Zento Kakusei Fu" (Ode on the Awakening of the Metropolis), which had received first prize in a poetry competition sponsored by Waseda Gakuhō (Waseda University Bulletin), appeared. The prominence given these two poems drew attention to the young poet.

For Hakushū, whose previous poetry had all been tanka, this was a period of experimentation in a new form of verse. Compared to the tanka, whose length and diction were relatively restricted, the shi allowed more freedom of expression. Although the shi Hakushū wrote during this period now appear to be more imitative than innovative, at least in terms of rhythm and diction, Hakushū seems to have been consciously exploring the boundaries of the form, particularly with respect to length, the most obvious difference between the thirty-one syllable tanka and the shi. He published

13

forty-two shi in *Library of Literature* during the period from December 1903 to April 1906, using the pen name Hakushū 薄 愁 , meaning "faint grief," for a short time during 1904. Some years later, however, when he went through his early works to choose poems for his first book, he did not see fit to include any of these. In 1931 he dismissed them with the following comment: "These poems with their flowery language and beautiful phrases were products of my youth. Now, I feel that the urge to compose such long poems helped me to discover myself."[3] Apparently Hakushū grew convinced that a shorter form of the shi was more suitable to his purposes. After this, he used it consistently, with the exception of the long poems in his last collection of shi, published almost forty years later.[4]

THE NEW POETRY SOCIETY AND *MORNING STAR*

In the spring of 1906, Hakushū received a postcard from Yosano Tekkan, the leader of the Shinshisha (New Poetry Society)[5] and editor of their journal *Morning Star*. In poetic refrains, Tekkan urged Hakushū to visit him, which Hakushū, it seems, had promised to do.

A songbird, it is said,
Keeps its listeners waiting.
Yesterday, today.[6]

Hakushū immediately paid a call. Tekkan and his wife Akiko, a prominent poet in her own right, were more than cordial to the young poet, and he gladly accepted their invitation to join the New Poetry Society. In April, *Morning Star* published "Hana Chiru Hi" (The Day Blossoms Fell) together with poems on the same subject by other members of the group as part of a poetry competition.[7] In May, it published another ten poems, ones which Hakushū had shown Tekkan at his first visit.[8]

Hakushū had been eyeing *Morning Star* for some time. As early as October 1904, six of his tanka had appeared in the magazine. Probably much to Hakushū's dismay, they were not listed in the table of contents or printed with poems written by members of the New Poetry Society, but instead relegated to the section reserved for readers' contributions.[9] Hakushū seems to have interpreted this as a rejection, and being a stubborn young man, he kept his distance from the group until he could be sure that Tekkan would treat him as an equal. He did not attempt to publish in *Morning Star* again until his two long poems in *Library of Literature* induced Tekkan to invite him to join his group. Still, when he did finally join the New Poetry Society, the fact was not announced in *Morning Star*—an omission which could not have been accidental.[10]

At the time, the New Poetry Society had become an important force in the movement to create modern poetry in Japanese. Yosano Tekkan's leadership was seminal. In 1894 at the age of twenty-two, Tekkan had published "Bōkoku no On" (Ominous Sounds of National Ruin),[11] which criticized contemporary tanka poetry for being ineffectual and effeminate. He felt that the tanka was doomed to extinction unless younger poets of his generation wrote bolder, more forceful poems, poems which would speak to a wide audience on topics of universal importance. His call for a revolution in the tanka marked the beginning of modern verse in this form.

In his first collection of poetry, *Tōzainanboku* (North, South, East, and West), published in 1896,[12] Tekkan attempted to exemplify his ideas in verse. But more significant than these tanka in his *masuraoburi* (masculine) style, so different from the traditional approach of his contemporaries, was his attitude. In his preface to the volume, he stated: "In my shi, be they tanka or shintaishi, I do not idolize anyone; I do not slobber over anyone's dregs. My shi are completely my own."[13] First of all, he refused to pattern himself on older models and took pride in expressing his own individual concerns. Secondly, he referred to all his poems, which were primarily tanka, as shi. These two ideas would become fundamental principles of the New Poetry Society.

Tekkan could not effect revolution by himself; that is why he established the New Poetry Society. He hoped to assemble poets of like interests, and together with them put his ideas into practice in the pages of *Morning Star*.

Although Tekkan had begun to formulate his ideas as early as "Ominous Sounds of National Ruin," he did not elucidate them carefully until he wrote the "Shinshisha Seiki" (Rules Governing the New Poetry Society) for the sixth issue of *Morning Star*, which appeared in June 1900.[14] Here Tekkan once again used the term "shi" to refer to poetry in general, whatever its form. For tanka in particular he coined the word "kokushi" (Japanese shi). Although this playing with terminology may seem rather forced, his assumption that the one word "poetry" (shi) included all the varieties of verse was of importance. It had traditionally been assumed that each type of poetic expression, whether tanka, renga, haiku, Chinese poetry, or shintaishi, was totally distinct, and no term embraced them all. To treat them together within one broad category was tantamount to poetical heresy.

The tanka could not become a vehicle for expressing the thoughts of modern poets while it was still loaded down under the weight of tradition. Neither could the traditional tanka masters be expected to initiate reform. By associating the tanka with the shintaishi, Tekkan gave it new life. He meant to liberate it from traditional diction and themes and make a means of expression for the modern age.

Masaoka Shiki (1867-1902) also began his reform of the tanka during this period. Although his conclusions would be different from Tekkan's, both men began with a similar assumption: that tanka had to be brought out of isolation and included in the broad category of poetry.[15] Shiki, however, stopped at this point; he did not suggest that someone who wrote tanka should also write shintaishi. In this sense, Tekkan's approach was more revolutionary. His ideas inspired poets such as Yosano Akiko, Ishikawa Takuboku, and Hakushū himself to produce fresh and bold new experiments in the tanka form. It was Tekkan who gave Hakushū the principle that the modern poet should not restrict himself to only one type of poetry, and that his work in one form should naturally enrich that in another.

Tekkan outlined one other important principle in his famous third rule: "We propose to create shi of our own. Our poetry will not imitate ancient poetry; it will be our own poetry. Or rather it will be the poetry of each one of us." Here he asserted the necessity and importance of individual experimentation. Along these lines he also rejected the traditional teacher-disciple relationship that had governed tanka composition up until now.

Although Tekkan proposed that the members of the New Poetry Society write in their own individual manner, in actual practice his own poetry and Akiko's set the tone for the group. Tekkan had met Akiko in 1900, and she immediately became an important member of his group. Their love affair and consequent marriage provided them both with important material for poetry. Love was the main theme in Tekkan's collection *Murasaki* (Purple), published in April 1901, and Akiko's *Midaregami* (Tangled Hair), published four months later.[16] As the name *Morning Star* suggests, much of the poetry published by the group was romantic and, at its worst, even sentimental.

The New Poetry Society, which at its inception was supported by older poets such as Mori Ōgai and Ueda Bin, soon became the gathering place for many talented young poets. Ishikawa Takuboku had joined this group in February 1903 at the age of seventeen, and Hagiwara Sakutarō, Takamura Kōtarō, Yoshii Osamu, and Kinoshita Mokutarō were among the other young poets of Hakushū's generation who started their careers here. As the interests of Tekkan and his group matured, *Morning Star* came to publish a variety of poetry, including shi as well as tanka. In January 1904, it introduced French symbolist poetry to Japan with "Sagi no Uta" (Song of the Heron), Ueda Bin's translation of Emile Verhaeren's poem "Parabole."[17]

The influence of Ueda Bin (1874-1916) in this period was pervasive. A scholar of unusual ability, he introduced European literature to Japan through translation and scholarly treatises and taught at the leading universities of the day. But he was not content to sit in his study. He participated in various literary groups and published in literary as well as academic magazines. His translations were addressed to the poetic community as much as to the academic. His renderings of French Parnassian and symbolist poetry changed the course of Japanese poetry.

During the two years following the appearance of Verhaeren's poem, Bin continued to publish other translations from French and Belgian symbolist literature in *Morning Star*. In June 1905, he published seven translations of poems by Verhaeren, Paul Verlaine, Henri de Régnier, and George Rodenbach under the title "Shōchōshi" (Symbolist Poems). Although *Morning Star* was not the first or the only magazine to publish Bin's renditions, the majority of the fifty-seven translations that were later included in *Kaichōon* (Sound of the Tide) first appeared there.[18] The symbolist poetry in particular received wide acclaim and gave Japanese poets of shi a new model which has proved influential down to the present day.

When "The Day Blossoms Fell" was published in the April 1906 issue of *Morning Star* and Hakushū became a member of the New Poetry Society, the two most active poets of shi publishing in *Morning Star* were Kanbara Ariake (1876-1952)[19] and Susukida Kyūkin (1877-1945).[20] An examination of the poems submitted for the poetry competition reveals the extent of their influence. Hakushū was no exception. His poem could easily be mistaken for one by Kyūkin and shows no similarity at all to his own later style. The same was true of the poem Ishikawa Takuboku submitted.[21]

The ten shi which Hakushū published in the next issue of *Morning Star* were more original. They were later included in his second collection of shi, *Memories*, and rank among its best works.[22] Written from the point of view of the child, they are based on his childhood memories.

Red Fruit

I don't remember when.
I don't remember where.
Crawling with a pretty child, I think.
Peaches? Apples?
Only that they were piled on an orange tray.

I don't remember anymore.
I don't remember his name.
Was it a dream?
Ah. Vaguely
Only that they were piled on an orange tray.
All I saw
Was the red fruit.[23]

Hakushū's subject matter was refreshingly novel, his language simple and lyrical. In short lines of five and seven syllables, he recalled some red fruit seen in his childhood. The circumstances were indistinct; only the red fruit piled on a tray came into clear focus, suggesting both the vagueness of a lingering memory and the strong impression left by the fruit on the child. On another level, the red fruit symbolized the poet's longing for his lost youth or perhaps the unconscious sexuality of a young child.

Hakushū termed these "poems of reminiscences" *(tsuioku no shi)* and later remarked that "after this I did not compose any more poems of reminiscences, but began to create impressionist-style poems and after that the symbolist-style verse of *Jashūmon* (Heretical Faith)."[24] His reasons for temporarily abandoning this type of verse which, as his later work would show, was in fact a more congenial form of expression, had much to do with the popularity which Bin's translations and Ariake's poetry enjoyed at the time. These men seemed to hold the key to the future of Japanese poetry. At least to Hakushū's eyes, his ten poems did not compare favorably with their more ambitious experiments. Hakushū's high expectations for himself impelled him to attempt to write in the new style.

Although Bin is usually credited with introducing French symbolist poetry to Japan, it was Kanbara Ariake who actually wrote the first symbolist poems in Japanese. In July 1905 he published *Shunchōshū* (Spring Birds),[25] which contained thirty-four shi of his own as well as three translations from Paul Verlaine. This volume, which appeared three months before Bin's *Sound of the Tide,* marked the beginning of Ariake's career as a symbolist poet. Ueda Bin, Yosano Tekkan, and Baba Kochō (1869-1940) reviewed "Asa Nari" (It Was Morning), a verse in it for the September issue of *Morning Star.* Their discussion reveals one problem which worried poets then. What indeed was a symbolist poem? Did Ariake's poem fulfill the requirements of a symbolist poem or should it instead be considered merely a lyrical description?

Scholars today still debate this question, a matter which is perhaps not as significant as the fact that the attention which greeted the appearance of *Spring Birds* and *Sound of the Tide* seemed to proclaim a new age in poetry. Along with other young poets, Hakushū began to explore the symbolist style. The laxity with which he and others used terms such as "impressionist poetry" and "symbolist poetry"—the former was regarded as inferior to the latter and frequently seems to have been used to designate verse which did not fulfill the writer's requirements for a symbolist poem rather than designating a specific style[26]—indicates that there was still wide disagreement about what constituted a symbolist poem.

Ariake was the first Japanese poet to recognize the importance of the synthesis of sense perceptions, a technique much used in French symbolist poetry. In his Preface to *Spring Birds*, he wrote:

> When various sense perceptions blend together, mingling with the emotions of modern man, sounds seem silver bright and colors sonorous.
> Although it is common to regard the eyes and ears as leading to man's soul, we can also perceive man's spirit through taste and smell. Those who call these faculties inferior do not understand the importance of sense perceptions.
> On occasion, one's sense organs sleep from exhaustion and then awake to smell, as it were, the deep blue-green of an ancient copper vase recovered after being buried in ruins for one thousand years. Perhaps we understand beauty only when we "see red and express it as blue."[27]

Spring Birds and *Ariake Shishū* (Poems by Ariake),[28] his last and best collection of poetry, now considered a classic of Japanese symbolism, made masterful use of imagery of mingled sense perception. Of course, the technique was not altogether unknown in Japan, as Ariake went on to explain, citing several well-known examples from Bashō.[29] Hakushū, however, seems to have learned of it from studying Ariake's poetry, and in his work of this period, sense perceptions assume a new importance. Without Ariake's example, Hakushū probably would not have developed this aspect of his verse—one of his most significant contributions to modern Japanese literature.

The imitative qualities which had marked Hakushū's earliest contributions to *Morning Star* soon made way for more original verses, which Hakushū later included in *Heretical Faith*. Sixteen of the twenty-seven verses in the "Furuzake" (Old Wine) section, which contains the earliest poems in this collection, were written during the autumn of 1906, barely six months after Hakushū had joined the New Poetry Society. Although they do not compare favorably with the later works in *Heretical Faith*, some characteristics of Hakushū's more mature style may be traced back to a poem such as "Hizakari" (High Noon), written in September and first published under the title "Shōgo" (Noontime) in the October 1906 issue of *Morning Star*. Here are the first two stanzas of the poem:

The noon gun now sounds
Booming out placidly.
Here and there the hungry groans

Of sirens cease.
The hot streets of Yanagihara
Again grow quiet.

Red brick buildings line the river bank.
Within prisonlike factories
The clangor of printing and
The sound of shears cutting tin plate and
A hammer pounding on a coffin and files
Blend in melancholy harmony.[30]

In this poem, Hakushū described the noon scene along an old street by the Kanda River in Tokyo. Factories, second-hand clothes stores, street cars, and hungry mongrels contribute to the drab and melancholy atmosphere; silence when it comes is almost frightening. For the first time we see Hakushū exploring the theme of gloom through the tenors of his imagery—a technique that would mark his style in *Heretical Faith*. With its high incidence of nouns and abundance of sense imagery, "High Noon" is an early example of the type of verse that Hakushū would develop in the next few years. His rhythm, here in simple twelve-syllable lines, would become more complex, his description more symbolic and less pictorial. But his later style may be seen here in embryonic form. It is not suprising that the publication of poems such as "High Noon" brought recognition of the young poet's talents from Kyūkin, Ariake, and Bin.

"AMAKUSA ISLANDS"

One important turning point in Hakushū's attempts to create a style uniquely his own was the New Poetry Society's trip to Kyushu in the summer of 1907. More than six months earlier, several members had traveled together to Kyoto, Nara, Ise, and the Kii Peninsula.[31] These journeys served two purposes: getting inspiration for their own poetry and creating interest in their magazine in areas far from Tokyo. They met with local poets, composed verses, and kept journals. The success of the Kyoto trip encouraged Hakushū to invite the group to Yanagawa.

On July 28, 1907, five members of the New Poetry Society—Yosano Tekkan, Hakushū, Yoshii Osamu,[32] Hirano Banri,[33] and Kinoshita Mokutarō[34]—left Tokyo for Kyushu.[35] They intended to spend a month visiting various large cities but at the last moment changed their plans to include a side trip to the Amakusa Islands in northwest Kyushu, probably at the request of Mokutarō, who at the time was studying the history of the Kyushu Christian movement.

This area was rich in the historical remains of the early Japanese Christians who had been converted by Jesuit missionaries accompanying the European traders near the end of the sixteenth century. It was here that in 1637 the Japanese Christians of Amakusa and nearby Shimabara had revolted when Tokugawa Ieyasu imposed stringent controls over Christianity. After the revolt was crushed, the islands were placed under direct government control and prohibitions against Christianity severely enforced. Suspected believers were required to tread on a picture of the Virgin Mary to demonstrate their innocence. As a result many Christians had gone into hiding, concealed their religious artifacts, and practiced their faith in secret.

In April 1906, an exhibition of foreign articles, religious artifacts, paintings, and pottery imported by European traders and missionaries prior to 1848 had been held at a museum in Ueno, attracting the interest of many intellectuals including Ueda Bin.[36] Although the beginning of literature on this subject matter (*nanban bungaku*) is usually traced back to the New Poetry Society's trip to Kyushu in 1907—indeed all five poets immediately began to compose verses on the early Christians and foreigners,[37] and their enthusiasm quickly infected other writers—Hakushū's interest in fact preceded the trip and may in fact have been prompted by the exhibition. One year earlier, in August 1906, he had published the poem "Kairan" (Weighing Anchor), in which he used the imagery of foreign ships leaving Nagasaki to speak of death.

> Weighing anchor, many large ships.
> Like the blond pater and his believers,
> Who are taunted as they bear their cross down
>   the long black road,
> One after another the ships groan regret.
> Black smoke quivers like spilling blood.
> Although destined for India, Europe, and Rome,
> These ships, like man's life, all will vanish
> Into the nether world. 7 P.M.
> 7 P.M. on a sea of gloom.[38]

Hakushū's description of early evening in Nagasaki harbor incorporated imagery associated with the early Christians. The deep tones of horns blowing on departing ships recall the moans of persecuted Christians, and the smoke their blood. The tenors of his imagery join as symbols of the speaker's melancholy, as indicated in the final phrase of the poem, *utsuyū no kokoro no umi ni* (literally: on the sea of my melancholy spirit). Hakushū wrote this poem in July 1906, two months before "High Noon," and it was his first published poem in the style exemplified by *Heretical Faith*.

The five poets took turns writing a journal of their trip, which was published in a Tokyo newspaper.[39] Their first stop was Yanagawa, where Hakushū's family warmly welcomed them, bringing out sake made in the family brewery. They next toured Saga, Karatsu, Hirado, and Nagasaki[40] before heading at last to the Amakusa Islands, which for Hakushū and Mokutarō at least would be the most interesting part of their journey.

Most of one day was wasted meandering lost along the narrow roads inland to Ōemura, a small mountain village where many Christians had continued to practice their religion in secret after the government proscription. Hakushū seems to have been impressed with the unusual vegetation in the area: grapevines and fig trees figure in an impromptu verse written that day and recorded in *Tōkyō Niroku Shinbun*.[41] Their purpose in visiting Ōemura was to talk to the French priest of the local Catholic church. He answered their questions and brought out various crosses, medallions, and statuettes which had been kept by the Christians.

From Ōemura, they traveled to Shimabara to tour the ruins of Shimabara Castle associated with the rebellion of 1637. They also visited Mt. Aso before returning to Yanagawa, the last stop on their trip.

Three months after he returned to Tokyo, Hakushū published "Amakusatō" (Amakusa Islands), a series of fifteen poems inspired by his visit. From this series were taken all but one of the eleven verses which make up the "Amakusa Gaka" (Amakusa Songs) section of *Heretical Faith*,[42] whose heading is graced by an engraving of a Christian medal: "This Santa Cruz is a sacred cross kept hidden in a Christian home in Ōemura for over three hundred years. It was discovered in a field.—From the treasures of Amakusa Ōemura Catholic Church."[43]

The "Amakusa Islands" series represents Hakushū's first serious attempt to treat the early Christians and their culture in his verse. Later he would use Christian imagery—foreign priests, mysterious ceremonies, and unusual religious articles—to express the fearful and mysterious.[44] Here, however, his treatment was much simpler. He had not yet developed the speaker of his later poems, the melancholy young man who, wearied with mundane affairs, dreams of unusual, exotic, and sometimes frightening things. Instead, he sympathized with the Christian and his theme was love, in particular the conflict between Christianity and love, as in "Kugui" (Swan).

> Young men. Don't come too close.
> For there goes the heretical swan,
> Who seven times, eight times a day
> Bathes in the sea to beautify herself.
> The secret love of a priest.[45]

Or again in "Tada Hime yo" (Please Don't Tell).

> Please don't tell; keep my secret, until we die in worship.
> For there's the whip of persecution.
> Please don't tell; of my cross, the sign of our love.[46]

In the first poem, the priest had fallen in love with a young girl, who appeared in the poem as a swan. In the second, the young suitor's religion conflicted with his love for a non-Christian.

The style and diction of these poems were also remarkably different from either "Weighing Anchor" or Hakushū's later symbolist poems. Bin's and Ariake's examples had been temporarily discarded for another work, the Song of Solomon as found in the Japanese version of the Old Testament.[47] As many scholars have pointed out, some of Hakushū's imagery, fig trees and grapevines for example, is vegetation found in Amakusa. However, other words such as *tomo* (friend or beloved), *mitsu* (honey), *hato* (dove), *yuri* (lily), *motsuyaku* (myrrh), *keishi* (cinnamon), *rokuwai* (aloe), and *zōge* (ivory) cannot be explained so easily, unless we assume that Hakushū had recently read the Song of Solomon. In addition, Hakushū borrowed certain phrases, *motsuyaku no shiru shitarasu* (dropping sweet smelling myrrh)[48] for example, and constructions, *na ga kami wa karasu no gotoku* (her locks are black as a raven),[49] directly from the Song of Solomon. When he included these poems in *Heretical Faith*, Hakushū changed the title from "Amakusatō" (Amakusa Islands) to "Amakusa Gaka" (Amakusa Songs). In using the word *gaka* for "song," he implicitly acknowledged the influence of the Song of Solomon, translated as "Gaka" in the Japanese version.

The influence of the Song of Solomon on this series of poems has not been noted by Japanese scholars; however, it gives us indisputable evidence that Hakushū was actively exploring new subject matter and diction for his poetry from sources other than Bin and Ariake, in this way preparing himself to write the more difficult symbolist poems of *Heretical Faith*.

It was to "Amakusa Songs" that Hakushū referred when he entitled his collection *Heretical Faith*. But these poems are in fact different in style from most of the collection. This suggests that symbolist verse did not, after all, come naturally to Hakushū and helps to explain why his later style departed from it, even though certain elements of diction acquired during the trip and an interest in Christian priests and religious articles appeared in different form in his later poetry.

During his association with the New Poetry Society, Hakushū also wrote tanka; 180 verses in this form may be found in *Morning Star*.[50] Hakushū's interest lay mainly in shi during this period, however, and he did not write tanka regularly. Most of the ones printed in *Morning Star* were composed for all-night tanka marathons *(ichiya hyakushu kai)* sponsored by the New Poetry Society. Had it not been for these marathons, he probably would not have written any tanka at all. They reflect the same concerns as his shi, from which they also borrow their subject matter and diction.

Waga kugui	My swan
Asa no neisu o	Abruptly leaves
Tsuto hanare	Her morning couch.
Haya utaitsutsu	Singing, she quickly
Kewaiya ni yuku.	Proceeds to her dressing room.[51]

Needless to say, Hakushū borrowed his ideas for this tanka from his shi "Swan."[52] The fact that he included only one of these 180 verses in his first tanka collection indicates that he did not value them very highly.

Barely six months after Hakushū returned from Kyushu, he and six other promising young poets abruptly resigned from the New Poetry Society.[53] On January 4, 1908, Hakushū took a letter to Tekkan announcing their intention to withdraw as a group. Tekkan's attempts to dissuade them were fruitless, and the New Poetry Society was left with very few young poets of talent.[54]

The reasons for this drastic move were complex. Yoshii Osamu has stated that it was Tekkan's refusal to allow members of his group to publish in any other magazine.[55] Mokutarō and Hakushū were also annoyed by Tekkan's decision made for the New Year issue of 1908, when he printed contributions from such established writers as Mori Ōgai, Ueda Bin, Baba Kochō, Susukida Kyūkin, and Kanbara Ariake in large type but used small type for poems submitted by members of his New Poetry Society.[56] Tekkan's firm stand against naturalism, expressed in the same issue, also infuriated the younger poets of his group, including Ishikawa Takuboku, who felt that they could not so easily dismiss works like Tayama Katai's *Futon* (Mattress), published in 1907, or *Hakai* (Broken Commandment) by Shimazaki Tōson, which had appeared one year earlier.

Underlying their discontent with the New Poetry Society was dissatisfaction with its leader. Hakushū led the group in their action. His reasons, expressed in a letter to a friend dated January 15, 1908, show how harsh his judgment of Yosano Tekkan was.

Tekkan pretends to be sincere in order to get his own way. You would be surprised to see how cleverly he does this. We are younger than he is, so we have had to be as discreet as possible in approaching others concerning him or the New Poetry Society. When his actions have disturbed us, we have tried our best to see Tekkan's view. However, I refuse to capitulate to his demands anymore. His attitude toward literature is dishonest; he has been stealing our poems. (He does this every month, and we have been dearly victimized. If you speak your ideas, he immediately borrows them. If you bring him a finished poem, he somehow manages to steal it from you. He not only does not understand poetry; he plagiarizes.) I realize only too well that my reputation will suffer. Nevertheless, I cannot honestly remain in the New Poetry Society.[57]

Hakushū, just twenty-two years old at the time, was an obstinate young man. There is no other evidence that Tekkan was actually plagiarizing poems from other poets in the group. However, he was no doubt stimulated by their youthful enthusiasm and, as the leader of the New Poetry Society, felt justified in correcting their verses and perhaps even borrowing their ideas. In any case, Tekkan's attitude probably reminded Hakushū of his experiences with his father and later with Hattori Motoharu. In withdrawing from the New Poetry Society, he declared his independence, confident in his own talents and eager to prove to himself and others that he could make his way alone.

A perceptible decline in quality was apparent in the February 1908 issue of *Morning Star*, a clear indication of where the talent in the New Poetry Society had resided. The withdrawal of the younger poets speeded the demise of *Morning Star*, which folded in November 1908 with its hundredth issue.[58]

HERETICAL FAITH

Hakushū had not published any poems outside of *Morning Star* for a year and a half. His withdrawal might have meant that he had nowhere to publish his poetry. He had been careful, however, to prevent this from happening; in the January 1908 issue of *Shinshichō* (New Trends),[59] he published "Muhon" (Rebellion), one of the best poems in *Heretical Faith*. Literary circles were buzzing with rumors of the young poets who had so abruptly left the New Poetry Society, and the poem's title, which seemed to promise an insider's report on the incident, no doubt intrigued prospective readers. As Hakushū probably planned, it brought him the publicity he needed. The prominence which *New Trends* gave the poem showed that the editors considered Hakushū an equal of Kanbara Ariake and Susukida

Kyūkin, whose poems also appeared in the same issue. This was in marked contrast to the treatment he was used to in *Morning Star*. Henceforth, Hakushū was considered an established poet, and had no further difficulty in finding magazines to publish his work.

"Rebellion" also indicated a new maturity in Hakushū's style as a symbolist poet. Despite the imagined implications of the title, the poem did not specifically treat Tekkan and the New Poetry Society. It has been interpreted as a description of the growing anger he and his friends experienced during their last months with Tekkan, but even this interpretation is somewhat forced. The poem stands on its own terms and does not depend upon an understanding of biographical facts for its literary value.

Rebellion

Today, in the garden of my convent,
In the quiet sunset of late autumn,
'Midst the sighs of the pale yellow spray from a fountain,
Faintly, the strings of a violin,
With dreams and sadness, faintly wail in lament.

Smoke rises from the flames of candles for confession,
Indistinctly; white robes pass along a corridor,
Silent in the dusk, a long line of nuns.
Now again, the agony of the violin
Pierces with the fire, [the stinging taste] of liquor.
    The strings of the violin cry in pain.

Meanwhile, in the colorful sunset,
Among the sighs of the fountain, its spray red with
    burning dreams,
'Midst the grief of mute white birds,
The strong [odor] of gunpowder. Black flames.
A fuse burns underground. The violin sobs madly.

The sound of tanks reverberates.
Poison bullets, blood-colored smoke, flashing swords.
And then, bursting into flames: the fountain, the convent,
    the sky.
Vermilion. Trembling. At the last second,
The shrieks burn out. The violin grows dumb.[60]

"Rebellion" is constructed in terms of one long extended metaphor, a convent suddenly engulfed in insurrection. It describes the destruction of certain ideals, symbolized in the poem by the convent. Just as the quiet but fervently religious life of the nuns is ordered by the rule and regiment of their convent community, so is the mind described here governed by somewhat innocent and dreamlike aspirations, forces which, because of their spiritual nature, isolate the mind from reality and at the same time make it susceptible to destruction, represented by the military vehicles, bullets, bayonets, and finally the bomb that destroys the convent. The marked use of synesthesia, as for example when Hakushū compares the piercing sound of the violin to the stinging taste of liquor, and the juxtaposition of seemingly unrelated images strengthen the effect. Each stanza ends with a description of the playing of a violin, which serves both to symbolize intuitive self-knowledge and to give dramatic tension to the poem by the ominous connotations of the words used to describe it.[61]

The rhythmic scheme of the poem, built on a combination of phrases of five and seven syllables, provides the structure for a dramatic exposition of the situation.[62] Consider, for example, the first stanza:

Hito hi waga shōja no niwa ni
Osoaki no shizuka naru iribi no naka ni
Aware mata usugi naru fukiage no toiki no naka ni
Ito hono ni bioron no sono ito no
Sono yume no kanashimi no ito hono ni ureinaku

The second line has one more five-syllable phrase than the first; the third line one more than the second. The effect of the partial stops at the end of each line is strengthened by the final seven-syllable phrases. However, in the last two lines, this pattern is broken. The somewhat choppy effect of the repeated five-syllable phrases in these two lines, combined with a repetition of the possessive particle *no* and a subtle echoing of the word *ito*, creates a certain uneasiness in rhythm. The contrast between the quiet pictorial quality of the description in the first three lines and the ominous foreboding suggested by the violin in the last two lines is made more effective by similar rhythmic and sonic effects.

"Rebellion" was a good poem and quite representative of the type of symbolist verse then being written. The construction of the poem—the fact that its symbolic import depended on allegory—showed Hakushū's debt to Kanbara Ariake and Ueda Bin.[63] Hakushū had proved to his contemporaries that he could write the type of symbolist verse then most admired.

During 1908, the year following the publication of "Rebellion," as Hakushū composed the majority of the poems included in *Heretical Faith*, he discarded the allegorical techniques seen in "Rebellion" for more direct description. He also created new imagery characterized above all by highly acute sensual perceptions through which he explored new themes, in particular the ennui and melancholy of a modern young man.

In March 1909, Hakushū published *Heretical Faith*, half at his own expense. Stylishly bound in red, the title and Christian insignia IHS inset in gold, and containing several prints by Ishii Hakutei (1882-1958),[64] Yamamoto Kanae (1882-1946),[65] and Kinoshita Mokutarō, *Heretical Faith* startled the literary world by its format as well as its content, and set a high standard of luxuriance in layout which Hakushū would adhere to hereafter.[66] The poet Murō Saisei (1889-1962), who was twenty-one years old at the time, later recalled being enchanted by the magnificence of the copy of *Heretical Faith* that his local bookstore finally procured for him.[67] Saisei was not the only young man to be astonished by the novelty of Hakushū's first poetry collection—by the mysterious ambiguity of his language, the acuteness of his sensual perceptions, and the glitter of the red and gold cover.

Hakushū dedicated *Heretical Faith* to his father: "Father, although it was against your desires, your son was enamored of his talent for verse and spent his youth composing poems of this sort. Please forgive him."[68] He was referring of course to his father's anger at Hakushū's determination to become a poet rather than succeed to the family business. Following the dedication is an inscription that proclaims the special world Hakushū sought to create in *Heretical Faith*.

> Pass beyond here to a forest of melodic anguish.
> Pass beyond here to a garden of sensual pleasure.
> Pass beyond here into a bitter sleep of benumbed nerves.[69]

Hakushū's verse echoes the famous third stanza of Dante's *Inferno* as translated by Ueda Bin in *Shisei Dante* (Dante, the Saint of Poetry) of 1901.[70] As Hakushū warns the reader, the pages that follow would treat a world of acute sensual perceptivity and languid weariness with life.

In the prose section following the inscription, he described his understanding of a symbolist poem.

> The soul of a poem is by nature abstruse. Poetry cannot be explained in terms of simple phenomena. The poet addresses himself to the indistinct sobbings of the spirit amongst the limitless vibrations of emotion, emotion which cannot be expressed with pen or speech. He is enamored with the pleasure

of inexhaustible music and also takes pride in the pathos of his own impressions. Is this not the true purpose of the symbol? We value the mysterious, we rejoice in visions, and yearn for the putrefied red of decadence, for we are the disciples of a modern heretical faith, who cannot forget even in our dreams the laments of a marble stone that seems to sob in the pale white light of the moon.[71]

This rather excessively poetic explanation of the relation between the symbolist poem and the poet almost defies clarification,[72] but when set alongside Ueda Bin's famous explanation of the symbol in his introduction to *Sound of the Tide*, we can see that Hakushū and Bin were saying similar things.

The function of symbols consists in borrowing their help to create in the reader an emotional state similar to that in the poet's mind; they do not necessarily attempt to communicate the same conception to everyone. The reader who quietly savors symbolist poetry may thus, in accordance with his own taste, sense an indescribable beauty which the poet himself has not explicitly stated. The explanation of a given poem may vary from person to person; the essential thing is that it arouse a similar emotional state.[73]

For both men, the symbolist poem was a means by which the poet could communicate to his reader something inexpressible in the ordinary language of speech or prose. Hakushū elaborated on the object of this communication: his poetry told of "the limitless vibrations of emotion," "the pleasure of inexhaustible music," and "the pathos of his own impressions." This was where the most important difference between Hakushū and both Ueda Bin and Kanbara Ariake lay. Hakushū made his symbolist poetry a vehicle for expressing emotion or mood, particularly that of modern youth, whereas Ariake and Bin felt that symbolist poetry should treat ideas.

Recent research has shown that Bin's understanding of French symbolism was far from complete. The ideas in the passage quoted above were not his own but borrowed from Vigié-Lecocq's *La Poésie contemporaine*.[74] His own tastes tended toward the Parnassians rather than the symbolists. The example he gives of a symbolist poem in this introduction is Emile Verhaeren's "Parabole," which the reader will remember as his first translation of a symbolist poem. This verse was in fact allegory, a technique which at least in its cruder forms the French symbolists had rejected for a more allusive mode of verse, their aim being not to state or elaborate ideas but to suggest an inner state of mind through the arrangement and music of their words.[75] In his discussion, Bin in fact implied that the symbolist poem was fa somewhat sophisticated form of allegory. Ariake's verses in this form, which often treat the conflict between reality and an ideal, also relied heavily on allegory.

If Hakushū was at first strongly influenced by Bin and Ariake, he gradually evolved his own approach to symbolist poetry. As evocations of mood, his verses went beyond theirs. He was able to fuse French symbolism and certain concepts common to traditional Japanese poetry, the tanka in particular, in a rather unusual and particularly Japanese way.[76]

Hakushū's verse also revealed the marked influence of Baudelaire in his rejection of reality for imagination, narration for sense impression, the beautiful for the decadent. His subject matter contained much that was unpleasant if not outright morbid, all seen through a special lens colored by his sensual perceptivity. Although Baudelaire is not properly considered a symbolist poet, his poems had been translated alongside other symbolist poems in *Sound of the Tide*. An interest in Baudelaire and the concept of decadence seems to have been closely joined with symbolism in the minds of Japanese poets at this time.

Hakushū shared the symbolists' interest in the musical effects of poetry.

> My most recent poetry employs symbols in a musical fashion.
> I try to orchestrate tonalities to accord with the rhythms which
> vibrate faintly in the inner life of man. Therefore, I use the
> new forms of free verse to express this.[77]

As his later poetry would show, Hakushū possessed a particularly keen sense of rhythm. In *Heretical Faith*, he rejected the somewhat formal rhythmic patterns of Kyūkin, Ariake, and Bin for a more flexible combination of five- and seven-syllable phrases. He did not try to force his ideas into a set pattern but instead chose his rhythms in a way appropriate to his meaning; therefore he called his poetry "free verse." The term "free verse" is of course misleading, for he continued to use the literary language *(bungo)* and the five- and seven-syllable rhythms of classical Japanese poetry.

Hakushū's approach was strikingly different from either Ariake's or Bin's. His language in particular must have seemed remarkably modern especially when compared with their refined phrases, filled with overtones of diction derived from classical sources. Hakushū's poems contain many more nouns than verbs, and he chose his imagery not so much to describe as to suggest, through the compounded associations of his words, a strange new world. The publication of *Heretical Faith* signaled the beginning of a new era in Japanese symbolist poetry and is as well an important milestone in the development of truly modern verse in Japanese.

Heretical Faith opened with "Jashūmon Hikyoku" (Secret Song of the Heretics), the most celebrated of Hakushū's poems today. Hakushū took the title of his collection from this verse, which was written in August 1908 to preface the volume.

Secret Song of the Heretics

I believe in the heretical teachings of a degenerate age,
   the witchcraft of the Christian God,
The captains of the black ships, the marvelous land of the Red Hairs,
The scarlet glass, the sharp-scented carnation,
The calico, arrack, and *vinho tinto* of the Southern Barbarians:

The blue-eyed Dominicans chanting the liturgy who tell me
   even in dreams
Of the God of the forbidden faith, or of the blood-stained Cross,
The cunning device that makes a mustard seed big as an apple,
The strange collapsible spyglass that looks even at Paradise.

They build their houses of stone, the white blood of marble
Overflows in crystal bowls; when night falls, they say, it
   bursts into flame.
That beautiful electric dream is mixed with the incense of velvet
Reflecting the bird and beasts of the world of the moon.

I have heard their cosmetics are squeezed from the flowers of
   poisonous plants,
And the images of Mary are painted with oil from rotted stones;
The blue letters ranged sideways in Latin or Portuguese
Are filled with a beautiful sad music of heaven.

Oh, vouchsafe unto us, sainted padres of delusion,
Though our hundred years be shortened to an instant, though we die
   on the bloody cross,
It will not matter; we beg for the Secret, that strange dream of
   crimson:
Jesus, we pray this day, bodies and souls caught in the incense of
   longing.[78]

On the surface, this poem described the curious fascination which met the Spanish and Portuguese priests and traders to late sixteenth-century Japan. Fundamentally, it was a catalogue of the exotic articles which the Europeans brought with them. The Japanese of this period, who had heretofore had no contact with European culture, could not help but be impressed by its telescopes and microscopes and by the religion that its priests so fervently preached.

Hakushū purposely chose difficult and sometimes bizarre diction, much of which dates back to the sixteenth century, in order to suggest the exoticism of European culture for Japanese of the time. By using circumlocutory expressions, for example, "the cunning device that makes a mustard seed big as an apple" to describe a microscope, he conveyed the bewilderment that early Japanese experienced when first confronted with Western artifacts.

The strange diction was carefully incorporated into a simple but powerful rhythmic scheme, made up of alternating five and seven syllables, and the effect is incantatory. The rhythm does not allow the reader time to ponder over difficult vocabulary; indeed, the meaning of the words is not as important as their sounds and the unusual smells, tastes, and colors that they evoke, intoxicating the reader and producing an emotional state similar to that attributed to the speaker of the poem.

In the introduction to *Heretical Faith*, Hakushū referred to himself and other modern poets as "disciples of a modern heretical faith."[79] When viewed in this light, the poem, particularly the last stanza, takes on a different nuance. It can be interpreted as a statement concerning the complex relationship between the modern poet and his art. He is fascinated by the mysterious, the exotic, and the unattainable which in his verse he tries to approximate. Like the speaker of the poem, he is willing to sacrifice himself for "the Secret, that strange dream of crimson." The fact that Hakushū identified the object of his art with religion, an heretical type of Christianity whose secrets were open only to those initiated in its occult and mysterious rites, shows an affinity with French symbolism. His interest in decadence and illusion must also be traced back to these sources. In this sense, "Secret Song of the Heretics" was Hakushū's manifesto as a modern Japanese symbolist poet and stands as an important document for his age.

"Secret Song of the Heretics" was a symbolist poem, but it was not an entirely representative example of Hakushū's poetry in this style, developed most fully just before he published *Heretical Faith*. In "Kumoribi" (A Cloudy Day), the latest poem in the collection, Hakushū conveyed the melancholy of a cloudy day in spring through a description of the animals at a zoo.

A Cloudy Day

In the air of a cloudy day,
I go mad with melancholy at the smell of the buds
  on a camphor tree.
A paulownia tree blooms.
The astringent, sad smell of whiskey.

Here and there, the heavy breathing of camels,
The dull, dirty color of sheep,
The souring sick odor of straw.
Flowers lie scattered in the wet mud.
Their light purple color brings sharp grief.
The oppression of the young leaves in the sky overhead.

There, I hear it again,
The fearful screams of hungry pelicans.
The restlessness of a mountain lion. A bush warbler
  wails.
In a putrid pond, water seems to steam.
Paulownia flowers fall....The strong sadness of
  whiskey.

A sweet wind blows with sultry warmth
As animals pace lewdly in their cages.
A lazy monkey hangs idly from a branch,
And with staring eyes, searching for bugs in his
  feathers,
The African pheasant calls out destitutely.

And flowers fall...the purple of paulownia.

Is this the way the day will end...one more day?
The dread of the patient who escaped from his hospital,
The agony seen in the eyes of a baby, a laughing savage,
The wild roaming of a drunken dissipate.

From the sky, paulownia flowers fall...a new
  astringence, sadness.

And outside the gate,
The black uneasiness of march music descends as night
   begins to fall.
The animals become unaccountably restless.
Suddenly, from somewhere,
The trembling wail, like ice, of a polar bear gone mad.

In the dark, flowers fall...the astringent smell of
   whiskey...purple paulownia.[80]

There are four images at work here: the oppressiveness of a cloudy day in late spring, the falling flowers of the paulownia tree, the smell of whiskey, and the restless animals. All are joined as symbols for the speaker's melancholy. Hakushū's symbolist poetry with few exceptions attempted to describe mood or emotion; most often as is the case here his theme was ennui.

The first half of the poem describes the speaker's melancholy in terms of images which bring all the senses into play: sight—in the dirty white of the sheep's wool and the color of the paulownia flowers; smell—in the odor of the camphor tree and the stinking straw; sounds—in the heavy breathing of the camels and screams of the pelicans; and taste—in the astringence of whiskey.

In the last half of the poem, the speaker's melancholy is compounded by fear. This change is signaled by the line: "Is this the way the day will end ...one more day?" All the images which follow serve to symbolize the speaker's emotional state. The day grows dark, and the animals become restless. The falling flowers and smell of whiskey take on new poignance. The poem crescendos at its end with the wail of the mad polar bear—a cry of futility and dread which might be the speaker's own.

The majority of the poems in *Heretical Faith* were symbolist poems in this vein. Their subject matter varied, but in nearly all Hakushū tried to describe an emotion, most often ennui or melancholy, through the layering of images based on sense perception together with what might best be termed imagery of decadence. The hospital; the sick, blind, or mad person; the stench of decay; blood, and other images of this sort recurred frequently. Hakushū seemed unable to relax his pose of nervous awareness or to stop his uneasy search for new stimuli. His sensual imagery broke new ground, making his poems seem unique and particularly modern to his contemporaries. In the words of one poet and critic, "for the first time we could hear a new music, played on the keyboards of our bodies."[81]

THE PAN SOCIETY AND *PLEIADES*

By 1909 when he published *Heretical Faith*, Hakushū had become a leading member of contemporary literary circles. At about this time, his interest in the exotic gained new dimension with the discovery of old Edo culture, which still flourished in some sections of Tokyo. Hakushū and the other young poets and artists of "Pan no Kai" (The Pan Society)[82] shared a fascination with the incongruity between the modernity of new Tokyo and the remains of Edo culture, and also a love for French poetry and art.

Kinoshita Mokutarō was the leading force behind the establishment of the Pan Society. In his words,

> We took pleasure in reading about Impressionist painting and the history of the movement. Ueda Bin was also active at that time; under his influence, we imagined the life of artists and poets in Paris and yearned to imitate them. At the same time we were also fascinated with the old Edo culture seen in Ukiyoe woodblock prints. In the final analysis, the Pan Society was the product of our longing for the atmosphere of both Edo and Paris.[83]

Mokutarō's interest in Impressionist painting and his friendship with the artists associated with the magazine *Hōsun* (Square Inch)[84] led to talk of organizing a group of poets and artists whose members would meet regularly to discuss subjects of mutual concern.

The first meeting of the Pan Society was held on Saturday night, December 12, 1908, at a Western-style restaurant near the Sumida River with six people in attendance: Ishii Hakutei, Yamamoto Kanae, Morita Tsunetomo,[85] Yoshii Osamu, Mokutarō, and Hakushū. In starting the Pan Society, these young men, all in their twenties, sought to stimulate communication between artists and poets. Besides sharing an interest in the French Impressionists, they yearned to imitate the café discussions of art common to France, which Iwamura Tōru had described in *Pari no Bijutsu Gakusei* (Art Students of Paris) of 1903.[86] This popular book demonstrated to the younger generation of Meiji artists that art did not have to be pursued in the deadly earnest manner of rigid groups formed about a particular poet or artist, the normal practice in Japan where master and disciple relationships still prevailed. Because there were no cafés in Tokyo, Mokutarō settled for a Western-style restaurant along the bank of the Sumida River, an approximation of the Seine. They took the name of their group from Pan, the Greek god of flocks and shepherds often represented playing a shepherd's pipes. Pan also bestows fertility and is therefore known for his vigorous and even lustful disposition. His boisterous character and love for music endeared him especially to the young men of the Pan Society.

In January 1909, the month following the first meeting of the Pan Society, Hakushū and a number of other young poets began a new magazine, *Subaru* (Pleiades),[87] which flourished concurrently with the Pan Society. Although there were no official connections between the two, they shared similar concerns: a belief in the supremacy of art for its own sake, a fascination with the exotic and foreign, and a yearning for old Edo culture. In 1910, Shiga Naoya (1885-1971), Mushanokōji Saneatsu (b. 1885), and other writers who were graduates of the Peers School began publishing the literary and art magazine *Shirakaba* (White Birches).[88] This year also marked the publication of *Mita Bungaku* (Literature from Mita)[89] at Keiō University by Mori Ōgai and Nagai Kafū, who at the time was a professor of French literature there. The Pan Society served as a meeting place for members of all these journals as well as many others who shared their distaste for the naturalist literature then enjoying great authority thanks to the writings of Tayama Katai (1871-1930), Tokuda Shūsei (1871-1943), Masamune Hakushō (1879-1962), and Iwano Hōmei (1873-1920).

Every meeting saw an increase in the number of participants, especially after the publicity received in May 1909, when one meeting was investigated by police who mistook the group for a society of anarchists by misinterpreting *pan* for its alternate meaning "bread." The group sponsored two large meetings this same year; special invitations were sent out to various musicians, playwrights, critics, and journalists. From this time, larger gatherings eclipsed the original intention of intimate meetings between poets and artists. The character of the evening get-togethers also changed accordingly. Socializing over food and drink often in the company of geishas called in to provide entertainment became more important than literary matters, and liquor flowed freely late into the night. The participants often sang this verse by Hakushū either at the meetings or while wending their way home in varying degrees of intoxication; it became the unofficial theme song for the society:

In the Sky, Deep Red

In the sky, deep red are the clouds.
In my glass, deep red is the whiskey,

Why do I feel so sad?
In the sky, deep red are the clouds.[90]

One major reason for the decline of the Pan Society was the lack of
any defined principles or consensus of purpose to bind the group together.
In addition, the second issue of *Okujō Teien* (Roof Garden),[91] a publication
which Nagata Hideo, Mokutarō, and Hakushū had begun in October 1909
and which they intended to be the official publication of the Pan Society,
was banned by the government for corrupting public morals.[92] What had
promised to be both the epitome of a literary-arts journal and a means of
giving purpose to the Pan Society was destroyed in its bud. As the novelty
of socializing with contemporary literary figures wore off, attendance began
to dwindle. At the last meeting of the Pan Society, held in February 1911,
only fourteen people were present.

The years when the Pan Society flourished had, however, been pro-
ductive ones for Hakushū. During them he wrote most of his next two
collections of shi, *Tōkyō Keibutsu Shi Sono Ta* (Scenes of Tokyo and Other
Poems),[93] and *Memories*. The former contains the poetry which relates most
directly to the Pan Society. He dedicated it to "my friends of the Pan Society
and *Roof Garden* in remembrance of the banquets of our youth."[94]

Wearing a Light Jacket

Wearing a light jacket, tonight, too,
I go to the Miyakogawa.
Is it love or jealousy? On a suspension bridge,
The faint yellow of the gaslights
Troubles me.[95]

Gold and Green

A nocturne of gold and green,
A duet of spring and summer,
The samisen tunes of Edo in young Tokyo,
The light and shade of my soul.[96]

Scenes of Tokyo contained many poems of this type—short non-
serious lyrics which sing of modern young men of Meiji and the exotic
attraction they felt toward old Edo. In the first example, Hakushū made
direct reference to a restaurant where the Pan Society often assembled. Its

description of the melancholy young man setting out for an evening in an old section of Tokyo expressed the charm of this remnant of the past, especially when combined with the fin de siècle sense of ennui which characterized the young poets of the Pan Society. In the second poem, the differences between old Edo and new Tokyo were expressed in a series of contrasts, both parts of which make up the poet's soul.

The poems in *Scenes of Tokyo* were written for the most part during the same period as the latest poems of *Heretical Faith*. Both collections contained symbolist poems in which Hakushū used imagery of sense perception to convey an emotional state of futility, gloom, and weariness with life, the only difference being that the poems found in the later collection all concerned Tokyo in one way or another.

In the following poem, the setting was the present-day Tokyo University of Science, known as the School of Physics in Hakushū's time.

Behind the School of Physics

Borum. Bromun. Calcium.
Chromium. Manganum. Kalium. Phosphor.
Barium. Iodium. Hydrogenium.
Sulphur. Chlorum. Strontium.....
(A sad voice is heard, and mysteriously....)

The day grows dark, faint silver and purple—
In the steaming June sky,
The gloom of the hemp palm flowers in the dusk.
Yellow. The clusters of new blossoms
Shine suffocatingly from beneath the dark fissured leaves.
They let forth a deep sigh and the smell of sweat.
The yellow of a toothache, the yellow of iodoform, the powdered
    yellow of excitement.

$C_2H_2O_2H_2 + HaOH = CH_4 + NaCO_3$....
The mood of the pale incandescent gaslight flows out through
    the frosted glass door.
Inside one of the square windows,
The dull blue flames of burning methane.

On the Tokyo School of Physics with its pale ashen walls
    like a sanitarium,
The moonlight falls eerily.
....

A train whistle blows....Into the faint purple silver sky near the
  moat,
A waiting train spurts green-white steam.
Three minutes of quiet.

A sweltering anesthesia now entangles
The sense of gloom of the hemp flowers.
A silver melancholy drips from the edge of the dark
  fissured leaves,
An elusive passion coloring their shade.
Iodoform yellow as a toothache, the powdered yellow of excitement.

Neon. Flourum. Magnesium.
Natrium. Silicium. Oxygenium.
Nitrogenium. Cadimium or, Stibium
  etc, etc......[97]

The list of chemicals at the beginning and end of this poem were spelled out
in roman letters in the original,[98] another example of Hakushū's use of
language, here the unfamiliar scientific diction of a chemistry lab, for special
effect. The arrangement has no scientific meaning, of course; in fact,
Hakushū seems to have made up a number of the terms. Nevertheless, the
sight of the roman letters on the page and the sound of the special vocabu-
lary, served as effective background for the description of the speaker's
melancholy which the lists enclosed.

    The speaker's mood is evoked through the hemp palm, whose yellow
flowers and strong odor symbolized his gloom. The stifling heat of dusk, the
pale light shining through the frosted glass door, and the gray walls of the
school all have the common tenor of melancholy.

    The use of color is striking. The yellow of the hemp palm flowers is
the major image of the poem. The gloom which the flowers symbolize is an
acute and painful emotion; their yellow color reinforces this and is echoed
in the images which conclude the second stanza: the yellow of a toothache,
the yellow of the powdered chemical iodoform, and the yellow of excite-
ment. Other colors in the poem—the ashen school walls, the purple-silver
sky, and the green-white steam of the train—are more subdued, serving to
accent the yellow.

    The use of color was another facet of Hakushū's imagery of sense
perception. *Heretical Faith* and most of his early verse had been dominated
by red, black, and gold, but in *Scenes of Tokyo* Hakushū began to experi-
ment with a variety of colors, including silver, gold, and green. By the time

of *Kiri no Hana* (Paulownia Flowers),[99] his fourth poetry collection and first volume of tanka, these had become the colors he used most.

Red and gold were found in "Katakoi" (One-sided Love), which critics agree to be the best poem in *Scenes of Tokyo*.

One-sided Love

The acacia leaves fall red and gold.
In the autumn twilight, they are falling.
My anguish, a thin flannel of one-sided love,
As we walk along the towboat canal.
Your gentle sighs are falling.
The acacia leaves fall red and gold.[100]

The acacia leaves are falling, tinged red and gold in the autumn sunset. The speaker, whose sorrow cannot shelter him from the coolness of the autumn evening, walks along the water, hearing his beloved's sighs echoed in the rustling of the falling leaves.

The beauty of the poem is reinforced by the gentle lyricism of the Japanese original.

Akashiya no kin to aka to ga chiru zo e na.
Kawatare no aki no hikari ni chiru zo e na.
Katakoi no usugi no neru no waga urei
Hikifune no mizu no hotori o yuku goro o.
Yawaraka na kimi ga toiki no chiru zo e na.
Akashiya no kin to aka to ga chiru zo e na.

Four of the six lines end with the same refrain *chiru zo e na*. The predominance of "a" sounds *(akashiya, kawatare, yawaraka)* and the frequent use of the particle *no* give the language a rhythmic softness.

This type of lyricism was not found in *Heretical Faith* and is unusual even for this collection. In the afterword written in 1916 for *Yuki to Hanabi: Tōkyō Keibutsu Shi* (Snow and Fireworks: Scenes of Tokyo), the revised edition of *Scenes of Tokyo*, Hakushū wrote:

I would like to make special mention of the fact that the poem "One-sided Love" brought about an important change in my poetic style....All of the new ballad poetry which I later wrote grew out of this poem.[101]

He went on to divide his verse into three types.

If I retrace the roads that I have walked up until the present time, I can distinguish three different styles in my poetry. The first is the symbolist poetry found in *Heretical Faith* and in this collection. The second is...the tanka of *Paulownia Flowers*. The third is the new ballad-style verse in this volume and *Memories*.[102]

The distinction Hakushū made here is very instructive.

"One-sided Love" was first published in *Pleiades* in April 1910. It was probably composed in October 1909, the date given after it in *Scenes of Tokyo*. The praise which greeted it encouraged Hakushū to write other poems in the same style, most of which were later included in *Memories*. Strictly speaking, its beginnings must be traced back to the ten shi which Hakushū submitted to *Morning Star*, one of his first contributions to the journal.[103] Soon after writing them he had turned to symbolist verse, and it was not until around the time he wrote "One-sided Love" that he began once again to seriously explore the lyrical possibilities of the Japanese language, discarding the theme of ennui and his imagery of decadence for a more simple, natural, and poignant style.

Hakushū's term "new ballad style" (*shin zokuyō shi*) is, however, a somewhat misleading way to characterize this style. Although the last section of *Memories*, "Yanagawa Fūzoku Shi" (Yanagawa Folk Songs), did in fact contain several shi with subject matter drawn from Yanagawa customs, diction incorporating Yanagawa dialect, and rhythms of local folk songs, those are the only poems which can strictly be termed "new ballads." *Memories* is more aptly characterized as a "collection of lyrical songs," which was its subtitle.

MEMORIES

Hakushū published his second collection of shi, *Memories*, in June 1911, two years after *Heretical Faith*. The title of the volume appeared in roman letters, 0·MO·I·DE, under a picture of the Queen of Diamonds. The inside pages were outlined in red, and Hakushū's own drawings graced many of the pages.

As its title suggests, this collection contained poetry inspired by Hakushū's memories of childhood. For the introduction he wrote a long prose poem about his youth in Yanagawa, "Growing Up," which contained important biographical information necessary to understand the poems which followed. The rests of the volume was divided into seven sections. The dates for most of the verses coincided with the years of the Pan Society, years when Hakushū was also writing the poems later found in *Scenes of Tokyo*.

Two sections, however, did contain earlier works: "Memories," with the verses composed before Hakushū began to write *Heretical Faith*, and "Danshō" (Fragments), written during 1908, which also marked the date of the latest symbolist verse in *Heretical Faith*.

The verses of "Fragments" were not extracts from longer poems but short lyrical statements describing the poet's mood. Hakushū may have chosen the title to indicate the works used minimal language and imagery to suggest the feelings of one moment; indeed, in comparison with the careful explication found in his symbolist poems, they do seem somewhat fragmentary. Nevertheless, despite their brevity, they display a lyricism heretofore not found outside the tanka in modern Japanese poetry.

The sixty-one poems of "Fragments" provides an important stepping-stone between early poems such as "Red Fruit" published in the May 1906 issue of *Morning Star* and the other poems of *Memories* written in 1910 and 1911. The first thirty-one were with two exceptions published in June, August, and September 1908 in the tanka magazine *Kokoro no Hana* (Flowers of the Heart).[104] The rest appeared first in *Memories*.[105] At the time of their composition, Hakushū probably did not regard these works as highly as his symbolist verse. Even when he discussed them in the preface to *Memories*, a slight note of disparagement appeared.[106] However, as is the case with all the poems in *Memories*, these verses deserve to be considered in their own right. Through such works Hakushū had begun to develop a new style more original and in fact superior to that of *Heretical Faith*.

10

Aware, aware, iro usuki kanashimi no hakage ni,
Honoka ni mo miidetsuru, ware hitori miidetsuru,
Aoki mi no urei yo.
Aware, aware, aoki mi no urei yo.
Hisoka ni mo, hisoka ni mo, ware hitori miidetsuru
Aware sono aoki mi no urei yo.

Ah, alas, beneath some pale green leaves, sad leaves,
I made a quiet discovery, all alone I discovered,
The grief of green fruit.
Ah, alas, the grief of green fruit.

Quietly, quietly, all alone I discovered,
Alas, the grief of green fruit.[107]

24

Nakamahoshisa ni ware hitori,
Hiyaki harido ni te mo atetsu,
Mado no kanata wa aka aka to shizumu irihi no no zo
    miyuru.
Nakamahoshisa ni ware hitori.

All alone wanting to cry,
I press my hands on a cold glass door
To gaze through the window at fields reddened in the setting sun.
All alone wanting to cry.[108]

Both poems above portray mood or emotion—in one case, grief, and in the other, melancholy—through the lyrical description of a scene from nature. He does not tell us the significance of these scenes, although there can be no doubt that they affected him deeply. Yet they would be less effective had Hakushū chosen to draw his pictures more precisely. The unripened fruit found midst the leaves on a tree somehow gives concrete form to his sadness, and in a similar way the view of fields crimson in the sunset makes his melancholy more poignant.

Hakushū was not the first Japanese poet to use ambiguity, suggestion, and lyricism to describe atmosphere or symbolize mood. These are the very aesthetic foundations upon which the classical tanka tradition had been built. Viewed in this light, the works in "Fragments" can, in fact, perhaps be best characterized as a cross between the shi as it existed in Hakushū's day, and the traditional tanka. Hakushū would later use the same motifs found in these verses in his first tanka collection *Paulownia Flowers* and in doing so change the direction of Japanese tanka poetry.[109]

The most striking characteristic of these poems, the lyrical beauty of their language, also derives from the traditional tanka. Hakushū is using language in a very different way here than he had in either *Heretical Faith* or *Scenes of Tokyo*. Rather than choosing bizarre words for poetic effect, as he had in those collections, Hakushū employed *yamato kotoba*, the soft, fluid language of the classical tanka. He carefully avoided words which would clash with the sound of this diction. For example, in the second poem, he created a new word *harido* (glass door) to replace the more common *garasu do*.

Itō Shinkichi credits Hakushū with developing a new form of poetry, *jojō shōkyoku* (the lyrical song), in *Memories*.[110] Whether we choose to view this as a separate verse form or instead as one of the many variations possible within the larger category of shi, Hakushū did bring a new lyricism to the shi in *Memories*. Once again Ueda Bin's *Sound of the Tide* was the most direct influence. However, this time it was not Bin's renditions of French symbolist poetry, but the more lyrical verses in the collection, works such as "Vergissmeinnicht' by Wilhelm Arent, translated as "Wasurenagusa" (Forget-me-nots), and "Chanson d'Automne" by Paul Verlaine, found as "Rakuyō" (Falling Leaves). Although critics often ignore this facet of *Sound of the Tide*, it was lyrical works that accounted for its immediate popularity.[111] They were committed to memory and recited by many young people of Hakushū's generation. Under their influence, Murō Saisei, still an unknown poet in Kanazawa, had begun to write the lyrical poems later found in *Jojō Shōkyoku Shū* (Collection of Lyrical Songs).[112]

Although the thoughts expressed in many of the poems in "Fragments" may seem overly sentimental, especially to a modern reader, Ishikawa Takuboku immediately singled them out for praise.

> Poems in which Kitahara used mingled sense perception, such as that one describing the scent of glass, are after all little more than kineorama. However, the short lyrical verses of "Fragments" which have been appearing monthly in *Flowers of the Heart*—these are real poems, truly real poems. They are irresistibly fine works. There is only one man in the contemporary world of poetry [worthy of admiration], and his name is Kitahara! However, Kitahara does not treat love. I am going to devote all my efforts to lyrical verse from henceforth. I want to write of youthful love.[113]

Takuboku found these works far more appealing than the technical ingenuity of Hakushū's verses in *Heretical Faith*. His views no doubt also reflected the opinion of many others. The truth was Hakushū's use of imagery of mingled sense perception made his symbolist poems seem somewhat artificial, a quality not found in "Fragments."

Takuboku himself immediately began to compose lyrical verses, marked perhaps too clearly by the influence of "Fragments."[114] In June 1908, the same month in which seven works from "Fragments" first appeared in *Flowers of the Heart*, he had already started to write the experimental tanka later included in *Ichihaku no Suna* (A Handful of Sand).[115] The new form for these tanka—three lines instead of the traditional one line—and his frequent use of the colloquial revolutionized modern tanka poetry. When compared to other tanka of this period, his works are indeed unique. Nevertheless, one cannot help but wonder, as Itō Shinkichi has, if Hakushū's verses in "Fragments" did not provide inspiration for the form of Takuboku's tanka and for many of their sentiments.[116]

Not all the poems in *Memories* were short lyrical songs like those in "Fragments." In the "Preface Poem," for example, Hakushū attempted to evoke the feeling of remembrance in a rather long verse of five stanzas.

Preface Poem

Memories are like red-ringed fireflies
Glowing green, as soft as
The uncertain feel of afternoon.
Light which is not seen as light.

Or better yet, flowers in a field of grain.
Or the song of a gleaner.
Or, south of a warm liquor warehouse,
The white heat on the feathers of a dove preening
  herself.

Expressed as sounds, they are like flutes,
Or the croaking of toads
Heard one night long ago following the doctor's
  medicine,
An harmonica playing in the morning twilight.

Expressed as mood, they are velvet,
Or the look in the eyes of the Queen in a pack
  of cards,
In the face of a foolish pierrot,
A feeling of loneliness.

Not the pain of a day of debauchery,
Not the clear ache of fever,
But as soft as late spring.
Memories? Autumn legends of myself.[117]

This poem, the most celebrated one in *Memories*, clearly draws on Hakushū's own memories. One of his earliest was of a firefly, as recorded in "Growing Up": "Although I felt intimidated by the fearful darkness of the night, I stretched out my hand from my position on nurse's back and caught that red-ringed firefly."[118] The storehouses for sake, the flute which his uncle Michizane played,[119] a night after recovering from illness—these are all images that Hakushū recalled from personal experience.

The success of the poem, however, does not depend on these associations but on Hakushū's superb use of sensual imagery. Each stanza layers images to create what might best be called "mood." He carefully plays off the vague against the concrete, as in the first line where the startling equation of memory and firefly contrasts with the careful detail about the red ring on the firefly's neck. Again, in the third stanza, he talks of sounds. The flute and the croaking toads are specific images, but in the third line, there is a sudden switch to evoke the feeling on a night after recovering from illness. This, in turn, is followed by an even vaguer image—an harmonica being played early in the morning. There is also a mingling of sensual perception here: in the first two stanzas, memory is compared to fireflies, the feeling of afternoon, light, flowers, a song, and heat. All of these images relate to each other because they are in fact part of the poet's memories of his youth. However, more important to the effect of the poem, they join to describe the feeling—soft, imprecise, and sad—of the past as it lingers in memory. Had Hakushū chosen only visual images, for instance, the atmosphere conveyed here would not have been as full.

The techniques Hakushū used here, particularly the layering of images of sense perception to describe mood, displayed an affinity to the symbolist verses in *Heretical Faith* and *Scenes of Tokyo*. Unlike his earlier poems, he had, however, discarded the theme of ennui, and his language was strikingly lyrical. Although the diction was not as pure as that of "Fragments," the composition of those poems seems to have influenced his style. Consider, for example, the first stanza of the "Preface Poem":

Omoide wa kubisuji no akai hotaru no
Hirusugi no obotsukanai tezawari no yō ni,
Fūwari to aomi o obita
Hikari to mienu hikari?

The "o" and "i" sounds of the first word, *omoide*, reverberate softly throughout the verse. The rhythm, which may be diagrammed as follows—

5, 5, 7
5, 6, 8
5, 7
7, 3

is based upon the five- and seven-syllable phrases used heretofore. Yet Hakushū no longer strictly maintains a single rhythm. The expanded phrases of six and eight syllables in the second line and the final phrase of three syllables help to emphasize those portions of the poem. The "h" sound of *hotaru* (firefly), the poem's central image, and the assonance of the "i" sounds echo in the final three-syllable phrase *hikari*, which because of its brevity—the reader would expect a five-syllable phrase—reflects the fact that the last line is a question.

Hakushū's subject matter, recollections of childhood, was also new. He was not, of course, the first modern Japanese poet to write of childhood. However, earlier verses had taken the standpoint of an adult, to portray nostalgia for the rosy days of youth. In this sense, Hakushū's poems where he adopted the viewpoint of the child were altogether original. Moreover, he did not shirk from portraying the less appealing aspects of the child's psychology. Fear, the awakening of sexual instincts, sadism, and sibling rivalry were all recreated vividly.

In "Night" Hakushū described a child's fear of the night and the fantasies that plague him in the dark.

Night

Night is colored black.........the black behind
    silver foil.
The slippery black of the sand by that bay,
The black of the final curtain of a play,
The black hair of a phantom.

Night is colored black.........snake eyes glitter wetly,
Unpleasant odors of black tooth-dye,
The wandering bag filled with Taoist cure-alls.
A black cat slinks by..........Night is colored black.

Night is colored black.........fearsome, the stealthy
    black of a robber,
The bull's-eye umbrella of wicked Sadakurō,
As if someone touched the nape of your neck,
Like the powerless wings of a dead firefly.

Night is colored black.........the strange black of
    the numbers on that clock.
Blood drips
From the pale white scissors carried by
The man who peers in to take my liver.

Night is colored black........even though I shut my
   eyes, shut them tightly,
Numberless spirits, red and blue, drop through the
   night.
Night rings without end in my ears.
The dark night.
Alone at night.
Night............night.............night.[120]

Night is black in contrast to the glitter of daylight, here compared to silver foil. Moreover, for the child, the black of darkness harbors a number of fearful associations: the slippery black of the sand, the wet black of a snake's eyes, the smell of black tooth-dye, the slinking walk of a black cat, and most frightening, the man who comes to cut out livers (*namagimotori*), imagined by the sleepless child.

The child here was, of course, Hakushū in his youth. "Growing Up" helps to identify the origins and the meaning of many of the images. For example, he recorded viewing the bay near his home in Okinohata from the back of his nurse: "The inclination of the sand by the bay at low tide was slippery smooth and a frightening color, which together with the navy blue luster reflected from the sky, intimidated me; the extent of my fear would be incomprehensible to someone who had never seen a bay of this type."[121] "Growing Up" describes in great detail the fear of the dark that Hakushū felt as a child. The sound of a clock near his room helped to magnify his anxiety. "The sound of the clock in the middle of the night marked with its ticking the bloody footsteps of the liver man (*namagimotori*), carving their impressions into Tonka John's imagination, benumbed with fantasy."[122]

Dramatic spectacles, probably Kabuki, also seem to have been associated with the young boy's conception of night. We know from Hakushū's brother's description of their childhood that the family often attended local plays in the evening.[123] Imagery related to Kabuki provides the central theme of the poem: the blackout after the final curtain, the black dye used to color the teeth of those taking women's roles, the black hair of a ghost—probably a woman returned from the dead to take revenge on her murderer, a stock character in Kabuki ghost plays—and Sadakurō, a villain in the masterpiece of the puppet theatre and Kabuki *Kanadehon Chūshingura*.[124]

Some years later, in 1918, Hakushū was one of the founders of *Akai Tori* (Red Bird),[125] a magazine for children, and he wrote many verses for it intended to be read by the young. The poems of *Memories*, by contrast, were not meant for children, but the first beginnings of his verses for children can be traced back to it. In 1925, on the occasion of the publication of the new revised edition of *Memories*, he wrote:

> It can be said, without much doubt, that *Memories* lies at the source of my present interest in children's verse. Of course, prior to that, I had written crude poems based on reminiscences, but *Memories* gave me my first chance to make them public, as a volume of lyrical verses where childhood feelings predominate. The poems included are not nursery rhymes in a language for children; however, their subject matter is such that with some change in rhythm they could be made suitable for children. I feel that my real nature can be found in this verse.[126]

Hakushū's real nature does seem to lie in the poetry of *Memories*. Aside from the fact that the subject matter is biographical, there is an honesty in tone and treatment that *Heretical Faith* and *Scenes of Tokyo* lack. *Memories* also seems to show more of Hakushū's natural poetic inclinations and less of the influence of earlier poets. Critics today are in accord in their preference for *Memories*.

The publication of *Heretical Faith* in 1909 and *Memories* only two years later created a sensation in the Japanese literary world. Takamura Kōtarō's astonishment at the appearance of *Heretical Faith* no doubt reflected the opinion of many of his contemporaries: "I was completely taken aback when Kitahara Hakushū published *Heretical Faith*. I marvelled that he could use Japanese so freely and yet so richly."[127] The reception of *Memories* was even more cordial. Hakushū's friends held a banquet in September 1911 to celebrate its appearance, incidentally setting a precedent for the publication parties now customary in Japan. Ueda Bin gave the main speech, which moved Hakushū deeply.

> I still cannot forget my happiness and pride that evening. When we began the dessert course, Ueda Bin stood up and spoke to extol *Memories* in the highest terms. He called it a collection which joined the long tradition of the Japanese ballad and contemporary French poetry. Moreover, he characterized its style as innovative for liberating sense perceptions through its use of sense imagery. He singled out the preface "Growing Up" for special praise. Reading it, he said, brought tears to his eyes. He finished the speech by telling of his

admiration for the poet Kitahara Hakushū of Yanagawa. I was
deeply moved. I wept profusely.[128]

The publication of *Memories* in June 1911, this reception, and Ueda
Bin's outspoken praise established Hakushū as a leading young poet of his
times. His reputation was confirmed in October in a poll of "The Ten
Greatest Literary Masters of Meiji," sponsored by the magazine *Bunshō
Sekai* (World of the Written Word). He took first place in the category of
contemporary poets of shi.[129] In November he began his own magazine,
Zanboa (Shaddock).[130]

Success had come easily to Hakushū. All signs pointed to a brilliant
career ahead of the young poet. However, complications in his personal life
were to mar the glitter of this success, forcing him to reconsider the very
foundations of his poetry.

3

PERSONAL TRIBULATIONS
1912-1914

One important motive for writing *Memories* was Hakushū's love for his birthplace, Yanagawa. The economic difficulties his family experienced there while he was working on this collection in Tokyo intensified his desire to recapture the nostalgic memories of his youth. "Hardly had I started work on *Memories* than I received a distressing letter from my mother telling of her humiliation at the public auction of our family valuables under the shade of the familiar willow trees near the canal where we had set off fireworks."[1] The money raised by the auction could not save the family business, which had never recovered from the debts incurred when it was rebuilt after the Okinohata fire. For several weeks in December 1909, Hakushū returned to Yanagawa to be present at the bankruptcy proceedings. Creditors took possession of their house and land, and divided the contents of the warehouses. In *Memories* Hakushū recalled Yanagawa, his home, and his family all the more poignantly because of this crisis.

> I intend this small collection of lyrics as a gift to my family, who have just lost their home. That is why I have used the Queen of Diamonds, so full of memories, on the cover and have included my own crude sketches of a red-ringed firefly, the liver man, "John," and "Goshan"....With these *Memories*, I resolutely bid farewell to my birthplace and my youth.[2]

Until the bankruptcy, Hakushū had been receiving a monthly allowance from his parents. Now, not only did he have to support himself with the income from his poetry, but beginning in January 1912, he also had to take care of his mother and sister Ie, who moved to Tokyo from Yanagawa. His father and two brothers followed soon after. These added responsibilities

51

were compounded by personal difficulties of a much more serious nature. His relationship with Matsushita Toshiko, the wife of a newspaper photographer who lived next-door, was exposed by a major newspaper when the husband brought the matter to court, with a disastrous effect on Hakushū's reputation and self-esteem.

On the morning of July 6, 1912, the *Yomiuri Shinbun* carried an article accusing Hakushū of adultery under the sensational headline:

POET HAKUSHŪ INDICTED
A PAGE TO DISGRACE THE ARTS[3]

The article, far from being an objective report of the indictment, painted a very distorted picture of the case. Nevertheless, there do seem to have been grounds for the indictment of July 5,[4] and on July 6 he received a summons to appear the same day in court, where a preliminary cross-examination found him suspect of adultery, a crime punishable by imprisonment. The law of the times stipulated confinement pending trial and Hakushū was immediately transferred to the Ichigaya House of Detention by police wagon, together with common criminals.[5]

Kanashiki wa	How sad is
Ningen no michi	The road man must take.
Hitoya michi	The road to prison.
Basha no kishimite	The pebbled road down which
Yuku koishimichi.	A police wagon creaks.[6]

By all accounts, Matsushita Chōhei was a disagreeable man and an unfaithful husband who openly flaunted his relationships with other women. His marriage to Toshiko was strained, despite the birth of a son, even before Hakushū met Toshiko. Hakushū's sympathy for her predicament soon developed into an attraction that proved to be mutual.

Hakushū was a sincere young man, but also remarkably naive. Toshiko, on the other hand, was coquettish and vain, though quite attractive.

She reminded me of a red cockscomb: capricious, deceitful, sometimes clever and at other times foolish, vain, and crazy, with an appeal at once frightening and bewitching, beautiful to look at.........all of which allured my artistic desires, only to deceive them. She possessed a mysterious quality that held me in sway....I don't really understand it, except that I was hypnotized by my belief in the supremacy of art amidst a lovely world of indulgence and illusion.[7]

Hakushū justified his illicit love for Toshiko in terms of his art. Love opened up a new world of sensual pleasure, necessary to the poet even if society disapproved.

During the two weeks Hakushū was kept in the Ichigaya House of Detention, he was once again taken by police wagon for preliminary cross-examination on July 16. Four days later he was released on bail into the custody of his younger brother Tetsuo. Soon afterwards, Tetsuo contacted Toshiko's husband, who agreed to an out-of-court settlement of three hundred yen, an extremely high figure for the day. On August 10, Hakushū was again ordered to appear in court, where he was informed that Matsushita had withdrawn his charges.[8]

These events changed Hakushū's life and poetry radically. In the Afterword to *Paulownia Flowers*, he wrote:

> My life has been stained. All my dreams are doomed to perish. Youth, its griefs and pleasures, will now fade away like the purple paulownia flowers in May. To those who can understand my sorrow, I extend my warmest thanks. Tonka John, the criminal, whose very soul is scarred, must begin his journey. Can I ever expect to see this volume in print? How ephemeral is the road of inconsolable pilgrimage which lies ahead of me.[9]

Given the strict moral standards of the time, the publicity surrounding these events gravely damaged Hakushū's reputation. The dreams and aspirations of his youth seemed to have lost their validity, and he sensed a need to change his life. The next two years were ones of introspection whose fruit was a new style of poetry.

PAULOWNIA FLOWERS AND "POEMS OF GRIEF"

The two prose pieces which conclude the tanka collection *Paulownia Flowers*, "Shironeko" (White Cat) and "Fusagi no Mushi" (Worms of Discontent), tell us much about Hakushū's emotional state at this time. "Worms of Discontent," his first piece of prose following the ordeal, described his activities and thoughts on August 28, 1912, less than a month after his release from prison.

> You coward........Memories of my anguish and shame reappear in fragments. Barely a month has passed since I left the house of detention, a month when night and day have been indistinguishable, and my nerves, strained and tense, have

quivered continuously like the wings of a grasshopper. Insanity
and derangement laugh redly before my eyes. My life will
soon end. I have no choice but to continue to live each
moment as it comes.[16]

"Worms of Discontent" suggested that Hakushū's psychological condition
bordered on insanity; in subsequent editions of *Paulownia Flowers* the piece
was deleted. He even considered suicide, but his desire to live eventually
proved stronger than his feelings of shame. The piece ended with Hakushū
applying his sister's white makeup to his face, to achieve a close approxi-
mation of the "white death mask of an executed criminal I saw in an
anatomy specimen room."[17] Frightened by the resemblance, he put rouge on
his cheeks and black rings around his eyes, and performed somersaults like
a clown.

Hakushū felt compelled to give poetic expression to his prison experi-
ences; they became the material for "Aishōhen" (Poems of Grief), the last
section of *Paulownia Flowers*, which he had begun to write in 1909 after the
publication of *Heretical Faith*. The second part of "Poems of Grief" con-
tained tanka arranged chronologically: the journey to the prison, the flowers
in the prison garden he noticed when he and Toshiko emerged from the
police wagon, the first night in a cell, his meeting with his brother during
visiting hours, having his head shaved, comments on other prisoners, being
taken by wagon to court again, and finally being released. Here are excerpts:

Nakihorete   A bird
Niguru sube sae   Singing of love
Shiranu tori   Does not know to flee.
Sono tori no goto   Like that bird,
Toraerarenikeri.   I was caught.[10]

Donsoko no   Into the darkest
Soko no hitoya ni   Depths of the prison
Sashikitaru   Shines
Amatsu hikari ni   The light of heaven,
Mi wa nurenikeri.   Wetting me with its rays.[11]

Hahabito wa   If my mother
Kanashiku maseba   Feels sad,
Hōsenka   Please tell her for me that
Semete akashi to   The touch-me-nots at least
Iitsugeyaramu.   Bloom red.[12]

Onore akaki	Using the red liquor
Suimitsutō no	From a juicy peach,
Tsuyu o moto	I will draw a face.
Kao o kakamu zo.	Your face
Nakeru nare no kao	Crying.[13]

Hitoya idete	I leave prison
Jitto furuete	And quivering with emotion
Kamu ringo	Bite into an apple.
Ringo saku saku	The taste and crunch of apple
Mi ni shimiwataru.	Permeate my being.[14]

The most striking feature of these poems was their extremely personal tone. The sorrow expressed seems an unmistakably real emotion, which has pierced Hakushū to the depths of his being. The melancholy mood of *Heretical Faith*, though skillfully evoked, appears somewhat artificial when compared to the emotions found here. In the Postscript to the reproduction of the first edition of *Paulownia Flowers*, Hakushū wrote:

> The tone of the tanka in *Paulownia Flowers* changes in "Poems of Grief," for I could no longer be satisfied with only dreams. The time for spiritual testing had come. One dogmatic critic...accused me of having lost my humanity at this time. In fact, it was the exact opposite. I came, on the contrary, to understand reality. And at that point, I destroyed the style of the main portion of *Paulownia Flowers*. This was, indeed, the beginning of *Kirarashū* (Mica); it also indicated that I was still confident and healthy.[15]

When Hakushū characterized his poetry prior to "Poems of Grief" as dreams, he was referring, of course, to that dreamlike state he evoked by layering images of sense perception. His prison ordeal thrust him into reality, whereupon he promptly lost interest in "dreams" and "moods." In writing the tanka for "Poems of Grief," Hakushū clearly rejected the foundations upon which his poetry had been built.

The images of "Poems of Grief" functioned differently from those in *Heretical Faith*. As the subject matter came from prison life, so was the imagery dictated by Hakushū's experience there. If an image was symbolic, it served to deepen the emotional immediacy of the poem. Red flowers were the predominant image, their color signifying both the intensity of Hakushū's passion and the depth of his sorrow. The imagery of *Heretical Faith*, by contrast, had been highly imaginative in quality; its role was to further the poem's "mood" rather than to suggest the "reality" of the situation at hand.

"Poems of Grief" did indeed signal the beginning of a new style, particularly when considered alongside *Mica*, Hakushū's second collection. This group of tanka also resulted from an anguished sense of guilt over his responsibility for the affair and seems to have provided a catharsis for it as well.

The change in Hakushū's poetic style is best understood by comparing "Poems of Grief" to the other, earlier tanka in *Paulownia Flowers*. Hakushū wrote the majority of *Paulownia Flowers* during three years, from the last months of 1909 up until his indictment in July 1912—the years when the Pan Society was flourishing and when he was also composing most of *Scenes of Tokyo*. Most of the earlier tanka, not surprisingly, showed a stronger correspondence to his shi in *Scenes of Tokyo* than to the later parts of "Poems of Grief." Not only were there numerous poems on the same subjects, but Tokyo was also their setting.

Dusk in the Park

In the pale blue-silver air,
Somewhere water drips from a fountain.
The light of dusk remains unchanged for a moment.
A woman passes by, her fluffy feather boa the color
   of gloom.[18]

This was the first stanza of the poem which opened *Scenes of Tokyo*. The following tanka from *Paulownia Flowers* treated the same subject matter.

Fukura naru	The odor of
Boa no nioi o	Her fluffy feather boa
Atarashimu	Seems fresh,
Jūichigatsu no	This November morning
Asa no aibiki.	Of our rendezvous.[19]

The image of a woman in her feather stole suggests the season, early winter in both poems, as well as the atmosphere of Tokyo in late Meiji times.

However, there is an important difference in the tone of these two poems. "Dusk in the Park" is another example of Hakushū's symbolist poetry with its concomitant theme of melancholy, and the woman's stole is one of several symbols of gloom in it. The tanka, in contrast, has an appealing freshness. The gloom and melancholy of the shi have vanished, leaving only the "atmosphere" of a brisk November morning. This approach, for which *Scenes of Tokyo* offered little precedent, became an important characteristic of many tanka in *Paulownia Flowers*.

In May 1909, Hakushū had published sixty-three tanka entitled "Mono no Aware" (The Pathos of Things) in the magazine *Pleiades*, his first serious attempt to write tanka since his 1903 disagreement with the tanka editor of *Library of Literature*. The following poem, taken from that series, opened *Paulownia Flowers*. We know from Ishikawa Takuboku's diary that it was composed in July 1908 at a meeting of Mori Ōgai's Kanchōrō Kakai (The Kanchōrō Tanka Group).[20]

Haru no tori	Birds of spring,
Na naki so naki so	Cease your calling.
Aka aka to	The grass outside
To no mo no kusa ni	Glows crimson
Hi no iru yūbe.	In the sunset this evening.[21]

From inside his house, the speaker hears birds calling. The view from his window of the setting sun coloring the fields makes him feel a poignant melancholy, and he tells the birds not to interrupt his thoughts.[22]

Considering the early date of this poem, it should not surprise us to find Hakushū describing melancholy through imagery of sense perception. The poem's effect depends on its images: the sound of the birds' calls and the red color of the fields at sunset. Furthermore, it is obviously a variation on a subject treated earlier in a shi, number 24 of "Fragments."[23]

The tanka poets of Hakushū's day, most of whom devoted their energies exclusively to this form, felt strongly that modernization of the tanka had to be accomplished from within it. Hakushū's view of the tanka as a form complementary to shi seemed intolerably radical to them. For Hakushū, however, who had not written tanka seriously since he left Yana-gawa, incorporating the techniques and subject matter of shi into his tanka was a natural step—and one which Yosano Tekkan had encouraged during Hakushū's years with the New Poetry Society.

In "Kiri no Hana to Kasutera" (Paulownia Flowers and Sponge Cake), the introduction to *Paulownia Flowers*, Hakushū proposed a new theory of tanka.

The tanka is a small, green, antique jewel...old but still valuable. The beauty of the tanka form has been perfected throughout the two thousand years of its history in the East, giving it an inexplicable luster of sadness acquired through various memories of pathos.

....

I love the soft touch of this ancient jewel. Nevertheless, I wish to give it a keen and special brilliance, polishing its luster with sweat from the new and subtle sense perceptions of modern man and with the heartfelt breath of unsettled youth.[24]

In this passage, he compared the tanka to an antique jewel which through the years had acquired a special luster in the hands of its various owners, the poets of the tanka tradition. He respected its history but at the same time wished, as a modern owner of the jewel, to add in his own way to its brilliance.

Whether the tanka could be an effective form for expressing modern concerns was an important problem for poets of this period. Hakushū felt that modern tanka could and should be written, but he had certain reservations, which he indicated by comparing the tanka to an ancient Japanese instrument, the one-string *suma koto*.[25] Just as the music capable of being produced on this instrument was limited, so the tanka, too, could not be expected to give full expression to the "pathos of modern men."

If the tanka was a *suma koto*, he continued, then the shi was an orchestra. The poet directed this orchestra to reveal all the complexities of his modern feelings. Only when exhausted by this enormous task did he turn to the tanka for relaxation, "a glass of old champagne sipped when slightly ill."[26] The composition of shi was the poet's main work; tanka was secondary.

This view of the tanka naturally called forth some rather harsh criticism, but Hakushū's belief that shi was the main form in which the modern poet should express himself and that the poet had to accommodate his concerns in order to treat them in a tanka reflected his own experience in writing verse.

In terms of the poet's attitude toward his work, Hakushū drew a straight line between shi and tanka and then proposed to compose in both forms. His work in shi, whether the symbolist poetry of *Heretical Faith* and *Scenes of Tokyo* or the poems of reminiscence in *Memories*, had extended the boundaries of the shi form. His experiments with synesthesia and the layering of sense images had caught the attention of Japanese poets and readers alike. He turned to tanka at this time with similar intentions.

If my shi are the vividly colored oil paintings of the Impressionist School, then my tanka must be the moistness of the turpentine whose faint workings underlie them. Its sad wetness resembles the emerald color of the small jewel in my heart and the refined sobbing of a single-string koto.

The reverberations of my new imagery of sense perception are delicate, simple, and soft. I must take care that my sense perceptions tremble gently so as not to mar the innate dignity of this old form.

I will attempt to bring to the tanka the clear sorrow of paulownia flowers and the light floury texture of sponge cake.[27]

Hakushū proposed to treat the tanka as an adjunct to his shi. He intended to bring to it the same techniques of sense perception, taking care to adjust them to the form, and use them to describe "sorrow" and "texture." He would use the tanka to describe mood and atmosphere, as he had in his shi: "What I desire in my tanka are feeling, nuance, and the nostalgic sighs of mood."[28]

Feeling, nuance, and mood had always been proper concerns for the tanka poet, and imagery of sense perception can be found throughout the tradition. What Hakushū brought to the tradition was a new type of sense imagery and a completely modern subject matter. Hakushū treated some subjects previously avoided by orthodox tanka poets: sherry, whiskey, gin, milk, coffee, cocoa, forks, spoons, cuff links, and nail polish, to name a few.

Hitosaji no	The smell of
Kokoa no nioi	A spoonful of hot chocolate
Natsukashiku	Brings back the past.
Otonau mi to wa	You do not know
Shirashitamawaji.	That I will visit.[29]
Usuakaki	The drop of milk
Tsume no urumi ni	Which had fallen
Hitoshizuku	On the light red polish
Ochishi miruku mo	Of her nails
Natsukashi to minu.	Made me yearn for the past.[30]

The appeal of tanka such as these depended entirely on the nuances of images like hot chocolate and nail polish, which were part of the new culture imported from the West and for that reason appealing to young people of the day. This type of subject matter gave an additional freshness to the tanka in *Paulownia Flowers*.

In bringing to his tanka subject matter and techniques associated with modern European poetry and the shi form, Hakushū in fact brought the tanka back into the mainstream of modern Japanese poetry. However, when we consider this work together with his shi, it is clear that he merely transplanted ideas and techniques from one form into the other. Only the last section "Poems of Grief" documents a change in poetic style. This change, it will be remembered, was precipitated by personal difficulties resulting from his love affair with Matsushita Toshiko.

MARRIAGE AND MISAKI: *MICA, PEARLS, PLATINUM TOP, FESTIVAL IN THE FIELDS*

Hakushū's emotional instability following his release from prison continued for some time. Toshiko's whereabouts at this point are not known. After leaving prison, they had separated. On January 2, 1913, Hakushū went to Misaki, a fishing village on the southern tip of the Miura Peninsula southwest of Tokyo, to visit a Buddhist philosopher, Kōda Rentarō, determined to end his life. The last leg of the journey, from Yokosuka to Misaki, was by boat.

> On the second of January, I went by sea to Misaki. I had resolved to die. In my heart a terrible storm had brewed, plunging my feelings from gentleness into resentment. I looked out over the sea. Beyond the undulating waves, in the distance, were mountains covered with red camellias in full bloom. I could no longer despair. No matter how intently I brooded, I could not kill myself. The air was too warm and the sunlight too bright to die.[31]

During the twelve days Hakushū spent here, his resolve was shaken. Certainly the change in scenery and climate, which was much gentler and warmer close to the ocean than in Tokyo, was one reason. Another reason, perhaps more important, was the encouragement of Kōda Rentarō, who was living in a room at the Shinfukuji Temple in Misaki to pursue his studies of Buddhism. Hakushū's notes on the trip recall Kōda's cheerfulness. Although it is difficult to document, it has been suggested that Hakushū's interest in Buddhism, found in his next collections of poetry, awoke under Kōda's inspiration.[32] On January 14, a messenger came from Tokyo with the news that Hakushū's brother was ill, and Hakushū returned to Tokyo in a much stabler frame of mind. The same month *Paulownia Flowers* was published.

Sometime that spring Hakushū learned of the whereabouts of Toshiko, who had contracted tuberculosis soon after her release from prison. In May he married her and moved his family, Toshiko included, to Misaki.

> Our new house was in a fishing settlement called Mukōga-saki. It was commonly known as "the foreigner's residence," having formerly belonged to an old Frenchman, the consul at Nagasaki, who had installed his foreign mistress here....A large Western garden, one section of which was grass, faced the sea. From the front of a stone parapet, stone steps led down to the water, where a small boat rocked in the waves at a wharf.[33]

The warmth of the climate at Misaki, the abundance of nature, and the proximity of the ocean encouraged Hakushū to begin a new life for himself.

> My life was once again renewed. I absorbed intact the glittering sunlight and fresh air. The "Poems of Grief" which closed *Paulownia Flowers* had signaled an important turning point for me physically and spiritually. The clear southern ocean landscape gave my soul the freedom and courage to rebuild my life.
> Strength and brilliance. I jumped in search of this strength and brilliance.[34]

Strength and brilliance were the main themes of the tanka in *Mica*, which appeared in August 1915, and the shi in *Shinjushō* (Pearls) and *Hakkin no Koma* (Platinum Top), both published near the end of 1914.[35]

Although Hakushū's residence at Misaki lasted less than a year, his experience there created the foundations for a truly new style of poetry.

> Once I had left Tokyo, my life changed radically. The fresh vegetables sprouting forth from the earth and the fish animatedly flashing their scales in the sea were my true friends. I sculled boats, fished, and wandered over the fields and mountains and had very little time left for reading or writing poetry.[36]

It was not until after he returned to Tokyo in July 1914 that the results of his wanderings were revealed in several volumes of poetry quite unlike any of his earlier work.

The following two tanka from "Shinsei Joka" (Rebirth; Introductory Verses), the first section of *Mica*, treated the themes of strength and brilliance.

Kōkō to	In brilliance
Hikarite ugoku	The mountain
Yama hitotsu	Seems to shimmer
Oshikatabukete	And lean toward me.
Kuru chikara wa mo.	Strength.[37]

Ōkinaru te ga	A large hand
Arawarete	Appears
Hiru fukashi	At full noon.
Ue kara tamago o	From above
Tsukamikeru ka mo.	It grasps an egg.[38]

In the first example, the mountain shimmers in the sunlight and appears to move toward the speaker, intimating some inexplicable strength which nature possesses. The large hand in the second poem, which reaches down to take an egg from a nest, suggests the same strength. In these poems, man has no control over nature; he stands in awe before manifestations of an innate life force strong enough to move mountains. Hyperbole is a characteristic found in all Hakushū's verses from this period.

In Hakushū's early poetry nature had never been treated so directly. It had been perceived only through the poet's sensibility, which remained the primary concern. By contrast, in *Mica* nature seemed to dominate Hakushū.

Nami tsuzuki	Continuous waves.
Gin no sazanami	Silver ripples.
Hateshi naku	The ocean glitters
Kagayaku umi o	Boundlessly.
Himosugara miru.	All day I watch it.[39]

Urarakaya	What a glorious sight.
Konata e konata e	From offshore
Kagayaki kuru	The waves glitter
Oki no sazanami	And move toward me, toward me,
Kagiri shirarezu.	In infinite number.[40]

The frequent use of words such as *uraraka* (splendid) and *kagayaku* (to glitter), and the sunlight which brightens many of the scenes described served to suggest Hakushū's awe at the beauty and infinite power of nature. Even ordinary sights such as the flowers in a potato field inspired him with deep reverence.

Sakana katsugi	I climb a hill
Oka ni noboreba	With a fish over my shoulder
Jagaimo no	The purple flowers
Murasaki no hana	In the potato fields
Ima sakari nari.	Are now in full bloom.[41]

Platinum Top, Hakushū's fifth collection of shi, published in December 1914, also grew out of Hakushū's experience at Misaki. The Postscript to this volume told of a rather unusual religious experience which he had in the autumn of 1914.

I have spent the last three days and nights in extreme ecstasy. Everything is bright; my spirit rejoices in the infinite world of sentient beings which manifest the Buddha. I have not been able to eat and drink. This feeling is neither anguish nor joy—but rather complete ecstasy.[42]

Nearly all the ninety-five poems contained in *Platinum Top* were written during those three days.

Buddhism played a much larger role in *Platinum Top* than in *Mica*; its poems could, in fact, be characterized as paeans to Buddha, inspired by Hakushū's religious experience. Buddhism was also found in *Mica*, however, where it was clearly an extension of Hakushū's concept of the power of nature. All phenomena attested to this life force, which in turn manifested the existence of Buddha.

Ami no me ni	In the mesh of a net,
Enbudagon no	Sacred gold dust.
Hotoke ite	Buddha exists.
Hikari kagayaku	A glittering
Aki no yūgure.	Autumn evening.[43]

Moro no te ni	Glittering they fall
Terite koboruru	From my hands,
Sakana no kazu	Numberless fish.
Sukuedomo sukuedomo	I scoop them up, scoop them up.
Mata terikoboruru.	Glittering they fall again.[44]

Kaku nareba	Beyond doubt,
Kinkan no ki mo	The kumquat tree
Hotoke nari	Is also Buddha.

| Katajikinayana | Blessed joy. |
| Mi ga terikoboruru. | Its fruit overflows with brilliance.[45] |

The first two tanka are found together; the second one helps clarify the meaning of *enbudagon*, the "sacred gold dust" which is found in the river flowing through the Jambu Forest of India. The scales of the fish caught in a net glitter like gold dust, reminding Hakushū of a golden Buddha. A fish net sparkling with fish or kumquats glittering in the sunlight manifests the beauty and power of nature and by extension gives evidence of the presence of Buddha.

The tanka in *Mica* are arranged in twelve sections, within which they are again separated into subgroupings of several poems. In general, one tanka does not stand well alone and is best considered within the context of its group. The last one is found in the section "Hōetsu Sanpin" (Ecstasy: Three Parts), which also includes the following tanka:

Koko ni kite	Here
Ryōjin Hishō o	When I read the
Yomu toki wa	*Ryōjin Hishō,*
Konjikikō no	Golden light
Sasu kokochi suru.	Seems to pour down on me.[46]

In 1912, one year before Hakushū moved to Misaki, the tanka poet and scholar Sasaki Nobutsuna[47] had discovered and published the *Ryōjin Hishō,*[48] a Heian period collection of poems in the *imayō* style, many of which were Buddhist hymns.

The strong Buddhist overtones of the *Ryōjin Hishō* no doubt encouraged Hakushū to put Buddhism into his own work.[49] Many tanka in *Mica* also show an affinity with the *Ryōjin Hishō* in subject matter and style.[50] The numerous poems on children, in particular, seem to be influenced by it.

Isshin ni	The voices sound
Asobu kodomo no	Of children
Koe sunari	Absorbed in their play.
Akaki tomaya no	A grass-thatched cottage
Aki no yūgure.	Red on an autumn evening.[51]

One of the most famous verses in the *Ryōjin Hishō* also treated children at play. Hakushū probably had it in mind when he composed his own tanka.

For sport and play
I think that we are born.

For when I hear
The voice of children at their play,
My limbs, even my
Stiff limbs, are stirred.[52]

The poems on children, in whose purity and innocence he also saw the manifestation of Buddha, are the only examples in *Mica* where human beings were his subject.

In *Platinum Top* Hakushū experimented with a new verse form, a variation of the *imayō* found in the *Ryōjin Hishō*. Most of the poems were in lines of twelve syllables (7, 5), although some ran longer than the four lines which characterize the *imayō*. A *katakana* script was used throughout, which together with the Introduction written on blue paper dusted with gold, suggested the layout of texts of the Buddhist sutras—a fitting form for this collection.

The poem which opened *Platinum Top* and from which the collection took its name expressed the religious ecstasy that was a central theme of this volume.

The Platinum Top

My tears fall in gratitude. I merge into Buddha.
A top revolves on my fingertips.

Glistening fingertips point to heaven.
Never ending, the top spins unseen.

Smoothly spinning in a world of impassivity,
The platinum top whirs clearly.[53]

Simplicity of form and clarity of diction cloak a rather obscure and personal description of nirvana. The speaker imagines himself to be Buddha balancing a whirring platinum top on his fingertips. The glittering top spinning infinitely symbolizes the perfection of the mind that has reached nirvana.

Unlike the tanka in *Mica*, the shi in *Platinum Top* generally did not have a specific setting. The religious ecstasy that each poem expressed was often suggested by the use of light.

Two Poems on the Rose

I

On a rose bush
A rose blooms.
Why should I marvel at this?

II

A rose.
Why should I marvel at this?

Glittering splendor spills from the bush,
Spills from the bush.[54]

The fact that a rose bloomed on a rose bush should not occasion amazement; yet to Hakushū, it was an example of the mysterious power of nature, which ordered that rose bushes always bore roses. The rays of light that pour down from the bush clearly symbolize this life force, before which man can only stand in awe.

Pearls, published three months before *Platinum Top*, contained sixty-eight one-line verses, which Hakushū termed *tanshō*, and twenty tanka.

> The sixty-eight short verses *(tanshō)* in *Pearls* were first conceived of in September 1913, during my residence in Misaki, and were written at various times after that. In these tanshō, which are my own invention, I have developed a new poetic form, different from haiku or tanka. The poems are extremely short, and the form as such is not fixed to allow me to employ the natural rhythms of language more freely. In these poems, which might best be likened to real pearls, I have sung my heartfelt exultations genuinely yet subtly.[55]

Although this short verse form was Hakushū's creation, it was remarkably similar to the poems in "Fragments,"[56] except that he printed each tanshō in one line rather than dividing the poem into several lines as he had earlier. Furthermore, its brevity, if nothing else, made the tanshō seem quite close to the tanka. Had Hakushū's conception of the tanka been less rigid, he might have successfully published these verses as experimental tanka. However, because their form was not fixed—he frequently expanded the syllabic count in a phrase or altered its position—he felt obliged to create a new name for them. On the other hand, in both subject matter and diction, these tanshō showed stronger affinity to the shi in *Platinum Top* than to the tanka in *Mica*, where Hakushū had toned down his language and made less obvious use of hyperbole. Frequent repetition of words or phrases, one characteristic of these verses, was also not a common technique in the tanka.

Had Hakushū added one more five-syllable phrase at the beginning and expanded the last line of five syllables into seven syllables in the first and third poems quoted below, they would have become full-fledged tanka. The majority employ classical diction *(bungo)*, but there are several instances, such as the fourth poem here, that have ended up in the colloquial —more by accident than intention, it would seem.

Ningen nareba	How unbearable it is,
Taegatashi,	If one be a man,
Shinjitsu hitori wa	A man all alone,
Taegatashi.	To face up to truth.[57]

Mezurashiya,	How extraordinary
Sabishiya,	How lonely
Ningen no tsuku iki.	Is the breath of a human being.[58]

Isokusamura no	In the beach grass,
Kirigirisu	Grasshoppers, unable to
Nakazu ni irarede	Restrain their calls,
Nakishikiru.	Incessantly chirp.[59]

Yama ga hikaru	The mountains glitter.
Ki ga hikaru	The trees glitter.
Kusa ga hikaru	The grasses glitter.
Tsuchi ga hikaru.	The earth glitters.[60]

The first two poems tell of Hakushū's anguish and loneliness during this period; the last two extol the power of nature. They are similar in conception to "Two Poems on the Rose" in that both express admiration for the mysterious force that orders nature.

Mica, Pearls, and *Platinum Top* occupy a unique position in Hakushū's poetry; their style and subject matter are patently different from the verse either preceding or following them. *Mica* sheds much light on the process which led to the religious exaltation found in *Pearls* and *Platinum Top.* However, we search in vain if we wish to find correspondences of the type that existed between the tanka of *Paulownia Flowers* and the shi in *Scenes of Tokyo.* The shi in *Pearls* and *Platinum Top* are characterized by religious ecstasy, often expressed through the use of light (causing Hakushū to later term this his "period of brilliance"), a lack of specific setting, and simplicity of diction; these qualities set them apart both from *Mica* and from the rest of his poetry. Nevertheless, a tendency to write shorter verses, even in his *shi*, would eventually lead Hakushū to a deeper appreciation of the tanka.

Hatake no Matsuri (Festival in the Fields),[61] one other collection that resulted from Hakushū's life at Misaki, was never published on its own. In 1920 it was included in the first volume of *Hakushū Shishū* (Hakushū's Poetry), in which Hakushū stated:

> *Festival in the Fields* contains poetry about Misaki and should be considered a companion volume to the collection of tanka, *Mica*. I became interested in this subject matter while I was living in Misaki; however, the poems were not written at that time. Most of them were composed after I moved to Ogasawara and the rest completed after that. They should, in fact, have been made public prior to the second volume of *Indian Cotton* [i.e. *Platinum Top*]. However, I have not had the chance to do so until now.[62]

Festival in the Fields did contain poems on the scenery and people of Misaki; however, this was the only feature that it shared with *Mica*, despite Hakushū's assertion that the two should be considered companion collections. There was little evidence of the exaltation in nature found in *Mica*. Instead, the subject matter was rather ordinary. The most interesting poems were those which drew on folk-song rhythms, often making use of local dialect. Their neo-folk-song style suggested a closer affinity to "Yanagawa Folk Songs," the last section of *Memories*. Throughout his life Hakushū composed poetry in this folk-song style, and his folk songs seem to form a separate stream of poetic composition not always reflecting the concerns of his other poetry written at the same time.[63]

The most famous poem in this collection, "The Rain on Jōgashima Island," was the first of Hakushū's verses to be put to music. The music was composed by Yanada Tadashi (b. 1885) for a concert held in October 1913. The song enjoyed immediate popularity throughout Japan and even today remains one of the classics of modern vocal music.

The Rain on Jōgashima Island

> The rain falls, falls on the sand of Jōgashima.
> The rain falls gray-green

Like pearls or early morning fog
Or my sobbing.
Your boat leaves, leaves—wet with its sail raised—
And passes by the tip of Tōriya Island.

Oars guide the boat, a song guides the oars,
The captain's whims lead the song.
The rain falls, falls; the day clouds over.
Your boat leaves, leaves; its sail disappears.[64]

From Hakushū's house at Misaki, the view of the sea, which provided the setting for this poem, included the island of Jōgashima as well as Tōriya Island in the harbor of Misaki. Hakushū described a fishing boat disappearing out to sea in the rain. The speaker is a woman whose lover has just departed on the boat. Colloquial dialect, strong rhythm, and repetitions suggest a boatman's song.

Despite the large volume of poetry which resulted from Hakushū's residence in Misaki, he actually spent only nine months there. Soon after he arrived in May 1913, the salary he had been receiving as editor of *Shaddock* stopped because of the discontinuance of the magazine following a disagreement between Hakushū and his publishers.[65] To support his family, Hakushū started a wholesale business with his brother and father, selling fish from Misaki to markets in Tokyo. By September of the same year, however, this business had failed. He sent his family back to Tokyo and moved with Toshiko into a rented room in the Kentōji Temple at Misaki.

In March 1914,[66] Hakushū moved again, this time to Chichijima Island in the Ogasawara Islands south of Hachiōjima Island off Tokyo, in hopes that the warm climate close to the sea would benefit Toshiko's tuberculosis. No doubt Hakushū himself was also allured by the prospect of finding new inspiration for his poetry in the unspoiled natural surroundings of this small island. However, their hopes were dashed by the cold reception of the islanders, who were extremely wary of Toshiko's illness. Hakushū sent her back to Tokyo three months later.

Aru ka naku   I remain behind
Ikite nokoreba   Barely alive
Arisobe ya   On this rocky shore.
Shunkan naranu   Like Shunkan
Mi wa yasenikeri.   I have grown thin.[67]

This poem contains an allusion to the famous episode in the *Heike Mono-gatari* in which Shunkan, a high priest exiled to a small island for his complicity in a plot against the Heike, is left behind after his two companions in exile are granted pardon and return to Kyoto. Comparing himself to Shunkan, Hakushū expressed his regret at not being able to go back to Tokyo immediately. He finally procured money for his fare home in July.

TOKYO AND DIVORCE: *SPARROW'S EGGS*

Hakushū returned to Tokyo in extreme poverty in July 1914. He divorced Toshiko that same month. In the following passage, which opens "Rinne Sanshō" (Transmigration: Three Parts), the earliest section of his third tanka collection, *Suzume no Tamago* (Sparrow's Eggs),[68] he explained his reasons for the separation. The fact that Toshiko and his parents, who were living together, did not get along seems to have precipitated his decision.

> In June 1914, I was still residing on a small island in the Ogasawara group. My wife, who had already returned to Tokyo, was not getting along well with my parents. In July, when I too went home, their relationship was still strained. I was poor, yet I myself had chosen poverty. Destitute as I was, I understood this to be my fate....After all, as a devoted disciple of poetry, I could be content with a life of honorable poverty. I came to my senses; my wife remained obsessed by lust. If I became genuinely apprehensive, Toshiko would be frantic. When I wept for my parents' sake, she slandered them. I disciplined myself determinedly. I aimed for the heavens; she did not understand how far away the azure sky extends. My tears fell sincerely, but she did not understand earthly sorrow. I searched for eternal truth; Toshiko treasured mundane vanity. Although I honestly pitied my wife, I could not give up my career, leave my parents, and ignore myself, all for her sake. There was only one step to take. Therefore I made up my mind, and we separated.[69]

Hakushū had married Toshiko without much forethought, and after his initial passion cooled, he found himself burdened with a woman incapable of assuming the responsibilities expected of the wife of the oldest son in a traditional Japanese extended family. She did not understand his commitment to poetry, nor did she want to share his life of poverty. He had tried to augment the family's income by opening the wholesale fish business in

Misaki, but his failure demonstrated that he had no aptitude for any profession other than being a poet. If being a poet meant hardships, he willingly accepted them as his fate. Toshiko, it seems, could not; Hakushū was no longer the celebrated young man who had originally attracted her, and his ideals alone were not enough to sustain her. Hakushū, for his part, found that Toshiko's presence had become an obstacle to his career. Divorcing her renewed his commitment to poetry.

Nevertheless, his decision to divorce Toshiko caused him much anguish, which is described in "Betsuri Shō" (Separation), the second part of "Transmigration." As the title "Transmigration" suggests, his divorce signaled the beginning of a new period in his life.

Tarachine no	Between my beloved parents
Oya to sono ko no	And their son's dear wife,
Hashizuma to	Why should there be
Arubeki koto ka	Such friction?[70]
Naka tagaitari.	

Ima sara ni	How much better
Wakare suru yori mo	Than parting now
Kurushiku mo	Would be the anguish of
Hitoya ni futari	Being in prison
Koishi masareri	Longing for each other.[71]

Hoto hoto to	Just as she was
To o sari aezu	Going out the door,
Nakishi wagimo	She wept unbearably.
Haya sarikerashi	My wife has left.
Hi no katamukinu.	The sun has set.[72]

Hisakata no	Flying
Mangetsukō ni	In the light
Tobu karasu	Of the full moon
Iyoyo ichiwa to	Only one crow
Naritekeru ka mo.	Now is left.[73]

The deep sadness and extremely personal tone of the tanka in "Separation" remind the reader of "Poems of Grief," the last section of *Paulownia Flowers*. Just as the latter foreshadowed the change in style that would result in Hakushū's Misaki collections, so the former was also the prelude to a new approach to poetry. The third tanka quoted above ends with the statement "The sun has set," suggesting both Hakushū's sad relief at the divorce and the promise of a new day. The last poem, one of three on "Mangetsu to Karasu" (The Full Moon and Crows), concluded this part. The speaker is watching several crows flying in the moonlight. All but one disappear. Hakushū, like the crow, has chosen to pursue his career alone.

.

4

SPARROWS
1914-1923

Hakushū's decision to divorce Toshiko was symptomatic of his realization that poetry would be the central element in his life, and he was fully aware of the hardships that lay ahead. After his divorce in July 1914, he continued to live with his mother, father, Tetsuo, and Ie in the Azabu section of Tokyo. The two years there were bleak not only for Hakushū but also for his aging parents.

> The adversities we endured during the winter of 1914 defy description. Whenever our eyes met, they seemed to appeal for help. At breakfast, our chopsticks moved from bowl to mouth, but we remained silent. My father looked irritated. My mother, who never began to eat at once, would let out a deep sigh. At such times, not surprisingly, I would feel myself consumed with pity for her. My spine felt as if it were about to crumble within me. It would have been better if we were spiteful, cynical, or accusing to one another; anything would have been preferable to that ominous silence. Suddenly a sparrow would tumble down from the eaves. I would notice it first and smiling, point it out. Then my father, mother, brother, and sister would laugh in spite of themselves. We owed a lot to those sparrows.[1]

This description is somewhat exaggerated, but life for the Kitaharas was far from carefree, and no doubt it seemed almost unbearable when compared to their happy life in Yanagawa. They had no steady income, but Hakushū objected when his parents started to take in boarders.[2] He was aware that he was to blame for the unhappiness of his family, but he could not see any

73

way out of their difficulties; he chose instead to accept these circumstances as his fate. He derived consolation from watching sparrows play in his garden, and these drab little birds figured prominently in his poetry of this period.

Although Hakushū's reputation had suffered because of the publicity surrounding his indictment for adultery, many young poets, including Murō Saisei and Hagiwara Sakutarō,[3] gathered around him. In November 1913, while he was residing in Misaki, he formed the Junrei Shisha (Pilgrim Poetry Society).[4] After his return to Tokyo, he established a new poetry magazine, *Chijō Junrei* (Pilgrimage on Earth), as the official organ for this group. Many of his Misaki shi and tanka, later included in *Mica*, *Pearls*, and *Platinum Top*, appeared here first. An examination of the contents reveals how many young poets looked up to Hakushū as their mentor. Murō Saisei, Hagiwara Sakutarō, and Ōte Takuji,[5] who had published their first verses in Hakushū's journal *Shaddock*,[6] figured so prominently in this group that they were nicknamed "Hakushū's three crows." Kōno Shingo,[7] Murano Jirō,[8] and Yashiro Tōson[9] also began their careers as tanka poets here. *Pilgrimage on Earth* ceased publication after barely half a year, however, with the sixth issue in March 1915.

In April Hakushū helped his brother Tetsuo to establish the small publishing firm Oranda Shobō. Their first venture was a new magazine, *Ars*, luxurious in its layout and often running to several hundred pages.[10] *Ars* published works by Mori Ōgai and Ueda Bin (whom Hakushū had persuaded to act as honorary advisers for the publication), Kanbara Ariake, Tanizaki Jun'ichirō, and Takamura Kōtarō, as well as poetry by Hakushū himself and the younger poets of the Pilgrim Poetry Society. Because of its high price, however, the circulation decreased with each issue, and *Ars* ceased publication with its seventh issue, in October 1915.

Oranda Shobō also published Hakushū's own poetry, beginning in May 1915 with *Wasurenagusa* (Forget-me-not), a selection of lyrical poems taken from *Memories*, *Scenes of Tokyo*, and *Platinum Top*, and followed in August by *Mica*. In addition, the firm published more than twenty books by such distinguished writers of poetry and prose as Mori Ōgai, Ueda Bin, Yoshii Osamu, Yosano Akiko, Tanizaki Jun'ichirō, and Akutagawa Ryūnosuke, including Akutagawa's first collection of short stories, *Rashōmon*.

The luxurious format and impeccable layout which characterized the books published by Oranda Shobō were reflected in their high cost. The market for such deluxe editions being extremely limited, Tetsuo was forced to sell Oranda Shobō in July 1917. That month he set up the new publishing firm Arusu, which derived its name from the defunct magazine *Ars*.

In May 1916 Hakushū married Eguchi Ayako,[11] and the newly married couple moved to rented quarters at the Kamei-in, a Nichiren temple in Higashi Katsushika, Chiba Prefecture. However, the constant noise of services being conducted at the temple and their distrust of the priest made them seek other lodgings after only two months.[12] Their new abode, a thatched house in Minami Katsushika (part of Edogawa Ward in present-day Tokyo), was situated in the midst of rice paddies. The house stood out so much from its surroundings that it was visible from a distance, and smoke from the kitchen fire could be seen circling up into the evening sky. Hakushū aptly christened the house "Shien Sōsha" (Thatched House of Purple Smoke), and at the same time changed the name of his poetry group from Pilgrim Poetry Society to Thatched House of Purple Smoke. In November the group began a new poetry magazine, *Tabako no Hana* (Tobacco Flowers), but the journal folded after its second issue.

The move to Katsushika did not alleviate Hakushū's poverty. If anything it was worse than during his two years in Azabu. Hakushū and his wife gradually sold off their possessions to purchase food, which they shared with their dog, pet crow, and the sparrows. During the winter months, the sparrows sought haven under the eaves of his house, providing Hakushū with an opportunity to observe their habits even more closely. Hakushū's own life became intimately entwined with these birds, and he continued to spend hours attempting to portray them faithfully in his tanka.

SPARROW'S EGGS

Despite the hardship and poverty of the three years from 1914 to 1917, Hakushū's life in Azabu and Katsushika was made tolerable by the new interest in nature learned in Misaki and it was a productive period for his poetry. In Azabu he had quickly finished editing the tanka and shi written in Misaki and published *Pearls, Platinum Top*, and *Mica*. In these collections, as related in Chapter 3, Hakushū had boldly discarded the approach so successfully employed in his earliest collections, namely the description of moods, dreams, and reminiscences through the layering of sense imagery of a characteristically decadent turn. He had found inspiration instead in direct contact with nature, notably its "strength" and "brilliance." He had also experimented with shorter forms such as the imayō of *Platinum Top* and the tanshō in *Pearls*. His decision after moving to Azabu to turn from the shi back to the tanka was in some sense the logical result. He returned to the tanka with increased respect for the form and a new determination to develop his poetry in that medium. From the tanka written in Azabu and Katsushika, Hakushū planned to publish new collections. A determination to set to work on this task prompted him to move once again in June 1917, this time back to Tokyo from Katsushika.

During the next five years, Hakushū revised his tanka, intending to publish three separate volumes, one of tanka first written after he had left Misaki, and two others of tanka written in Azabu and Katsushika. He finally decided to publish them all together in one collection. The "Suzume no Tamago" (Sparrow's Eggs) section contained the Azabu poems and the "Katsushika Kangin Shū" (Katsushika Poems) section contained the Katsushika verses; together with the earliest part, "Rinne Sanshō" (Transmigration: Three Parts), they made up the three sections of *Suzume no Tamago* (Sparrow's Eggs), Hakushū's third tanka collection.

Hakushū spent a total of seven years, 1914-1921, writing *Sparrow's Eggs*. The difficulties he encountered during this time are recorded in the "Daijo" (Introduction).

> I wagered my life on this volume of poetry *Sparrow's Eggs*. While bringing it to completion, I struggled against all manner of hardship. I lived in such extreme poverty that I was threatened with imminent starvation. Many times I defied death, only in the end to withstand the worst, all for the sake of these verses.[13]

Although Hakushū's description sounds overstated, the years spent writing *Sparrow's Eggs* were indeed hard, lean ones. Had he not chosen to devote most of his time to the tanka, he could undoubtably have devised other ways to earn extra income through his writing. He would later term this period a time of "discipline" (*shugyō*), for he voluntarily chose to experience hardship, hoping that a life of honorable poverty spent concentrating on his poetry would help him to develop a totally new style of verse.

Hakushū set such high standards of perfection for these tanka that he felt compelled to make four complete revisions of them. This in part explains why seven years elapsed between the first versions made at Azabu and the final publication of *Sparrow's Eggs*.

> My poetry was inept. The more I refined and polished these verses, the more desperate I became. I could not let pass the defects I noticed in a single word or phrase. At one point, I discarded ninety tanka out of a hundred, nine tanka out of ten. On another occasion, I spent seven days and seven nights laboring over the wording of one phrase. Only today, after three years, have I at last found the appropriate expression for a word in a certain tanka.[14]

While laboring over these revisions, Hakushū's understanding of the tanka deepened. This in turn led to further revision, eventually resulting in the new approach to poetry elucidated in the Introduction to *Sparrow's Eggs*.

Hakushū's new approach to poetry developed gradually and not without interruption. From June 1917, having moved back to Tokyo, he devoted himself to preparing the tanka written at Azabu and Katsushika for publication. He even dissolved his poetry group, Thatched House of Purple Smoke, in order to have more time for his task. As soon as the first draft of *Sparrow's Eggs* was ready, he gave it to his brother Tetsuo at Oranda Shobō. Dissatisfied with the tanka as they appeared in the first set of proofs, he at once revised them all. The second set was still unsatisfactory; once again he set about reworking them. In July, as already related, Tetsuo sold Oranda Shobō and founded the new publishing house Arusu. The following month, in extreme poverty, Hakushū moved from his temporary quarters in Tsukiji to rented rooms at Hongō, bringing with him the unfinished manuscripts.[15]

Hakushū continued to work on the manuscripts through the winter.

> At this time my tanka began at last to show promise. Their tone had changed completely. I felt that a stern unnaturalness, resulting from early attempts to force my verse to be clear, had disappeared. However, just as they were beginning to show promise, I suddenly found myself mute.[16]

Just as his careful revisions were at last beginning to bear fruit and his efforts to eliminate affectation and a forced unnaturalness had finally produced tanka of promise, Hakushū suddenly stopped writing.

He discussed the reasons in the Introduction to *Sparrow's Eggs*. First of all, about this time a strong disagreement had occurred between Hakushū and the young poets who gathered in the Thatched House of Purple Smoke. Following the dissolution of this organization, his disciples split into two groups. Hakushū helped the tanka poets begin their own magazine, *Mandara* (Mandala), in September 1917, and the poets of shi begin *Shihen* (Poems) in December 1917.[17] He served as adviser for both magazines and published in them as well. Nevertheless, he wanted to dissociate himself from both groups in order to concentrate on his own work. He also felt strongly that their dependence on him was hindering their own development as poets. His views can be found in "Shien Sōsha Kaisan no Ji" (On the Dissolution of the Thatched House of Purple Smoke), published in the first issue of *Mandala*.

Why don't you dissociate yourselves from my verse? Why don't you rely on your own efforts? Why don't you wave the flag of rebellion? Why don't you conquer and humiliate your great Hakushū?

Think of me as your enemy. Bring your spears; thrust them at me.

In poetry there are no teachers, no disciples, no fathers, no sons, and no friends. Only here is it beautiful to fight blood with blood. Honest and correct. Anything is permitted for the sake of poetry. There is no need to vacillate.

I will happily feed you all that I have. You must swarm about me and suck my blood and chew on my bones. And then you must go forward anew. The reason I have severed the bonds of teacher and disciple between us is to keep you from hesitating. My desire is not to make pretensions of modesty, but to arouse within each of you an innate fierce will to fight for what is yours.

Rebel, rebel. If you do not rebel, I will cut you down.[18]

Japanese poets at this time rarely wrote in isolation. Teacher-disciple relationships served to group poets of similar interests and provided the opportunity for younger poets to have their work continually evaluated by a successful older poet. Hakushū's severance of this relationship no doubt seemed to his disciples an expression of dissatisfaction.

Although the passage was strongly phrased, however, Hakushū felt no animosity toward his disciples. On the contrary, it was his sense of responsibility for their development as poets that prompted his outburst. Like a mother bird eager to see her fledglings fly, he pushed them out of the nest. The push was strong, but it was well-intentioned.

In another passage of this piece, Hakushū spoke of his strong affection for these poets, most of whom, as already related, had first published with his support. He urged them to rebel as poets, not as friends, and he was therefore deeply hurt when soon afterward they turned against him personally. In the Introduction to *Sparrow's Eggs*, this discord is cited as one reason for his long silence.

However great his distress at his disciples' betrayal, this fact alone does not fully explain his temporary inability to write tanka. In the same Introduction he gave two more reasons, which touched more directly on his attitude toward the tanka at this time.

First of all, although I was living in extreme poverty, my life had become more complex. I found it increasingly difficult to write alone, to discipline myself for the sake of my tanka. Secondly, while devoting my life to the tanka, I came to understand quite naturally the value of silence. I felt then that even the thirty-one syllables of the tanka were too lengthy, that the tanka itself contained too many words.[19]

Hakushū's devotion to the tanka had begun, by his own reluctant admission, to produce work of promise. But this made him all the more critical. Despite the deceptive simplicity and brevity of the tanka, fulfilling his own high standards seemed an enormous task. This, coupled with the difficulty of concentrating on his work, seems to have decided him. He sensed that a period of silence, time to gain self-composure and a new perspective, was needed. When *Sparrow's Eggs* was finally published, Hakushū expressed relief at having waited and not forced himself to publish these tanka before he felt confident of their value.

By comparison, his two earlier tanka collections, *Paulownia Flowers* and *Mica*, had been composed with much less effort. He had regarded the tanka as an extension of his shi, often treating the same material in both forms, and enthusiasm for his subject matter had made the verse form a secondary consideration. By this time, however, Hakushū was consciously attempting to develop a deeper mastery of the tanka form. The difficulty of the task temporarily discouraged him. And yet, although Hakushū stated that he did not write tanka for four years, his silence did not actually last that long. He stopped revising the manuscripts for *Sparrow's Eggs* in the winter of 1917-1918 and began work again in the early months of 1921—a little more than three years of interruption.

MISCELLANEOUS REMARKS ON CONCENTRATION

In June 1917, while still working on *Sparrow's Eggs*, Hakushū began to publish short essays on the tanka in the magazine *Sangoshō* (Coral Reef).[20] Ten in all, they continued to appear until July 1918, by which time he had already stopped composing tanka. In 1921 he collected and published them as *Senshin Zatsuwa* (Miscellaneous Remarks on Concentration).[21]

Hakushū discoursed on the tanka in a rambling fashion in these essays, which reveal that his understanding of the tanka was changing radically and suggest what had stimulated the change. The essays contain the first exposition of ideas which later would be reworked, developed, and, in final form, stated in *Sparrow's Eggs* as Hakushū's theory of tanka.

In *Concentration* Hakushū discussed the relationship between a poet's technique and his attitude toward the tanka. Although he allowed himself numerous anecdotes and digressions, his remarks were on the whole much clearer than the abstruse metaphors he had used to compare the tanka and the shi in *Paulownia Flowers.*

He asserted the importance of poetic craft; however, it must not be ostentatious or in any way impede the natural flow of the poem.

> Words in poetry—at times they flow forth effortlessly from the start, as natural as breathing. Such poems, willed by heaven, are beyond criticism. In most cases, however, considerations of diction impede the composition of a verse. Or, rather than language, the egotism of the poet himself as he takes up his pen to write distorts what should have been natural in the verse. The value of the poem that results depends, then, upon the personality of its writer. The labors we expend over a phrase or the rhythm of a verse should be aimed at ridding the poem of egotistical concerns and removing unnecessary ornament in language so that the verse reflects genuine feeling.[22]

A good poem, he declared, was completely natural in its rhythm, wording, and feeling.

The private concerns of the poet, in particular his overwhelming desire to compose a good poem, marred the naturalness of his verse. To prevent artificiality, the poet had to cultivate an attitude of reverence for his surroundings, especially the phenomena of nature. A good poem, in turn, communicated this attitude of reverence to the reader.

The second half of *Concentration* was devoted to Hakushū's discussion of *warabe kokoro* (naiveté), by which he meant the purity of heart, unstudied reactions, and self-oblivion of the child. The poet absorbed in his contemplation of nature shared much with the child intent on his play.

> You must forget personal concerns. Become like the child absorbed at play, in love with what fascinates him. After all, art is play, but play deeper and broader than the play of a child.[23]

When Hakushū declared that the poet had to contemplate nature both intently and reverently in order to produce verse that conveyed genuine emotion, when he asserted that ostentatious diction or the poet's private concerns marred the naturalness of his tanka, he was taking a completely different approach to poetry than he had heretofore, and its implications for his own verse, which changed radically as a result, would be far-reaching.

The ideas Hakushū expressed in *Concentration* were not completely his own. He incorporated fundamental principles of traditional Japanese aesthetics into his own approach, repeatedly singling out for praise two poets, Matsuo Bashō (1644-1694)[24] and Ryōkan (1758-1831).[25]

Hakushū related many anecdotes describing Ryōkan's love for children and his ingenuous approach to life in order to illustrate the importance of *warabe kokoro* for the poet. To some extent Ryōkan's tanka no doubt also served as models for Hakushū, although his verse as such was not dealt with in detail.[26] In 1916 Saitō Mokichi (1882-1953) had published a selection of Ryōkan's tanka, which may have aroused Hakushū's interest.[27]

Bashō's influence was far more seminal. Not only did Hakushū repeatedly mention him as the prime example of a poet who embodied the attitudes Hakushū himself advocated, but Bashō's views on *haikai* provided the basis for Hakushū's own theories of tanka composition. The *Sanzōshi* (Three Copy Books),[28] in particular several pages of the second section "Akazōshi" (Red Copy Book), reveal such strong similarities to Hakushū's opinions that it is hard to avoid the impression that Hakushū's readings in Bashō occasioned the change in his approach to the tanka. Bashō warned against the poet's allowing his personal feelings to intrude into his verse; only when the poet had projected himself into nature was a poem the natural result. Bashō was also reported to have taught his disciples "Let a child of three feet tall compose *haikai*. Nothing is more precious than the poetry of the inexperienced."[29] Only five years earlier, Hakushū had dismissed Bashō in "Hiru no Omoi" (Thoughts at Noon), a prose section in *Paulownia Flowers*, with these strong words: "We who are young cannot get excited about Bashō's elegant simplicity *(sabi)*."[30] Now Bashō had become Hakushū's model.

POEMS FOR CHILDREN: *RED BIRD*

During the three years when he stopped writing tanka, Hakushū turned to other forms of expression: essays, including *Concentration*, short stories, folk songs, and poetry for children. His interest in writing poetry for children dates from his association with *Akai Tori* (Red Bird),[31] a literary magazine for children begun in July 1918 by Suzuki Miekichi.[32] Distressed at the poor quality of children's magazines in his day, Miekichi published original poems, songs, stories, and art work and encouraged children to contribute as well. The magazine exercised an important influence on the creative education of children. The best writers of the day, including Akutagawa Ryūnosuke, Izumi Kyōka (1873-1939), Tokuda Shūsei (1871-1943), Shimazaki Tōson, Takahama Kyoshi (1874-1959), and Kikuchi Kan (1888-1948), all contributed to *Red Bird*, and their stories and poems mark a high point in modern children's literature. Miekichi placed Hakushū in charge of children's poetry for the magazine. For the first issue of July 1918, Hakushū wrote "Risu Risu Korisu" (Squirrel, Squirrel, Little Squirrel).

> Squirrel, squirrel, little squirrel.
> Darting about, little squirrel.
> Red are apricots now.
> Eat, eat, little squirrel.
>
> Squirrel, squirrel, little squirrel.
> Darting about, little squirrel.
> Green is the dew on the pepper leaves now.
> Drink, drink, little squirrel.
>
> Squirrel, squirrel, little squirrel.
> Darting about, little squirrel.
> White are the blossoms on the grapevine now.
> Swing, swing, little squirrel.[33]

The repeated refrains, careful attention to sound patterns, and vivid color imagery are characteristic of many of these poems.

As the result of his participation in *Red Bird*, Hakushū became involved in teaching children how to write poetry. He was convinced that children should not be forced to conform to formal rules and encouraged those who contributed to *Red Bird* to write free verse. In January 1921 Hakushū started a new magazine, *Geijutsu Jiyu Kyōiku* (Free Education in the Arts),[34] which was intended to transmit to teachers his views on education in the arts. Hakushū was also frequently invited to lecture on and read his poetry to children.[35]

Hakushū's had earlier composed poems based on reminiscences from childhood, especially those in *Memories*, but they were not specifically intended for children. In October 1919 he published his first and most famous collection for children, *Tonbō no Megane* (Dragonfly's Spectacles), bringing together the poems he had written for *Red Bird*. From then on, collections of children's poetry appeared almost annually up until his death, constituting a major contribution to this form of literature.[36]

His children's poetry provided Hakushū for the first time in many years with a steady income. About this time, he also began to write fiction, which he published serially in newspapers and monthly magazines.[37] These stories, all autobiographical to some extent, are not highly regarded; the verbose language, excessively complicated descriptions, and faulty plot structure mar what value they have as documents of Hakushū's life. Nevertheless, along with his children's verse and folk songs, they helped to alleviate Hakushū's straightened circumstances.

KOUTA AND FOLK SONGS

While he was living in Katsushika, Hakushū wrote a number of *kouta*, short poems in the style of folk songs, often extemporaneously, for young men of the area to sing.[38] Although his interest in folk songs can be traced back to the "Yanagawa Folk Songs" in *Memories*, Hakushū did not take up the form in earnest until this time. Even after he abandoned work on *Sparrow's Eggs*, he continued to compose in it.

His first collection, *Hakushū Kouta Shū* (Kouta by Hakushū), appeared in December 1919 and incorporated the kouta written from 1916 to 1919.[39] *Kouta* means merely "short song," but for Hakushū it meant specifically a four-line verse form derived from the twenty-six syllable *riyō* of the Tokugawa period.[40] The subject matter was varied, not necessarily in the tradition of earlier examples, and the poems were written in the colloquial, rather than in the classical diction Hakushū used in his shi and tanka. A number were about sparrows and there was one on Bashō.

After finishing *Sparrow's Eggs*, Hakushū once again turned to the folk song. He wrote over five hundred in late 1921 and early 1922.[41] From these verses he compiled a second collection, *Nihon no Fue* (Japanese Flute), published in April 1922.[42] The form, subject matter, and language of these verses differed from his earlier kouta; Hakushū termed them *minyō* (folk songs).[43] He patterned these poems on folk songs of the Japanese countryside, and employed the rhythms, local dialect, and nonsense refrains found in such songs. He chose subject matter suitable to the form: descriptions of local customs, harvesting, festivals, and country scenery. Needless to say, the folk song had heretofore been of anonymous authorship, passed down from generation to generation as a part of the daily life of a village. However, in Hakushū's hands, it was elevated into an art form. The same is true of his children's verse.

A number of Hakushū's children's poems and folk songs were immediately set to music by such contemporary composers as Yamada Kōsaku (1886-1965) and Yanada Tadashi, and are now among the most celebrated pieces of modern Japanese vocal music.[44] Hakushū's lyricism, known most widely through these songs, continues even today to touch the hearts of his compatriots. Although intellectuals are apt to scoff at his popularity, neither his readers nor Hakushū himself considered composing popular poetry reprehensible.

In "Minyō Shiron" (My Views on the Folk Song), the introduction to *Japanese Flute*, Hakushū outlined his approach. He felt that when composing folk songs the poet had to follow traditional forms, employing local, dialectical, colloquial language, and describing the concerns of the people who would sing them. The success of the poem would be determined by its popularity. In answer to those who looked down on the form as third-rate art and its writers as third-rate poets, he drew a firm line between his work in the shi and tanka forms and his folk songs, declaring that he was proud to be able to compose both literary and popular poetry.

Hakushū continued to write folk songs until his death; he published in all six large collections.[45] Judged by his own standards, his folk songs were certainly successful. A large number were incorporated into the existing repertory in various communities and are still sung today.

ODAWARA: *LIFE OF THE SPARROWS* AND *SPARROW'S EGGS*

In February 1918, Hakushū moved from Tokyo to Odawara, Kanagawa Prefecture. Ayako had a congenital lung condition, and the move was made in the hope that the warmer climate would be beneficial. By October of the following year, after several moves, Hakushū and his wife finally settled into a rustic dwelling and small studio house, both newly built for him in a bamboo forest belonging to the Denjōji Temple in Odawara.[46] He would live here for the next eight years; this was unusual for Hakushū, who rarely stayed long in one place.

With the money earned from his children's verse, folk songs, and fiction, Hakushū decided the next year to build a modern two-story house at the same site. Hakushū had always been fond of display, and he made elaborate plans for the traditional groundbreaking and purification ceremonies in June, hiring geisha from Tokyo and building a stage for entertainment. When his family arrived for the ceremony, they were shocked by his ostentation. Even more perturbed at Hakushū's display were those acquaintances who barely a year and a half earlier had contributed from their own pockets to help build the other two houses on the grounds. Tetsuo took it upon himself to rebuke Hakushū and Ayako before the others present.[47]

Ayako was noticeably upset by this criticism. She had justified the celebrations in her mind as marking an important turning point in Hakushū's life, the end of the poverty which had clouded their four years of marriage. In any case, the festivities were not her idea but Hakushū's, and she was indignant that in return for her efforts—she had supervised all the preparations—instead of thanks, she got a scolding. Her anger prompted her to make a rash decision. No sooner had she done what was expected of her as the hostess than she got into a taxi hired to take guests to the railroad station; she left her house and husband not alone, but with another man, Ikeda Ringi, a newspaper reporter who had often visited their home.[48]

After most of the guests had left, those remaining proceeded to a restaurant hired for the occasion. Once again animosity flared up between those who sympathized with Hakushū and those who felt the celebrations had been in poor taste. Someone switched off the lights, and a brawl ensued in the dark. When the lights were switched back on again, people were dismayed to see that Tetsuo was covered with blood. He was rushed to the hospital where three stitches were required for a cut on his face.[49]

Hakushū was thoroughly embarrassed by the whole affair. Ayako, still unable to forgive Tetsuo and the others for blaming her and too proud to attempt a reconciliation, refused to return home. Friends urged the couple to separate[50] and on June 25, 1920, Ayako and Hakushū were divorced.

The ostentatious manner in which Hakushū chose to celebrate the groundbreaking of his new house caused ill-feeling among his friends and family and precipitated events that neither Ayako nor Hakushū could have foreseen. There is no reason to doubt that the marriage would have lasted if the celebrations had not occurred. Nothing Hakushū wrote in the four years of their marriage suggests there was any strain in their relationship. Indeed, Ayako had uncomplainingly put up with the hardships of their life in Katsushika, and, as far as one can tell, had been a model wife until this point. Her sudden change of attitude remains an enigma.

Hakushū's marriage to Satō Kikuko in April 1921 at last brought stability to his life.[51] His son Ryūtarō was born in March of the following year, and a daughter Kōko in June 1929. For several months after his divorce from Ayako, he had been unable to concentrate on his work. However, during the winter before his third marriage, he took out the manuscripts for *Sparrow's Eggs*.

When he read these tanka, untouched for three years, Hakushū was understandably discouraged. Rewriting all the poems—he was satisfied with only five or six[52]—seemed a formidable task. Tetsuo was worried that if Hakushū did not begin work at once, he would never publish *Sparrow's Eggs*, and he sent a young man from Arusu to help with the copying and rearrangement of the verses. This enabled Hakushū to concentrate on the rewriting. Eight days of hard work resulted in a new manuscript which was sent to the Arusu Press.

Throughout the spring, Hakushū worked on further revisions and wrote more than one hundred new tanka for the "Katsushika Poems" section. By late May, *Sparrow's Eggs* was at last finished. The effort that went into these revisions helped to solidify his ideas on the tanka. He laid out his new approach in the Introduction to *Sparrow's Eggs*, his most important work of poetic criticism since "Paulownia Flowers and Sponge Cake" in *Paulownia Flowers*.

Another illuminating exposition of Hakushū's ideas was *Suzume no Seikatsu* (Life of the Sparrows), a loose poetic journal written a few years before he completed *Sparrow's Eggs*.[53] In this work (which is of far more interest than the fiction he was serializing at the same time) he meticulously recorded the activities of the sparrows he had become so fond of in Azabu and Katsushika. His identification with his subject matter made his descriptions of the sparrows—usually not a compelling subject—revelatory of his aesthetics at the time. The work was also intimately connected with the poems in *Sparrow's Eggs*. Many of the ideas later expressed in the form of tanka there were first expressed here in prose.

The years Hakushū spent at Azabu, Katsushika, and other places in Tokyo before starting work on the final revisions of the tanka for *Sparrow's Eggs* were unhappy. In his numerous accounts of this period, Hakushū described the consolation and diversion he found while watching sparrows near his house. His diversion soon evolved into absorption, and all his waking hours were spent contemplating their movements and attempting to capture his observations in verse or prose.

Why, the reader may justly ask, did Hakushū find the common sparrow so appealing? No doubt the fact that sparrows could be seen at any season outside his window was one factor. However, he could have chosen to write about other natural phenomena. More compelling reasons may be found in *Life of the Sparrows*.

Life of the Sparrows revealed that Hakushū was interested in sparrows precisely because of their drab coloring and unostentatious nature. Simplicity and unobtrusiveness, though often more refined than that of the sparrow, had been aesthetic ideals for many traditional Japanese poets, best expressed by the term *sabi*.[54] Hakushū described numerous scenes where the sparrow embodied this ideal. To cite one example, "Occasionally sparrows fly across a windless sky filled with the cold, icy clouds of midwinter, cutting the air with their wings—the epitome of *sabi*. Even more so if there is only one sparrow."[55] *Sabi*, a new word in his aesthetic vocabulary, occurred frequently in this work. It was probably derived from Bashō's use of the term to describe the restraint of a good haiku. For Hakushū, sabi also characterized scenes, such as the one quoted above, which symbolized the transience of life within nature. These scenes, most often lonely, seemed to capture the essence of his subject matter, in this case a winter day.

Hakushū's interest in sparrows was also related to his concept of the poet. "When you grow intimate with the simple life of sparrows, your heart becomes naturally humble. It becomes pure and simple. Gentle and honest."[56] Humility and simplicity, the traits by which Hakushū had distinguished the true poet in *Concentration*, came naturally to the poet who could give himself completely to observation even of sparrows.

Contemplation of such subject matter enabled the poet to understand the transience of nature. Hakushū, like Bashō, believed that change was the essence of nature and that the quality of a poem could be judged by its success in portraying the impermanence of life. Careful description of the scene at hand was, therefore, not as important as suggesting its significance. No matter how faithful the representation or how true the colors, an oil painting, for example, could never portray the fleeting existence of the sparrow as well as a few quick strokes in monochrome.

> Whatever others may say, I myself believe that the essence of the sparrow is best captured in *sumie*. Sparrows embody the transience of nature, the manner in which life forever changes. This constitutes the essence of the sparrow. All nature ultimately possesses sabi. Long ago Bashō found peace of mind by uniting himself with nature. No other man has experienced the profundity of serene solitude *(kanjaku)* as deeply as he.[57]

Hakushū obviously identified with Bashō during this period. He referred to his year in Katsushika as a period of "serene solitude."[58]

As its title suggests, *Sparrow's Eggs* was largely devoted to poems on sparrows. The following example, one of the "Katsushika Poems," expresses the same conception as the prose passage on winter sparrows quoted above.

Samuzora o	Cutting through the wind
Ichiwa kaze kiru	Of a wintry sky,
Tsubasa no hie	The cold wings of a single sparrow.
Sabi kiwamaru ka	The bird cries in flight
Suzume chichi to naku.	Is this not the essence of sabi?"[59]

This tanka, not one of Hakushū's best, seems to be stating observations which had been better expressed in prose, but its closeness to his stated beliefs reveals the preparation and thought behind each poem.

The numerous revisions to which Hakushū subjected all the *Sparrow's Eggs* tanka make it difficult to uncover now what must originally have been very great differences between the earliest section "Transmigration: Three Parts," based on tanka written just after Hakushū left Misaki; "Sparrow's Eggs," which treated his experiences in Azabu; and the "Katsushika Poems," half of which were composed during the few months before Hakushū completed the collection. Nevertheless, vestiges of the development in Hakushū's attitudes toward tanka may still be traced.

Certain tanka in "Transmigration: Three Parts" recalled *Mica*, particularly those describing the scenery, crops, and animals of Chichijima and those which, like the following poem, described Hakushū's awe at the beauty of natural phenomena, expressed through the use of light.

Tsuki no yo ni	An evening of moonlight.
Mizu o kabureba	I pour water over my head.
Atama yori	Gold, silver, and emeralds
Kongonruri no	Fall in drops
Tama mo koso chire.	Around me.[60]

A number of more lyrical tanka, describing his longing for his parents while on Chichijima or his feelings at the time of his first divorce, were reminiscent of the "Poems of Grief" in *Paulownia Flowers*. This type of lyricism, which directly expressed the poet's personal emotions rather than objectifying them into descriptions of scenery or external events, also characterized some of the tanka in the later sections of *Sparrow's Eggs*.[61] It is probably safe to assume that these works were not submitted to much revision. They remain somewhat out of place alongside his serious tanka on natural phenomena. Although often sentimental, they do seem to speak honestly of Hakushū's emotions and do not suffer from the hyperbole of his Misaki tanka.

By the time Hakushū completed *Sparrow's Eggs*, he considered that *Mica* had been a failure. His reasons reveal the basic difference in his approach at these two times. Fundamentally he felt that his attitude had been too self-centered. "In my haste, I had expressed too much of myself."[62] Because he had been absorbed with his own enthusiasm, his poems likewise failed to describe nature faithfully.

Although it embarrasses me to admit this, *Mica* was a failure. I was consciously trying to destroy the style I had perfected in *Paulownia Flowers*. Like a snake shedding its skin, I could not be satisfied unless once and for all I had effected a personal revolution of that sort. Vigorously and energetically I persisted in forcing everything. I indulged my egoism; exaggerated natural phenomena to an extreme; and used high-flown diction that did not reflect reality....Although these tanka were about Misaki, most of them were written after I had succumbed to the splendid, radiant brilliance of the sky, sunlight, and colors in the Ogasawara Islands. I pranced about, my eyes seeing everything sparkle. When I look back now, I feel that, even with its faults, *Paulownia Flowers* was the better collection.[63]

Although his criticism was rather extreme, *Mica* and the other collections from Hakushū's Misaki period did indeed express a very personal outlook, which took the form of affected language and distortion of the subject matter. Hakushū no doubt worked hard to rid "Transmigration: Three Parts" of these faults, as an examination of the following two poems, the first a shi and the second a tanka, will show.

Hikaru hi urara	The sun glitters brightly on
Mangō hetaru	A sea turtle
Umigame no	Come from eternity.
Kono akirame no	How great is his resignation
Ōkinaru ka mo.	to fate.[64]

—*Pearls*

Hi ni terare	The moss on
Nami ni sarasare	This sea turtle's shell
Umigame no	On which the sun has shone,
Kōra no koke mo	On which the waves have beaten,
Aosabinikeri.	Has taken on a deep patina.[65]

—*Sparrow's Eggs*

The version found in *Pearls*, probably close to Hakushū's original conception, was completely revised for *Sparrow's Eggs*. Both poems conveyed the strength of nature through the image of an ancient sea turtle. However, whereas the earlier version described the turtle in hyperbolic terms, concluding with an exclamation about the resignation to fate which the poet saw symbolized, the later version implied as much with greater subtlety. Words such as *kagayaku* (to glitter) and *urara* (bright), often found in the Misaki poetry, had been carefully eliminated. As an expression of sabi, the tanka compared favorably with the best poems in *Sparrow's Eggs*.[66]

As Hakushū's approach to poetry evolved, his views on language changed accordingly. By the time he wrote the Introduction to *Sparrow's Eggs*, he was taking great pains to make his diction appropriate, natural, and, above all, consistent with the content of his poems.

In a really good poem, the form and content must fuse into a perfect whole. True technique consists in faithfully expressing the contents of one's verse in the form so that the poem will approach that hallowed realm of the truly natural, unadulterated, absolutely essential, full, and purposefully honest and pure.[67]

A single word, if not absolutely necessary and suitable, would spoil the effect of an entire poem so that it failed to suggest sabi, the ephemerality of nature, and the essence of the subject matter.

The poet's success in using language of course depended upon his basic attitude. The poet who "let narrow personal views intrude, who lacked humility, assumed poses, indulged his emotions, or lacked moderation,"[68] —qualities which Hakushū felt had marred his verses in *Mica*—would produce poems that appeared empty and ostentatious.

Hakushū's new approach to poetry was inspired by his discovery of the traditions represented by Bashō and, to a lesser degree, by Ryōkan and other masters of the different Japanese arts.

I feel very close to Bashō, Kōetsu, Taigadō, Rikyū, and Enshū, and the secret principles of the traditional martial arts and Shintō. My earnest desire is to be included someday in their ranks. Artistic refinement is not enough; one must truly return to nature and place oneself within it as it is found in a tree or a flower. Following nature, entrusting oneself to it represents [the fundamental principle of] true art. I have adopted this attitude and can feel myself changing.[69]

Hakushū adopted an aesthetic principle which he recognized as central to certain Japanese arts whether it be Bashō's *haikai*, the pottery and screens of Honnami Kōetsu,[70] the scrolls of Ike no Taiga,[71] the tea ceremony of Rikyū[72] and Enshū,[73] or the teachings of the traditional martial arts. He believed that these artists had approached nature directly; their art resulted from a fusion of themselves with those elements in nature which they wished to portray. Hakushū clearly saw himself as a modern poet in this ancient tradition.

The influence of Bashō, noted in Hakushū's earlier discussions of theory, remained conspicuous. For example, the preceding description of the poet's attitude toward nature calls to mind two famous passages from Bashō on the theory of *haikai*: the opening of *Oi no Kobumi* (Letters from my Backpack) and Bashū's injunction to his disciples in *Sanzōshi* (Three Copy Books).

One fundamental principle is common to the *waka* of Saigyō, the *renga* of Sōgi, Sesshū's paintings, and Rikyū's tea ceremony. This principle—the essence of all art—consists of following nature and communing with the seasons. For the object of the artist's observation must be flowers; the subject of his thoughts the moon. The poet who does not appreciate the forms of flowers [and other natural phenomena] is no better than a barbarian. He whose heart is not moved by flowers is of the same species as an animal. You must leave the realm of barbarians, separate yourself from common beasts to follow nature, to return to nature.[74]

—Letters from my Backpack

Bashō taught that the poet understands pine trees by studying a pine tree in nature and about bamboos by studying a bamboo, by which he meant that the poet must rid himself of personal concerns. You will not comprehend these teachings if you interpret "studying" as meaning whatever you please it to mean. By "studying," Bashō meant that when the poet enters into his subject matter, its essence becomes apparent to him; at this point a poem naturally results.

—Three Copy Books[75]

Hakushū organized his ideas in the same manner as Bashō in *Letters from my Backpack*. His understanding of the relationship of the poet to nature, however, obviously came straight from the *Three Copy Books*, which, together with *Kyorai Shō* (Conversations with Kyorai), is the central source for Bashō's theories of *haikai*. Other principles—that personal concerns interfered with the poet's contemplation of nature, that the poetry of the young or inexperienced was often preferable because of its honesty, that the essence of nature could be found in its changeability—could also be traced back directly to the *Three Copy Books*, particularly the introductory section of "Akazōshi" (Red Copy Book), its second part. Bashō's teachings clearly became a poetic handbook of sorts for Hakushū during the seven years he was working on *Sparrow's Eggs*.

This is not intended to cast doubt on Hakushū's originality. In the process of expanding on the principles first enunciated by Bashō, he added many new conceptions. For that matter, he did not accept all of Bashō's theories; he chose only those which were helpful in developing his new aesthetic. The result was a theory of poetry founded on traditional aesthetics but applicable to modern tanka.

Most critics view the appearance of *Sparrow's Eggs* as an about-face in Hakushū's approach to poetry, as if he had at last reached the proper age—thirty-five—to appreciate Japanese poetic traditions. The return to Japanese traditions by middle-aged writers and others who in their youth were wholehearted admirers of Western culture is so frequent in ordinary Japanese society that it is now accepted as a behavioral stereotype. However, the process is not as simple as it sounds. The change in Hakushū's approach was radical, but not precipitous, as we know from the long time it took for him to complete *Sparrow's Eggs*. Bashō's theories provided a viable model for him but he worked to expand them into a view of poetry that was definitely his own. His tanka were certainly not mere copies of traditional verse. Moreover, his decision to emulate Bashō rather than the *Man'yōshū* or some other classical collection was distinctive; most tanka poets sought guidance from the tanka rather than the haiku of the past.

The Introduction to *Sparrow's Eggs* contained several carefully worded attacks on the Araragi school of tanka,[76] severing the loose ties Hakushū had formed with that group in his Misaki days.[77] Hakushū asserted that faithful description of natural phenomena (*shasei*), the main tenet of the Araragi poets, while a necessary component of good poetry, was by no means the most important.

> Candid observation and honest description is, of course, correct—correct as a basic principle of poetics, yet nevertheless merely a first step. It is from this point that one must start. No matter how honestly the poet observes a phenomenon and how keenly he reflects this in the form of his tanka, his verse, if it does not move the heavens, if it is static, commonplace, and indiscriminating, if it shows callousness of spirit and disregards true musicality, cannot be considered superior as a poem.[78]

The ideal poem had to be more than mere description.

> True art in absolute terms departs from *shasei* for a higher, deeper, and subtler realm. By partaking of true symbolism, it suggests something mysterious and refined. Subjective and objective elements fuse into one to communicate clear echoes of heavenly strains otherwise inexpressible.[79]

Hakushū asserted that the aim of true art was to echo the mysterious and profound, through the poet's penetration into his subject matter, the rhythms of his language, and the symbolism which enabled the brief tanka to suggest large concerns. Needless to say, this type of symbolism was different from that found in *Heretical Faith*, where Hakushū had layered images of mingled sense perception to suggest "moods" and "dreams" of a world divorced from reality. What he tried to express in *Sparrow's Eggs* was, by contrast, reality itself as revealed in nature. Throughout the tanka tradition, particularly in the *Shinkokinshū*, poets had described nature in a way that would evoke their own view of the world or their relationships with others.[80] This was the type of verse that Hakushū had in mind. The implications of these ideas would be explored more fully in the next period of Hakushū's poetry as *shin'yūgen* (new *yūgen*-style verse) and *shōchōka* (symbolist tanka), and would provide the aesthetic foundations for all of his later poetry.

This new attitude must be borne in mind when reading *Sparrow's Eggs*. Take the following tanka, found in "Katsushika Poems":

Hiru nagara	Faintly glittering,
Kasuka ni hikaru	Even though it is broad daylight,
Hotaru hitotsu	A single firefly
Mōsō no yabu o	Emerges from the bamboo grove
Idete kietari.	Only to disappear.[81]

A firefly, at first seen faintly glittering in a dark bamboo grove, flies into the bright sunlight, where it disappears from sight.

Fireflies are among nature's most ephemeral creatures; during their short life span of less than a month, their lights can be seen at evening around small rivers and irrigation canals. However, this tanka is interesting because it describes a firefly in daylight. By chance Hakushū discovered one in the shade of a bamboo grove, but almost before he could take in the fact, the firefly vanished into the sunlight, making his discovery seem even more precious.

At first reading, the poem seems to be purely descriptive. Had faithful description been his aim, however, Hakushū would have rejected such a scene as being too special to convey an impression of reality. The scene appealed to him precisely because it suggested more than what he actually described. It was the atmosphere, with its sense of transience, that interested him, more than the firefly itself.

Traditional Japanese poets had always found ephemeral beauty more appealing than obvious spectacle, all the more so if a scene in some way suggested an ineffable charm or fleeting mood. This aesthetic ideal, variously termed *yūgen* or *yōen* and most fully developed by poets associated with the *Shinkokinshū*, valued mystery, suggestion, and atmosphere. It was those qualities which Hakushū referred to in a later comment on this poem when he said:

> I do not wish you to think about this poem logically. Rather, I would have you approach it intuitively....This verse is not merely descriptive; it is symbolic. I am not saying here that the firefly is something moving or sad. All I have stated is that it emerged from a grove and disappeared. In order to grasp the meaning, you must let the faint, vague mood of the verse touch your heart and then savor this mood exactly as it stands.[82]

The construction of the verse is tight. There is not one word that is not appropriate, natural, and moreover absolutely essential to the meaning, just as Hakushū had advocated in his Introduction. In addition, Hakushū employed the musical qualities of his language, its sound patterns and rhythms, to emphasize the content of the poem. A strong stop at the end of the third phrase, *hotaru hitotsu*, effectively divides the tanka into two parts. In the first half, the vowel sounds "a" and "o" predominate, and this characteristic is carried over into the fourth phrase *mōsō no yabu o*, which ends with a secondary stop. The fact that the firefly could be seen glittering in the daylight created an unresolved question in the first three phrases of the tanka, the answer to which is given here; it was in a shaded bamboo grove. The last line with its "i" and "e" sounds contrasts sharply with the fourth line—strengthening the import of these words which tell of the firefly leaving the grove and disappearing—and at the same time faintly echoes the "i" of the "hi" sounds found in the first three lines in words such as *hiru*, *hikaru*, and *hitotsu*.

Although this is the most famous tanka in *Sparrow's Eggs*, it is not entirely representative, for sabi rather than yūgen best characterized the collection. The middle section, "Sparrow's Eggs," contained a number of nature poems, comparable to those found in the latest section but originally written in Azabu, as well as some very personal tanka where Hakushū referred to his life at home, his parents, and even to the difficulty they experienced in obtaining food. "Kiji no O" (Pheasant's Tail),[83] the best known of the five parts that make up this section, was devoted to poems about his elderly mother and father.

Anakasoka	I can hear so faintly
Chichi to haha to wa	My mother and father
Me no samete	Awake

Nani ka noraseri   Whispering.
Yuki no yoake o.   Dawn after a snowfall.[84]

Hakushū, who had probably been contemplating the serenity of the early morning snow, hears the soft whispers of his parents. Their voices, far from interrupting the scene and his mood, seem to blend into its tranquility. The stop at the end of the fourth phrase divides the verse into two contrasting parts. The sound of his parents' voices and the snowy scene outside at first seem unrelated. When we realize that they both join as symbols of sabi, which is also the mood of the speaker, we begin to see what Hakushū was attempting to say in this tanka.

     This, the first poem of this part, is one of the best. Other verses are more moving; however, it is difficult to avoid the impression that many are sentimental. Hakushū's remorse for causing his parents' suffering is understandable, but when transferred into material for verse, the result was not as successful as his nature poems. He conscientiously applied the principles developed during this period in all his poems except these, where the subjective concerns eliminated from other works were stated perhaps too clearly.

     The best tanka in *Sparrow's Eggs* were in the "Katsushika Poems." For this reason and also because these tanka most clearly illustrated the principles put forth in the Introduction, Hakushū placed them first, though they were written last. The following poem opened *Sparrow's Eggs*.

Susukino no   In the fields of pampas grass
Shiroku kabosoku   A faint white line
Tatsu kemuri   Of smoke rises
Aware naredomo   Poignantly
Kesu yoshi mo nashi. But shows no signs of disappearing.[85]

In its loneliness, subdued colors, simplicity, and suggestion of evanescence, Hakushū's description evoked sabi. The poem was also an excellent example of what Hakushū meant by the fusion of subjective and objective elements. The first three lines portray a winter scene, and the last two explain the poet's feelings about it. He finds the view moving *(aware)* but qualifies his emotions with the last phrase, *kesu yoshi mo nashi;* this line, because the Japanese original does not contain personal pronouns, is open to various interpretations that are not mutually exclusive. The white trail of smoke moves Hakushū because it does not disappear, even though it is so faint he feels sure it cannot last. At the same time, the conjunction *-domo* (but), which separates the last phrase from the rest of the poem, suggests that the scene would have been even more poignant had the smoke ceased while the poet contemplated the scene. A translation of the last two lines incorporating this interpretation would read "moving as it is, nevertheless, the smoke shows no signs of disappearing." Finally, one more problem remains. Why did Hakushū use the transitive form *kesu* (to blot out) rather than the intransitive *kieru* (to disappear)? If his aim was merely to convey the mood of this scene, the latter word would surely have been normal. The verb *kesu* suggests instead that Hakushū wished somehow to make the smoke vanish but could not.[86] Viewed in this light, the poem symbolizes the relationship between the poet and nature; it seems to imply that Hakushū's knowledge of his own limitations, of his inability to compel nature to conform to his expectations, though initially disappointing, in the end brings him closer to an understanding of the workings of nature. The poet must not adapt the reality he perceives in nature to reflect his own concerns—the approach taken in *Heretical Faith* and *Paulownia Flowers*—but instead contemplate it so deeply that his verse comes to convey the essence of what he sees.

Another tanka made bold reference to a haiku by Bashō. Hakushū's confident use of Bashō's turn of phrase seems an affirmation of his special affinity with Bashō.

Haru asami	Spring is young.
Sedo no mizuta no	The green-leaved watercress plants
Midoriha no	Lining the rice paddies
Nezeri wa uma ni	By my back door
Taberarenikeri.	Were eaten by a horse.[87]
	—Hakushū

Michi nobe no	The rose of Sharon
Mukuge wa uma ni	By the edge of the road
Kuwarekeri.	Was eaten by my horse.[88]
	—Bashō

Only a poet who had consciously incorporated so many of Bashō's principles into his own theory would have the daring to make such an obvious allusion to one of Bashō's most famous haiku. Despite the close similarity of the last phrases of both poems, however, the effects are quite different. Bashō's haiku seems more extemporaneous and lighter in tone. The speaker no sooner catches sight of a flower beside the road than his horse devours it, reminding him anew of the evanescence of beauty in nature. On the other hand, the first half of Hakushū's tanka successfully evokes the poet's joy at the arrival of spring through description of the young plants at the edge of the rice paddy, this joy being broken when a work horse eats them. The sight, however, does not so much discourage the poet as suggest the busyness of the farmers at this time of year. The poet Kimata Osamu believed that Hakushū's poem conveyed a deeper feeling for season and painted a fuller picture of spatial scenery than Bashō's, although he qualified his remarks by noting that the limitation of length in the haiku made this all but inevitable.[89]

A large number of tanka on sparrows were found throughout both the "Sparrow's Eggs" and the "Katsushika Poems" sections. During his solitary years of poverty in Azabu and Katsushika, Hakushū carefully observed the movements of the sparrows in his garden, sharing rice from his table with them when there was enough to spare. His tanka on sparrows described in minute detail their activities during each season, their nests, and the way they fly, chirp, feed, and alight on various trees and plants. The following is perhaps Hakushū's best known tanka on sparrows.

Tobiagari	He flies up
Chū ni tamerau	And pauses in midair.
Suzume no ko	A baby sparrow,
Ha tatakite mi ori	Fluttering as he watches
Sono yururu eda o.	The swaying branch.[90]

Here Hakushū successfully captured the vitality of a baby sparrow which pauses after taking flight. The poem comes to a stop at the end of the third phrase, creating dramatic tension which is held and further emphasized in the next phrase describing the sparrow's busy flapping to keep himself suspended as he watches something. The last phrase resolves this tension by at last revealing the object of his attention—the branch from which he had taken flight, still swaying after the thrust of his take-off. The passage of time, barely a moment, has been suspended. This suggests Hakushū's absorption in his subject as well as the young sparrow's as yet unformed approach to his surroundings. Besides being a technical tour de force, this tanka again illustrated the fusion of objective and subjective elements that Hakushū advocated.

In nature poems, such as those quoted above, Hakushū succeeded in putting into practice the views put forth in the Introduction. Although he was successful in that sense, the poems may seem somewhat artificial on closer examination. Those on the firefly and the baby sparrow, for example, both describe rather contrived situations; others can be justified only in terms of Hakushū's conscious attempt to portray sabi and to intimate the essence of nature and its phenomena. To prove that he had indeed penetrated into nature, he described his subject matter too closely, relying heavily on imagery of sense perception, and thereby forfeiting the possibility of portraying nature with a broader understanding.

Hakushū believed that his approach was the only valid way to produce modern tanka which could stand comparison to the verse of the classical tanka tradition. To this end, he consciously assumed the poetic stance of Bashō and adapted Bashō's poetics to the modern tanka. Yet Hakushū's poems do not appear in any way imitative or archaic, despite his adoption of Bashō's ideals and his use of the ancient classical language, a common practice at the time. If his subject matter was not markedly modern, it was certainly his own. No poet had described sparrows in such detail. His material was carefully chosen to accord not with traditional practices but with his own theories of tanka. His sense perceptions, furthermore, remained as acute as ever as he applied them to illustrate this new approach. The same may be said of his sensitivity to language.

During the seven years spent preparing *Sparrow's Eggs*, Hakushū had devoted himself to the tanka and, except for children's verse and folk songs, had refused to write any other form of poetry. If he was determined to create a new style, he was also committed to the tanka as the form in which this change had to occur. With the exception of this period in his life, Hakushū was always involved with both tanka and shi, in contrast to most Japanese poets, who concentrated on one or the other. In *Paulownia Flowers* he had asserted that the modern poet had no choice but to compose both shi and tanka. Cross-influences between the two forms gave his poetry a depth which it might not have achieved otherwise.

CHŌKA: THE ROAD BACK TO SHI

After he completed *Sparrow's Eggs*, Hakushū no doubt intended to expand his new approach to include shi. As early as 1920, the summer before he began work on the *Sparrow's Eggs* manuscripts after a three year hiatus, he found certain ideas that could not be expressed in the short tanka, yet he was not yet ready to write shi. At this time he started to write *chōka*.[91] He published five in June 1920 and another twenty-one in January 1921.[92]

Few Japanese poets had composed chōka during the previous thousand years, and it was all but extinct as a verse form. Hakushū's reasons for taking it up certainly related to its similarities to the tanka. Both forms employed classical diction and a similar rhythmic structure—a combination of alternating phrases of five and seven syllables, ending with an extra seven-syllable phrase. The chōka was thus both an extension of Hakushū's tanka and a logical alternative to shi.

Hakushū might not have noticed the chōka had it not been for the esteem in which his contemporaries, particularly the Araragi poets, held the *Man'yōshū*. It was the *Man'yōshū* tanka, however, not its chōka, which Saitō

Mokichi praised and took as his models. Few other poets actually composed in that form.

Recent scholars have given scant attention to Hakushū's chōka beyond remarking that he composed them and citing one or two representative examples. To write chōka was for a modern poet an anachronism; furthermore, the poems themselves are not particularly noteworthy. In his earliest chōka, Hakushū employed the same subject matter, diction, and tone as in his tanka. He did not try to imitate examples by predecessors like Hitomaro. The only other contemporary poet interested in chōka, Kubota Utsubo, published *Tsuchi o Nagamete* (Gazing at the Ground) in 1918.[93] This work, primarily a tanka collection, also contained some chōka, leading one scholar to credit Utsubo with reviving the chōka.[94] However, credit should in fact go to Hakushū, for his earliest experiments in this form, four poems written in 1916 and 1917, were published earlier than Utsubo's collection. Hakushū seems to have experimented with the chōka on his own, although *Gazing at the Ground* provided him with a precedent for including twelve chōka in *Sparrow's Eggs*.

In 1922, Hakushū published a slim volume of chōka, *Kansō no Aki* (Autumn of Contemplation). In the Introduction, he stated that he had chosen the chōka form because it was the most suitable for expressing what he wanted to say.[95] He also expressed distaste for the free verse being written by his contemporaries, deploring its lack of musicality and characterizing it as "prose divided into lines."[95] He did not approve of the directions shi had taken during the seven years he had spent composing tanka. This suggests another important reason why he took up the chōka.

Takamura (Bamboo Grove), published in 1929, contained all the chōka Hakushū wrote from 1915 to 1928, including a number already published in *Sparrow's Eggs* and *Autumn of Contemplation*. In the early examples in *Sparrow's Eggs*, he had faithfully employed the traditional chōka form. Each poem ended with several envoys, and his language was the classical diction of his tanka. However, by the time he published *Autumn of Contemplation*, more than half were in the colloquial and he had discarded the envoy altogether. The length also decreased. The latest chōka in *Bamboo Grove* were short ones. In several examples he even used a colloquial haiku for the envoy.

For Hakushū, the chōka was an intermediate step between the tanka and the shi. He chose it because he wanted to write longer poems but detested the kind of shi in vogue at the time. By 1922, when he published *Autumn of Contemplation*, Hakushū reluctantly admitted that his chōka could be classified as shi.[96] Furthermore, his first true shi of this period, "Karamatsu" (Chinese Pines), published in November 1921, shows a marked resemblance to his chōka.

Compare the first four lines of "Chinese Pines" with the first five phrases of the chōka "Mōsō to Tsuki" (The Moon and Bamboo):

Karamatsu no hayashi o sugite,
Karamatsu o shimijimi to miki.
Karamatsu wa sabishikarikeri.
Tabi yuku wa sabishikarikeri.

Passing the forest of Chinese pines,
I stared profoundly at the Chinese pines.
How lonely were the Chinese pines.
How lonely it was to travel.
"Chinese Pines"[97]

Sawasawa to yururu mono ari.
Sayo fukete yururu mono ari.
Waga mado no garasu to no soto,
Masukaseba tsuki ni kage shite
Kogoeyuki taezu hashireri.

Something moves and rustles,
At midnight moves and rustles
Beyond the sliding glass door of my window.
I peer out. Shading the moon,
The snow falls ceaselessly.
"The Moon and Bamboo"[98]

What should be evident by comparing the originals of these two poems—indeed, almost any of Hakushū's chōka could have been chosen to illustrate this point—is that Hakushū's metric pattern in "Chinese Pines," his use of repetition, and his diction have been adopted directly from the chōka. The resemblances are too strong to dismiss as merely another example of Hakushū's penchant for transplanting characteristics developed in one poetic form into another, such as we saw in the tanka of *Paulownia Flowers*. The metric pattern, alternating phrases of five and seven syllables, is identical to that of the chōka. "Chinese Pines" could have been included in *Autumn of Contemplation* without appearing to violate the chōka form if Hakushū had added only one more seven-syllable line at the end of the poem. "Chinese Pines" was the first shi Hakushū had published for seven years, but we can only conclude that it was originally conceived of as a chōka.

The five months from August 1921, when *Sparrow's Eggs* appeared, to January 1922, which saw the publication of twenty-one chōka in *Nikkō*

(Sunlight),[99] marked the high point of Hakushū's interest in the chōka. At no other time did he compose so many poems in this form in such a short period. His attention was focused on chōka, not shi, before the appearance of "Chinese Pines." Had Yosano Tekkan not asked Hakushū to submit a poem for the first issue of the revived *Morning Star*[100] in November 1921, "Chinese Pines" would probably have ended up as a chōka.

The fact that the poem appeared in *Morning Star* seems particularly significant. Hakushū might have hesitated to publish an experiment of this sort in another journal, but it was Tekkan who had taught Hakushū that the experience gained in writing one form of poetry could, and indeed should, be employed in other forms. The original *Morning Star* had often published tanka by poets who like Hakushū were concentrating on shi, and shi by tanka poets.

The basic rhythmic unit of Hakushū's chōka was identical to the twelve-syllable unit used as a line in "Chinese Pines." Groupings of four twelve-syllable phrases—the stanza form in "Chinese Pines"—constituted the most common natural unit within these chōka. In this sense, the opening of "The Moon and Bamboo," a five-phrase group, was not representative of Hakushū's chōka. Most of the chōka in *Autumn of Contemplation* did not have envoys. If, as I have suggested, "Chinese Pines" was originally conceived as a chōka, it probably did not have one either. On the other hand, the content of the fourth stanza of the final version (which Hakushū had placed last when he published the poem in *Morning Star*) and of the seventh stanza (the eighth was not added until later) are different enough from the rest of the poem for either one to have originally served as envoys. The envoys of a chōka function to give additional or concluding comments on the scene described in the body of the poem or to present this content from a different angle. Both these verses do just that.

In August 1921, the same month that *Sparrow's Eggs* appeared, Hakushū visited Hoshino Hot Springs at Karuizawa, Nagano Prefecture to lecture on children's poetry to a group of over one hundred teachers at the Summer Institute on Free Education.[101] He stayed with Yamamoto Kanae at his summer home, newly built nearby. This visit provided the inspiration for "Chinese Pines," and he probably wrote a first draft of the poem either in Karuizawa or directly after he returned home.

We know that Hakushū composed the version found in *Morning Star* in October 1921, one month before it was published.[102] There is no record of an original draft, but it is difficult to imagine that Hakushū wrote a poem in October describing impressions of two months earlier. Some sort of draft for "Chinese Pines" was surely written in August, presumably in the form of a chōka. When he received a request from Tekkan for a poem, his first inclination was probably to submit a chōka, but before long he realized that a chōka would disappoint the readers of *Morning Star* who remembered the shi he had published in that magazine some fifteen years earlier. As he worked over "Chinese Pines," he saw how easily it could be revised into a shi. Hakushū was thus induced by Tekkan's request to return to a form of poetry he had seemingly abandoned.

"Chinese Pines" received immediate acclaim, much to Hakushū's surprise. Its success, in Hakushū's own words, "prompted me to return once again to the shi."[103] He immediately began to write other poems in this form, and in June 1923, two months before *Autumn of Contemplation* appeared, he published his sixth collection of shi, *Suibokushū* (Poems in Monochrome).

"Chinese Pines" is known today in its final version, the form which appeared in *Poems in Monochrome*.

Chinese Pines

1

Passing the forest of Chinese pines,
I stared profoundly at the Chinese pines.
How lonely were the Chinese pines.
How lonely it was to travel.

2

Coming out of the forest of Chinese pines,
I entered the forest of Chinese pines.
Entering the forest of Chinese pines,
Again the narrow road continued.

3

Deep in the forest of Chinese pines,
There was the road which I would take.
It was a road of misty rain.
It was a road of mountain winds.

4

The road in the forest of Chinese pines
Had been traveled by others before me.
The road was narrow and forlorn,
A lonely road which bade one hurry.

5

Passing the forest of Chinese pines,
My steps grew stealthy. I cannot say why.

How lonely were the Chinese pines,
Whispering with the Chinese pines.

6

Leaving the forest of Chinese pines,
I saw the smoke rising from Mount Asama.
I saw the smoke rising from Mount Asama
Above the forest of Chinese pines.

7

The rain in the forest of Chinese pines
Was lonely, making the forest still.
There were only the calls of the cuckoos.
There were only the sounds of wet Chinese pines.

8

Oh world, how sad you are.
Inconstant yet joyous.
In the hills and rivers, the sound of mountain streams.
In the Chinese pines, the wind of Chinese pines.[104]

The most remarkable fact about this poem, when set alongside the tanka and chōka that Hakushū had been composing about the same time, is the clear description of the speaker that emerges. By endeavoring to fuse subjective and objective elements in his tanka, Hakushū had effectively blotted out almost any suggestion of his personal feelings about his subject matter. In this poem, however, we have a clear statement of the speaker's relationship to his material, a forest of larch (translated here as Chinese pines), over which he sees in the distance the outline of Mount Asama, an active volcano sending up plumes of smoke.

The poem describes the speaker, a visitor to Karuizawa, walking along a narrow path which winds in and out of the pine forest. In the fourth stanza, this path comes to symbolize for him the road of life—a road traveled by others yet nevertheless not an easy road to travel on, a road that "bade one hurry." Leaving the forest again, he looks back at it, this time sensing something mysterious and yet appealing in the solitude of the trees rustling in the wind. Suddenly his field of vision broadens to include Mount Asama, smoke rising from its peak, standing above the pine forest.

In the seventh stanza, the scenery changes again as it begins to rain, reminding the speaker once more of the loneliness of the forest. In conceits reminiscent of Hakushū's tanka, the rain is described as making the forest seem quieter; only the cuckoos' calling and the rain falling on the pine trees can be heard.

The statement which concludes the poem was not originally part of it; when the poem was first published in *Morning Star*, the fourth stanza had been placed last. Adding this last verse, in which the speaker comments on the significance of his walk, not only provided a fitting conclusion, but also gave an added dimension to the poem in the speaker's revelation of his joy at the inconstancy of the world. Although most Western poets would have felt grief at discovering the world to be transient, Hakushū felt pleasure, like any number of earlier poets in his tradition.[105] Up to this point, the loneliness of the scenery was stressed, although a strong argument could be made that in repeatedly using the word *sabishikarikeri* (was lonely), Hakushū meant in addition to emphasize the elements of sabi in the scene; he had frequently used the word in *Life of the Sparrows* to describe similar scenes which had moved him to thoughts of the transience of nature. But although this attitude was implied in the tanka of *Sparrow's Eggs*, nowhere had he stated it as strongly as in the last stanza of "Chinese Pines."

If Hakushū had published this poem as a chōka, no one would have been surprised by the archaic diction, but readers had come to expect shi to be written in a more modern idiom. Certain contemporaries objected to the poem because they felt that its diction proved that Hakushū had lost touch with the times.[106] Nevertheless, old-fashioned as his diction was, it was wholly appropriate for expressing the traditional approach to nature he had adopted. Such sentiments belonged to the world of the tanka or the chōka, and if he had attempted to treat them in free verse, the poem would have lost its effect. Furthermore, the archaic diction allowed Hakushū to explore the special musicality of the literary language. The mournful sound of long inflected words like *sabishikarikeri* and the soft flow of *yamato kotoba* (words of purely Japanese origins) in the use, for example, of *hayashi no michi* rather than *rindō* (both meaning "forest road") had no counterpart in the colloquial.

The sound of the words in "Chinese Pines," one of Hakushū's most celebrated poems and certainly the most famous of his later works, was at least as important as the meaning. Its strong rhythm was further emphasized by repetition, a technique Hakushū had employed in his chōka. The word *karamatsu* (Chinese pines) occurred in three out of four lines in each of the first two stanzas, in the beginning line of every other stanza but the last, and at the start of several other lines also. Furthermore, within each verse, the line endings were also frequently repeated. The climax of the poem, both in meaning and rhythm, comes in the sixth stanza with the repetition of the line *Asamane ni keburi tatsu mitsu* (I saw the smoke rising from Mount Asama), when the speaker leaves the forest and sees the mountain outlined against the sky above the pine trees.

A strong stop after *yo no naka yo* (Oh world) in the first line of the concluding stanza signals a change in tone here. The poem ends gracefully with the repetition of *yamakawa* (hills and rivers) and *karamatsu*, reminiscent of this tanka from *Sparrow's Eggs:*

Kono yama wa	On this mountain
Tada sōsō to	All I can hear
Oto su nari	Is the rustling of
Matsu ni matsu no kaze	Pine winds in the pines
Shii ni shii no kaze.	Oak winds in the oaks.[107]

Repetition was balanced by a soft lyricism made possible by the use of the literary language with its variety of inflections. The total effect was one of pleasing musicality. Many composers immediately petitioned Hakushū for permission to set the poem to music. In reply, Hakushū published an open letter "To Certain Composers" in the first issue of *Shi to Ongaku* (Poetry and Music)[108] in October 1922, declining these offers and expressing the belief that the effect of the poem would be diluted if made into a song. Hakushū also stated that "Chinese Pines" and his other shi were to be regarded as serious poetry, categorically different from his folk songs, which by their nature were meant to be sung.[109]

The short preface to "Chinese Pines" in *Poems in Monochrome* should be interpreted in the light of this episode:

> The haziness of the Chinese pines and the pathos of the lonely wind that faintly blows through them must touch your soul. Remember this. The wind and its whisperings are the whisperings of my soul. Reader, this poem should not be read aloud. Its reverberations and nuances must be appreciated as they are.[110]

Hakushū intended the sound of his words to reflect the loneliness and poignancy of the soft rustling wind in the pines. The rhythm was so strong that he feared it would prevent the reader from giving due attention to the meaning. This was the reason he did not want the poem to be read aloud or, for that matter, to be set to music.

Despite its success as a poem, "Chinese Pines" was in many ways a paradox. Employing to the fullest the musical qualities of the literary language, it expressed a traditional approach to nature. Yet at the same time, Hakushū warned against being carried away by the rhythm, thereby dismissing one important reason for the poem's success. The last stanza, moreover, concluded on a modern note, which reminds us that if Hakushū conceived of nature in the manner of traditional poets, he was consciously fitting himself into a role. Hakushū in 1921 was himself a paradox.

Although it was still possible to write tanka with these attitudes, the shi as a form had, during the seven years Hakushū stopped writing it, begun to show signs of full maturity. The first evidence came with the publication of *Tsuki ni Hoeru* (Howling at the Moon) by Hagiwara Sakutarō in January 1917, in which Sakutarō established once and for all that the colloquial Japanese language could be used sensitively and indeed musically to express modern thoughts.

Sakutarō was a poet in the symbolist tradition, although not himself a charter member of the symbolist movement, which in Japan primarily designated works by Ueda Bin, Kanbara Ariake, Susukida Kyūkin, Hakushū, and Miki Rofū[111] and coincided with the last flowering of poetry in the literary language. Working with the elegant diction of Bin and Ariake, which was weighted with words borrowed from the classics of Japanese literature, Hakushū had created a new poetic idiom to describe the emotions of modern youth. Sakutarō, however, went further, to express not only modern emotions but also to hint at the psychological workings which underlay these emotions in the free rhythms of his colloquial verse. With *Howling at the Moon*, which appeared eight years after *Heretical Faith*, symbolism entered the movement to develop a modern colloquial poetry, and it continues to this day to be an important aesthetic as demonstrated in the works of such poets as Hinatsu Kōnosuke (b. 1890), Yoshida Issui (b. 1898), and Kaneko Mitsuharu (b. 1895).

Hakushū wrote a long introduction to *Howling at the Moon*, expressing his admiration for Sakutarō as a person and as a poet.[112] He responded fully to the innovations in language and the depth of Sakutarō's probing into often neurotic themes. Yet at that stage in his life, Hakushū was no longer interested in writing Sakutarō's kind of poetry. Hakushū's experience writing tanka had confirmed in his mind the importance of traditional aesthetics. He could not share Sakutarō's enthusiasm for the colloquial language or modern subject matter. In the Epilogue to *Poems in Monochrome*, he included a paragraph explaining his position, which can be interpreted as an apology to poets like Sakutarō for his traditional approach to the shi.

> My style has undergone numerous changes. When I remember the wild period of *Heretical Faith* and *Memories*, I cannot help but wonder where the bewildering exuberance of those collections has gone. However, at this point, I have no intention of returning to the style of my youth. Not only would it be impossible but, should I try, my style would be fraudulent. In any case, I have arrived at my present approach

to poetry, finally reaching these conclusions after experiencing
many tragic and complicated vicissitudes as a man and as a
poet. Of course, today, I have gained the perspective to enable
me to look back upon myself in these years. (There are few
people who can truly appreciate the significance of this.) I
believe that my style in those days was completely appropriate
for that time. In that sense, my position today is also the only
one possible for me now.[113]

In his early poetry Hakushū had stood at the forefront of his age. *Heretical
Faith* had transformed symbolist poetry in Japan into a form which spoke of
and to modern youth and *Memories* had inspired a flowering of lyrical
poetry. When he chose, however, to take a more traditional approach in
Poems in Monochrome, Hakushū consciously allied himself with traditional
forces at a time when Japanese poets of shi were striving to create a truly
modern style. The paradox of this position, which Hakushū inevitably had
to take, would be reflected in *Poems in Monochrome*, where the colloquial
and the literary language, modern and traditional subject matter, and modern
and traditional viewpoints co-existed, often, as was the case with "Chinese
Pines," in the same poem.

POEMS IN MONOCHROME

Poems in Monochrome is a voluminous work, containing 176 poems,
divided into fourteen sections. Hakushū obviously intended to produce a
companion volume of shi to his tanka collection *Sparrow's Eggs*, where he
would put into practice the ideals learned from Bashō.

> My shi today are lonely (*sabishii*), the majority brushed in ink
> like *sumie* landscapes. In addition, I continue to be moved by
> the freshness of reality. The fact that I chose to express the
> spirit of my shi in the simple black and white of ink paintings
> was inevitable. At this point in my life, this is the only path
> left open to me. Needless to say, I am using the same brush
> in these ink paintings as I did for my former paintings in
> color, and these colorations lie intimately mingled deep within
> the black ink.[114]

Just as the colors, emotions, and tone of his tanka had noticeably softened
with *Sparrow's Eggs*, his shi would likewise be brushed in India ink instead
of the heavily colored oil paints and the bright red and glittering gold of his
early poetry. Nevertheless, despite this radical change in style, the poet

himself remained, of course, the same. His material was different; his approach had changed remarkably; however, his sensitivity to the sounds of language and his reliance on imagery of sense perception attest to the identity of the man whose brush produced such different pictures.

Most of the verses in *Poems in Monochrome* were cast in the colloquial; however, this fact alone did not make them modern. After the publication of *Howling at the Moon*, all but the most conservative poets of shi had abandoned the literary language, and the next five years saw enthusiastic experimentation in colloquial verse. It was not only a matter of the language of poetry; young poets had begun to demand that verse speak of contemporary concerns. For example, those in the Minshushiha (People's Poetry Group),[115] the most active group then, felt that poetry should treat the daily life of the ordinary citizen.

Switching to the colloquial presented no difficulty to Hakushū, for he had already written a large number of folk songs and poems for children in the modern language. The colloquial shi in *Poems in Monochrome* displayed the same lyricism and strong rhythmic sense found in his early verse. These qualities had been extolled and imitated a few years earlier, but the fast pace at which poetry was developing made them now seem dated. Young poets, led by those associated with the People's Poetry Group, condemned musicality in poetry, which they considered to be incompatible with their subject matter. Hakushū's opposition to their position was made clear in 1917 with his withdrawal from the Shiwakai (Group to Discuss Poetry), a loose federation of Taishō poets,[116] and again in 1922, when he took a stand against Shiratori Seigo and Fukuda Masao, two leaders of the People's Poetry Group, in the pages of *Poetry and Music*.[117]

Hakushū also defended musicality in "Geijutsu no Enkō" (Halo of Art), the long preface to *Poems in Monochrome*.[118] Free verse, he insisted, did not mean abandoning rhythm in poetry. Rhythm, of course, no longer conformed to set patterns; instead it had to reflect the content of the poem. Rhythm gave form to the poet's expression of his experience contemplating nature. Prose was like the ordered steps of a march; the movement of a poem had to be more subtle.[119]

Hakushū coined a new term, *kihin* (refinement), to describe a good poem. He also used this word to designate the essence of natural phenomena. A grasshopper or a snail, an apple or a tree, each had particular qualities innate to it alone. The poet's job was to capture this essence (kihin) in his poem; he could not do this if he had not developed the ability to forget himself and personal concerns in contemplation of nature.[120] Kihin, therefore, also characterized the true poet. It could not be imposed on a poem through its diction, rhythm, or techniques, but rather resulted naturally when the poet expressed his observations in truly appropriate language. A poem could suggest or symbolize something otherwise inexpressible, but only if the poet himself was able to view nature as if he had never seen it before and express his thoughts in language as fresh and vital as his experience.

Poems in Monochrome opened with a series of poems on the snow, inspired by an unusually heavy snowfall in Odawara in January and February of 1923—fitting subject matter for depiction in India ink. These poems, among the latest in the volume, proved that Hakushū's experience writing chōka continued to influence his shi. For example, the first poem in the series, "Yuki ni Tatsu Take" (Bamboo Standing in the Snow),[121] showed marked similarity to the chōka "Moon and Bamboo" quoted above. Both poems were lyrical descriptions of bamboo in the snow, although the chōka's focus was the sound of the bamboo rustling at night, whereas the shi's was the shadows cast by the bamboos on a sunlit expanse of new snow. Hakushū had abandoned a formal rhythmic pattern and the literary language in his shi, but his treatment and diction reflected the traditional approach found in his chōka.

In the second section, "Suibokushū" (Poems in Monochrome), from which the collection took its name, the influence of his chōka was less apparent, but his material was definitely traditional—the ancient sages, artists, and poets of China and Japan. His interest had broadened to include, besides Bashō, who was still an important influence, Saigyō, Sōgi, such painters who worked in India ink as Sesshū, Tanomura Chikuden,[122] and Wang Wei, and a number of Chinese poets and sages, including the Seven Sages of the Bamboo Grove and Lao Tzu.[123] In numerous poems about these artists, he praised their approach to art and the elegant simplicity of their works. These poems were in the colloquial, but it was the formal diction used in books and newspapers, distinguished from conversational Japanese by forms like *de aru* rather than *da* or *desu*.

The collection also contained a series of twenty-two tanshō, entitled "Gekkō Biin" (Soft Echoes of Moonlight). The form was, of course, the same as that found in *Pearls*.[124]

2

Tsuki no yo no	The smoke from my cigarette
Tabako no kemuri	On a night of moonlight
Nioi nomi	Purple
Murasaki nari.	In fragrance.[125]

7

| Tsuki no yo no | Under the moonlight |
| Shiroi shiroi mukuge ni | White, white mallow flowers |

| Kage sasu mono wa | On which bamboo leaves |
| Sasa no ha. | Cast silhouettes.[126] |

11

Chō no tobu	Butterflies wing
Mizuta akari,	Over luminous rice paddies
Sono sue wa	Beyond which lies
Tsuki no yo no umi.	The ocean on this moonlit night.[127]

18

Tsuki kage sura mo	Even the moonlight
Itakaramu,	Seems painful.
Asu hiraku akaki	The pointed tip of a red
hachisu no	lotus bud
Tsubomi no saki yo.	Which will bloom tomorrow.[128]

These poems displayed the same concern with atmosphere found in his tanka; however, here it was not sabi but kihin, the refined beauty of the moonlight, which Hakushū attempted to suggest. His language was closer to the colloquial than the examples in *Pearls*, but he did employ the literary language occasionally, as in number 18.

Hakushū's use of sense imagery was striking, although tempered somewhat in comparison with his early poetry. The bright moon illuminated the scenery, changing its appearance by accentuating the white color of the mallow flowers, on which could be seen the soft outlines of small bamboo leaves, or the whiteness of the butterflies fluttering over rice paddies glittering under the full moon. In the first and fourth poems quoted here, Hakushū employed imagery of mingled sense perceptions: the cigarette smoke was described as smelling purple, and the sharply pointed tip of a lotus bud and the bright moonlight seemed painful.

In "Setsugo no Koe" (Call after a Snowfall), another poem from the opening series on snow, Hakushū employed conversational diction; his imagery, techniques, and treatment were also distinctly modern.

Call after a Snowfall

A cicada is singing on this moonlit night
In the brightness of the snow.
How could that be? That
Unseasonal ringing, the sound of a call.

Everything is so silent,
So distant, so indistinct.
Once more, a string of gold snaps.[129]

The poem opened with a striking image—a cicada calling out from a snowy scene, bright under the moonlight. The piercingly clear sound of the call merges with the white glow of the snow to form an image of mingled sense perception; what it refers to is not stated. Cicadas sing not in winter but in late summer; therefore, the sound the poet hears must be imagined. He awakes from his reverie with a very apt and extremely colloquial expression in the third line: *Nan to shita koto da* (How could that be?). The second verse tells us the inspiration for his reverie—the overpowering silence of the night. The poet again begins to dream, and hears once more the sound, described this time as the snapping of a golden string.

Juxtaposition of unrelated images and synesthesia are techniques not found in Hakushū's tanka in *Sparrow's Eggs* or his chōka. These were techniques that he had employed in his early collections but discarded when he developed the new approach of *Sparrow's Eggs*. "Call after a Snowfall" was also distinctive because of its personal tone, which is related to Hakushū's use of a conversational diction. For example, in the opening phrase of the poem, *kanakana ga naiteru* (a cicada is singing), he employed a contraction of the verb *naite iru;* this is a form that occurs only in conversation. We seem, therefore, to be hearing Hakushū talk about a personal experience. Hakushū did not use this conversational style in his poems on artists or nature, but reserved it to relate the mundane events of his daily life: breakfast in his garden,[130] going out into a summer field without taking his cigarettes or a hat,[131] or burning leaves with his wife.[132]

Hakushū remained sensitive to the sounds and rhythms of language, and more often than not we find him singing rather than conversing about ordinary events. Of course, his poems were not written as songs, and Hakushū forbad composers to set them to music. However, many of the poems in *Poems in Monochrome* read as refreshing affirmations of lyricism in an age that had denounced this type of poetry.

Poems in Monochrome concluded with "Nobara ni Hato" (Doves and Wild Roses),[133] usually counted among the best two or three poems in the collection. Here Hakushū experimented using a lyrical style and colloquial diction to describe his despondency on a spring day. Each of the ten stanzas began with two lines of onomatopoeia, approximating the cooing of doves, and the language of the poem was almost distressingly rhythmical. It is a glorious spring day. Wild roses bloom in his garden, and the doves coo contentedly. However, these things only serve to make him more depressed, as he imagines how the flowers will wilt, the season will end, his dreams fade away, and finally, his own death.

"Doves and Wild Roses" was the only poem of its type in *Poems in Monochrome*. It was also a rare example of a modern Japanese colloquial poem that successfully treated modern concerns in a lyrical fashion. The poem was, nevertheless, an anomaly for its age and an anomaly even within the context of Hakushū's own poetry. To use the techniques of traditional lyricism to express traditional concerns was one thing; it was another to use these same techniques to treat the concerns of modern human beings.

The fact that Hakushū was able to do just that bespeaks the fundamental paradox of his position in modern Japanese poetry at this time. He represented in so many ways the very antithesis of all that his contemporaries valued. He advocated an approach based on traditional aesthetics, while they strove to formulate modern theories; he defended lyricism and rhythmic verse, while they were busy denouncing them. The fact that he succeeded in composing good poems, despite these handicaps, documents both his genius and his commitment to his ideals.

5

ODAWARA AND TOKYO
1923-1937

Four months prior to the publication of *Poems in Monochrome* in June 1923, Hakushū and Shimaki Akahiko (1876-1926), a leader of the Araragi Tanka Group, began a literary feud, their famous "Mohō Ronsō" (Argument concerning Imitation). The result would make Hakushū a major figure in the growing group of poets in the anti-Araragi camp.

Hakushū, as already related, had been close to Saitō Mokichi and the Araragi Tanka Group during his Misaki days. He had published a large number of his tanka from this period in their magazine *Araragi*, beginning in January 1914 and culminating with the appearance of 112 tanka in the May 1916 issue. The Araragi poets, particularly Saitō Mokichi, had actively sought Hakushū's friendship, urged him to publish with them, and written favorable reviews of his tanka. Hakushū and Mokichi's decision to bring out selected collections of each other's tanka attests to the depth of their friendship.

Before these collections could even appear in print, however, critics had begun to take notice of the association between Hakushū and the Araragi poets. The November 1916 issue of *Teikoku Bungaku* (Imperial Literature) stated bluntly that Akahiko and the other poets of the Araragi Group were being influenced by Hakushū.[1] Akahiko reacted strongly to this. In the January 1917 issue of *Araragi*, he asserted that his tanka and Hakushū's represented patently different approaches to the form and therefore defied comparison, ending his discussion with the famous remark: "Hakushū has his own way, and I have mine. By admitting our mutual incompatibility, we will show respect for ourselves and for the world of poetry."[2] This article announced in effect that the group no longer desired to associate with Hakushū.

Akahiko had become the leader of the Araragi Group after the death of Itō Sachio (1864-1913). As editor in chief of *Araragi* he developed his own theory of *shasei*, which expanded on Masaoka Shiki's much simpler advocacy of tanka that reflected reality and stressed the importance of studying the tanka found in the *Man'yōshū*. In the vacuum left by the decline of previously influential tanka groups, the Araragi Group assumed a central position in contemporary tanka circles. At the same time, Akahiko's sometimes dogmatic assertions and his concern for maintaining the purity of the Araragi Group gradually worked to isolate it. This background helps to explain why Akahiko desired Hakushū to keep his distance. To admit to any influence from a poet outside the group would threaten its autonomy, undermine Akahiko's own position, and cast doubt on the integrity of his theories.

Hakushū touched on this problem in the preface to his *Saitō Mokichi Senshū* (Selection of Saitō Mokichi's Tanka), finally brought out in January 1922.

> In his Introduction to *Kitahara Hakushū Senshū* (Selection of Kitahara Hakushū's Tanka), Saitō Mokichi seems troubled over irresponsible accusations that his tanka imitate mine. I feel sorry to see Mokichi put in such a position. Akahiko, too, was forced to defend himself several years ago when *Kiribi* (Flint Sparks) was criticized as being modeled on *Mica*. I also sympathize with Akahiko's plight. Nevertheless, we were all born in the same period, pursued similar careers as poets, and in a spirit of friendliness have exchanged verses and held many pleasant discussions. In this sort of relationship, we naturally influenced each other, inevitably so because of our sensitivity as poets.[3]

Hakushū's position was a logical one: poets of the same generation were necessarily influenced by common cultural undercurrents and when closely associated with one another, as he and the Araragi poets had been, were bound to exert a mutual influence. Hakushū contended that this did not damage their poetic integrity.

Saitō Mokichi, who might have tempered Akahiko's combative attitude, was studying medicine in Europe from 1921 to 1924. Meanwhile, Akahiko became increasingly offensive in his attempts to maintain the authority of Araragi, striking out at Maeda Yūgure[4] and other poets and groups, thereby earning criticism even within his own clique.

Then, in the February and March 1923 issues of *Araragi*, Akahiko openly attacked Hakushū's essay "Kōsatsu no Aki" (An Autumn for

Thought), which had appeared in the October 1922 issue of *Poetry and Music*.[5] The famous dispute had begun. During the rest of this year the two poets denounced each other in print, Akahiko publishing his attacks one month in *Araragi*, followed by Hakushū's response the next in *Poetry and Music*.

"An Autumn for Thought" was one of a series of essays by Hakushū on modern poetry, published monthly in his capacity as poetry editor for the magazine; it did not differ notably from others in the series. Why Akahiko chose to find fault with this essay in particular remains puzzling. He singled out one section in which Hakushū had compared several of his own tanka to some haiku by Bashō and upbraided Hakushū for likening himself to Bashō. His choice of examples was petty, and he even stooped to misquoting two of Hakushū's tanka in the process.

Except for his carefully worded remarks in the Introduction to *Selection of Saitō Mokichi's Tanka*, Hakushū had disdained to respond to Akahiko until then, although he had no doubt been perplexed by Akahiko's abrupt severance of ties in January 1917. The appearance of Akahiko's two attacks, however, brought forth a vigorous response. In "Donguri no Kotoba" (On Acorns), which appeared in the April 1923 issue of *Poetry and Music*, Hakushū answered all of Akahiko's points of criticism, quickly reaching the conclusion that Akahiko's attacks stemmed from a deep-rooted desire to discredit him. The essay concluded with the assertion that if Araragi tanka suffered from rigidity and unoriginality, it was thanks to Akahiko's policies. The Araragi Group, Hakushū concluded, was losing its appeal and influence in tanka circles because of Akahiko's intolerance toward poets who did not conform to his standards.[6]

As Akahiko and Hakushū continued their dispute, Akahiko became increasingly dogmatic and kept on misquoting Hakushū's tanka, seemingly on purpose. The content of the dispute did not change in these later exchanges; both participants stubbornly defended their established positions. The argument was followed closely by contemporary tanka poets, and most of those who did not belong to *Araragi* sided with Hakushū.

The Araragi Group continued to occupy a central position in the tanka world. Its policies toward outsiders did not become less belligerent until after Akahiko's sudden death in 1926. But by 1924, Akahiko's readiness to sacrifice personal associations with poets inside and outside the Araragi Group and to condemn, for the sake of maintaining the authority of his group, any tanka that did not comply with his rigid views of poetry created such animosity that it led to the creation of *Nikkō* (Sunlight),[7] a new magazine.

Sunlight AND THE Colloquial Tanka

Sunlight was begun by a large group of tanka poets who were weary of the endless controversies associated with the Araragi Group and sought more relaxed relations with other poets, as well as an organ where they could freely express their individual poetic styles without fear of censure.

Their purpose, stated in the first issue, was deliberately vague: *"Nikkō, our Sunlight,* whose radiance is all-pervading. Today we join hands in friendly association under this sunlight, and bathed in its warmth, we breathe the pleasant fresh air of our various artistic fields."[8] The group did not profess any common principles aside from optimism about the value of the tanka and a desire to publish its members tanka freely. Beneath a surface friendliness, however, lay very real differences; discord between major poets and their factions over how much space to allow to one member or another was to force the magazine to stop publication and the group to disband after barely three years.

Two months after *Sunlight* began, Hakushū, who was both a founder and editor of the magazine, wrote an essay on its purpose, stressing its differences from the ordinary tanka magazine, which published only the poetry of the faction that supported it.

> The poets of the Sunlight Tanka Group did not unite for the purpose of forming one more faction among tanka circles. What we desired was, in fact, a magazine of standards that would allow us to be sincere in our verse and relaxed and open in our relations with others. This sort of tanka publication has never existed before. There have been many magazines for factions centered about one teacher and many trade publications directed toward novices. The former represents a faction; the latter is a composite publication directed at the general public. Our group, founded on mutual friendship between all the members, fully recognizes the right of each poet to develop freely and at the same time desires to foster each member's individuality in a relaxed and genial manner.[9]

Sunlight published tanka of literary merit, regardless of the author's poetic principles. Poets were respected as individuals, exchanged their views concerning the tanka, and stimulated one another to produce a wide range of tanka of high literary value in both the colloquial and the literary languages. The formation of this group, which included three former members of Araragi—Koizumi Chikashi, Ishihara Jun (1881-1947), and

Shaku Chōkū (Origuchi Shinobu, 1887-1953)—and others, such as Hakushū, Maeda Yūgure, and Toki Zenmaro, who openly opposed it, reflected the widespread resistance among poets to Araragi's inflexibility and belligerent policies.

Hakushū occupied a central position in the Sunlight Tanka Group from its inception to its demise in December 1927. During this period, he wrote monthly essays on poetry, later collected and published as *Kisetsu no Mado* (Window to the Seasons),[10] and a large number of tanka, many of which were inspired by the numerous excursions he took during these years. He also embarked upon and some important experiments in colloquial tanka.[11]

Hakushū had first become interested in writing colloquial tanka in the early half of 1923, when he was particularly friendly with Maeda Yūgure. It was Yūgure's enthusiasm for three tanka, written in a conversational style and divided into lines, which Hakushū sent to him in July 1923, that stimulated Hakushū to publish a series of colloquial tanka in the August 1923 issue of *Poetry and Music*.[12]

In April 1923, Hakushū visited the town of Ōya, in Nagano Prefecture, to attend the ceremonies for the opening of the Nōmin Bijutsu Kenkyūjo (Research Institute of Peasant Art) managed by his brother-in-law, Yamamoto Kanae. After the ceremonies he spent two weeks traveling in the area with his family. The August 1923 issue of *Poetry and Music* contained a long series of traditional tanka, "Shinano Kōgen no Uta" (Tanka concerning the Nagano Plains),[13] 267 poems in all, followed by a series written in the colloquial, "Nōmin Bijutsu no Uta" (Tanka on Peasant Art),[14] concerning the ceremony he had attended, the participants, and the rural scenery.

The contrast between the two series was striking. The tanka in the first were written in the literary language, printed in the traditional one-line form, and arranged in sections with headings to designate the places they treated. Those in the second were remarkably original experiments in colloquial tanka, each printed conspicuously in three to six lines. These justly famous poems, which described Hakushū's impressions at the ceremony in a refreshingly intimate manner, astonished readers, just as they had surprised Maeda Yūgure, bringing Hakushū to the forefront of the colloquial-tanka movement.

Kaze da, shigatsu no	Feel the wind, the fine sunshine
Ii kōsen da,	Of April.
(Miro, Kikuko yo)	(Look, Kikuko!)
Shinsen na ringo da,	It's a fresh apple.
Tabi da,	We've been traveling.
Shinano da.	We're in Shinano.[15]

In these verses, Hakushū freely added extra syllables to the thirty-one syllables of the traditional tanka and cut his poem into lines where a phrase came to a natural stop. His use of *da*, the conversational form of the verb *de aru* (to be), not only strengthened the colloquial flavor of the poem but by being repeated five times made the poem quite rhythmic. Hakushū was using the colloquial language both naturally and poetically, with a facility that must have surprised those who knew only his more traditional poetry. This facility with the colloquial, the most striking feature of these tanka, was no doubt developed while writing folk songs and children's poetry. In *Window to the Seasons* he also advised serious poets of colloquial tanka to study the folk songs of the Tokugawa period, the language of which was closer to the modern colloquial than to the classical literary language of poetry.[16]

Prior to this time, the colloquial-tanka movement had been torn by disputes between those who felt that the traditional form of the tanka should be maintained and those who were ready to sacrifice it in order to employ modern Japanese more freely. The dispute was further complicated by the consideration of lines: some poets wished to print their poems in the traditional one-line form, others favored a set number of lines, most often three, and still others divided their poems into lines according to the natural dictates of sense. Proper subject matter was also a matter of much debate, with poets at one extreme writing on traditional subjects only, even though they used the colloquial, and poets at the other extreme insisting that modern tanka had to deal specifically with the daily life of modern people.

In this context, Hakushū's experiments startled his contemporaries by their refreshing naturalness. He was the first tanka poet to employ completely colloquial diction, and his flawless use of language demonstrated once and for all that the tanka form would have to be expanded to allow for extra syllables if poets were to employ the colloquial naturally.[17]

Hakushū wrote a large number of colloquial tanka for *Sunlight* and together with Maeda Yūgure, Shaku Chōkū, Ishihara Jun, Yashiro Tōson, and other poets associated with the magazine who were experimenting in this idiom, gave *Sunlight* a significant place in the history of the modern colloquial tanka. In June 1924, he published "Kōgoka ni tsuite" (Concerning Colloquial Tanka) in *Sunlight,* explaining his ideas on the form.

> The traditional tanka of thirty-one syllables in the literary language of course deserves our respect.
> However, colloquial tanka will and must evolve, if only because it is the kind of verse demanded by our times.
> Unfortunately, the majority of those who advocate colloquial tanka do not understand the fundamentals of the

colloquial language—its nature, its rules, and rhythms—and do not clothe their ideas in appropriate expressions. For these reasons, their poetry is in effect a wasted effort. I speak here of those colloquial tanka that read like translations.

If one merely changes classical language into colloquial, this is after all simply translation.

In order to write a colloquial tanka, the ideas for one's poem must be conceived of in the colloquial. There is no reason, therefore, for a poem to read like a translation.

A colloquial tanka will not necessarily conform to the thirty-one syllables of a traditional tanka; the majority of colloquial tanka contain too many syllables. This is because our modern language is not as concise as the literary language, in essence making extra syllables inevitable. From my own experience, I have found that three syllables soon become four, seven become eight.

To force the language to conform to thirty-one syllables kills the rhythm.

The form of a poem necessarily grows out of its content. Most contemporary poets of colloquial tanka ignore this and instead try to bend the colloquial language to fit into a traditional form. This is pure ignorance.

Those who assert that modern tanka must be written in the colloquial but do not understand the importance of this fact seem to be racking their brains over a task which, contrary to their expectations, can only damage the colloquial language.[18]

Hakushū understood the demands of the colloquial language more clearly than most of his contemporaries. To make it conform to rules established for tanka in the literary language was, he realized, impossible. The only justification for colloquial tanka was that the poet had subject matter which, by its very nature, could not be expressed except in that form. Hakushū's experience writing folk songs and poems for children in the colloquial gave him a decided advantage. His colloquial tanka were far more fluent than those composed by poets with less experience.

OUT OF THE WIND AND EDGE OF THE SEA

Hakushū's interest in colloquial tanka did not preclude composition of tanka in the literary language. On the contrary, during his last three years in Odawara, from 1923, when he published *Poems in Monochrome*, to 1926, when he moved back to Tokyo, he wrote a great many traditional tanka, stimulated by the exchange with other poets in the Sunlight Group, encouraged by the happiness of his home life after so many years of hardship and poverty, and motivated by a strong desire to break away from the constraints he had placed upon himself in *Sparrow's Eggs*.

Hakushū did not publish the tanka from this period as separate collections. It was not until several years after his death that Kimata Osamu compiled and published two volumes: *Fūinshū* (Out of the Wind),[19] containing tanka, originally published in contemporary magazines, which described Hakushū's life at Odawara from 1923 to 1925, and *Unazaka* (Edge of the Sea),[20] containing travel poems and colloquial tanka published in magazines from 1923 to 1927. Hakushū had published a small portion of these tanka in the third volume of *Hakushū Shiikashū* in 1941 and in his comments there explained his reasons for not publishing these two collections of poetry.

> I have easily more than two thousand tanka for this period. I wrote many verses, in fact overproduced to a large extent. For this reason, the long time later required for revising the poems in the end so overwhelmed me that they got quite out of hand.[21]

In later years Hakushū, confronted with the task of rewriting and editing the immense number of tanka he produced during these years, found it increasingly difficult to assemble them into collections that would meet his high standards. It is also true, as he said, that during the years in Odawara, encouraged by a happy home life and a secure position in poetry circles, he wrote excessively. Very few of these tanka merited inclusion in a collection.

At 12:58 P.M. on September 1, 1923, a tremendous earthquake struck the Tokyo area, and its powerful tremors caused untold damage. The epicenter of the earthquake was close to Odawara. Hakushū's house was partially destroyed: the tiles were knocked off the roof, and a main pillar split, causing the whole structure to list. Hakushū and his family immediately set up temporary living quarters in the bamboo forest adjoining the house. One part of *Out of the Wind*, "Taishinshō" (Earthquake Poems), records the tanka from this period of his life.

Taishō jūninen	On the first of September
Kugatsu tsuitachi	In the twelfth year of the Taishō era,
Kuni kotogoto	All of Japan
Furue tōreri to	Trembled under an earthquake.
Nochiyo imashime.	Let later generations be forewarned.[22]

Meushi tatsu	Cows graze
Mōsō yabu no	In the sunlight
Hi no hikari	That filters into our bamboo grove.
Kasukeki jishin wa	Faint tremors from the earthquake
Mada tsuzukurashi.	Still seem to be continuing.[23]

Hakushū also wrote haiku recording these events.

Takebayashi no	The eyes of cows
Ushi no me yo yoshin	In our bamboo forest. After-tremors
Shikiri furu.	Continue without interruption.

Hi wa kasuka ni	In the faint sunlight
Shingo no fuyō	After the earthquake, the rose
Nao akashi.	mallow flowers
	Seem redder than ever.

Takebayashi no	In the cool
Hiyayaka no ko to	Of a bamboo forest
Suwatteru.	I sit with my child.[24]

Although the tanka are in the literary language and the haiku largely in the colloquial, they describe the same scenes: the cows who shared the bamboo grove with Hakushū and his family, and the red mallow flowers that bloomed, unaffected by the quake. The fact that the earthquake had all but destroyed his house, far from discouraging Hakushū, obliged him to live, as he had desired, in closer contact with nature.

Even these poems, which were among the earliest in *Out of the Wind*, contrasted sharply with the tanka in *Sparrow's Eggs*. This was due, first of all, to the different subject matter. In *Sparrow's Eggs*, Hakushū had treated primarily "poetic" subject matter, lonely scenes that expressed the impermanence of nature. The poems in *Out of the Wind*, however, concerned the mundane events that made up his daily life. He did not attempt to suggest that these events had wider significance than what they described. In place of the cold sketches of scenes epitomizing sabi, he wrote warmer, more human, and more spontaneous verse.

Out of the Wind contained a number of poems about Hakushū's son Ryūtarō. The pleasure Hakushū took in life during this period derived in no small part from his relationship with the four-year-old boy.

| Hashiru kisha | "Draw a moving train |
| Kureon de kake | With my crayons," |

To iu ko yue	Said the child,
Ware wa kaki ori	So I am drawing
Hi o taku tokoro.	By the lighted fire.[25]

Sora wa mite	A child,
Atamagachi naru	Only his head showing,
Ko ga hitori	Looks up at the sky
Arakusa no ka no	In the sunny stillness
Teri no shizukasa.	Of a field of fragrant wild grass.[26]

The language used in the first example is very close to the colloquial, and the predominance of "k" sounds suggests the crackling of the fire beside which father and son play. The second poem is the first in a series "Kusa no Kaori" (The Smells of Wild Grass), which begins the "Sansō no Kisshū" (The Beginning of Autumn at Our Mountain Home) section of the collection. Hakushū's portrayal of this autumn scene—the large head of his son conspicuous in the wild grass of a field—shows subtle use of sense perception. In the last two phrases, *arakusa no ka no teri no shizukasa*, Hakushū employs the possessive particle *no* to connect images of sight and smell with the silence of the sunny field.

The tanka found in *Edge of the Sea* were written during approximately the same period as those in *Out of the Wind*. The formal division of the tanka from this period into two volumes was not, in fact, made until many years later, in 1941. *Edge of the Sea* and *Out of the Wind* are in every sense companion volumes, remarkably similar in style, approach, and subject matter.

The second section of *Edge of the Sea*, "Shinano Ryojō" (Traveling in Shinano), contained poems inspired by Hakushū's trip to Nagano in April 1923. After attending the opening ceremonies of Yamamoto Kanae's Research Institute of Peasant Art, described above, Hakushū and his family spent several weeks relaxing at hot springs in the area. On the way back to Tokyo, they stopped at Usui Pass, beyond Karuizawa. His family then went on to Sakamoto to wait for Hakushū, who had decided to walk the six kilometers along an old road over the mountain.

In Oiwake and Kutsukake in northern Nagano, the new green buds on the larch trees had barely begun to show; the wind whistled in the dry brushwood and pampas grass; and the sun shone on the dreary decay of winter. However, to my surprise, when I reached the south side of Mount Usui, there were eddies of new leaves in reddish gold and vivid green. From the north side of Mount Myōgi back to where I was standing, numberless mountains rose up from the smoky mist, sparkling together. Here and there rock azaleas wove their blazing colors into the scenery. In one place the azaleas formed a mountain peak of flowers; their red and purple colors cut the intense blue expanse of sky. I stood, amazed at the remarkable transformation from winter to spring.[27]

Although the various places where Hakushū stopped all provided inspiration for tanka, the most famous poem in this series—indeed for this period—resulted from his experience walking over Usui Pass to find spring waiting in all its glory on the other side.

Usuine no	I have reached
Minami omote to	The southern face
Narinikeri	Of Mount Usui.
Kudaritsutsu omou	As I walk down the mountain,
Haru no fukaki o.	I ponder
	The intensity of spring.[28]

The stop at the end of the third phrase helps to emphasize the poet's joy at having reached the southern face of the mountain. The object of his thoughts as he starts on his way down is not revealed until the final phrase, so that the poem's construction accentuates the dramatic quality of his experience. The value of this and many of Hakushū's other travel poems is greatly enhanced if the reader knows the area. In this case, without the background provided by Hakushū's description of his walk, one cannot fully appreciate the poem's import.

The title *Edge of the Sea* was taken from the section of the same name, which contained tanka written about a trip to Hokkaido and Sakhalin in July and August 1925. The tanka poet Yoshiue Shōryō (1884-1958),[29] who through friends had learned of this trip sponsored by the Ministry of Railways, induced Hakushū to accompany him. Hakushū's observations during the trip provided inspiration for the tanka found in this section, for a number of poems in his next collection of shi, *Azarashi to Kumo* (Seals and Clouds),[30] and for a travel diary entitled *Fureppu Torippu* (Raspberries and Blackberries).[31]

RASPBERRIES AND BLACKBERRIES, SEALS AND CLOUDS

Hakushū's purpose in traveling to northern Japan, as recorded in *Raspberries and Blackberries*, was not originally to gather subject matter for his poetry.

> On this voyage, my interest was not necessarily either in places of poetic association where I could ponder the sadness of things or in the attitude of the poet of elegance who searches for signs of poignancy in the world. My only desire was to lose myself, body and soul, in the smoky mists of the north, which I had not yet seen. I wanted to satiate myself with a feeling of carefree travel.[32]

During this trip, indeed during this period of his life, Hakushū firmly rejected the attitude toward poetry he had developed while writing *Sparrow's Eggs*. Although in his criticism he continued to laud Bashō, Ryōkan, and the concept of sabi, Hakushū was no longer attempting to imitate the poets of the past either in his personal life or in his tanka. Confidence in his established position and optimism concerning the new directions his poetry was taking allowed him to relax his stance and react more naturally to his environment.

> The artist should maintain an attitude of confidence. He should not compromise when compromise is not required. Those who yield ground in their dealings with others are weak, and their remarks and behavior can easily become tainted. However, if despite their weakness, they persevere, the situation will resolve itself. By vacillating they become impure. Self-composure and steadfastness should mark the artist's relations with others.[33]

If he had become introspective while working on *Sparrow's Eggs*, his attitude changed once the collection appeared in print. By attacking Shiratori, Fukuda, and the People's Poetry Group and standing his ground against Araragi, particularly Shimaki Akahiko, he had recovered the position of leadership relinquished while writing *Sparrow's Eggs*. His self-assurance no doubt encouraged other poets like Maeda Yūgure to share his enthusiasm for the tanka.

The tanka inspired by Hakushū's trip to Hokkaido and Sakhalin treated subject matter that would later be seen in the shi in *Seals and Clouds*. The following poems were from two subsections, "Kamo" (Wild

Duck) and "Dattan Kaikyō" (Tartar Straits). The Tartar Straits, or Mamiya Straits, are Japanese names for the body of water separating Sakhalin from the Siberian mainland, otherwise known as the Gulf of Tartary.

Dattan no	The black horizon
Unazaka kuroshi	Of the Tartar Sea.
Harobaro to	A steamship crosses
Koeyuku fune no	Into the distance,
Fue hibikasenu.	Sounding its horn.[34]

Tsuratsura ni	Smoothly
Kamo no ukikuru	A wild duck comes floating
Ao no nami	On a green wave.
Uneri ōkiku	How huge they seem now,
Mienikeru ka mo.	Those undulating breakers. [35]

Uneri no	A wild duck slides down
Fukaki kubomi e	Into the deep hollow
Suberu mishi	Behind a breaker,
Moriagaru nami no	And then comes riding up the wave
Kamo no norikuru.	As it surges.[36]

The shi "Kamo" (Wild Duck), found in *Seals and Clouds*, treated the same subject matter.

Wild Duck

1

A duck. A duck. A duck
Comes sliding up
From the hollow behind a large swell.
From the deep deep bottom of the sea,
A massive wave surges up.
On the incline of the wave, the duck rolls and is rolled.

2

The duck, look.
How yellow his bill is! Vivid yellow.
Facing sideways,
He stops. The peak of the wave reaches its height
And without forming a whitecap descends broadly.

Horizontally
The world stretches into the distance.

3

The duck sliding
Falls suddenly into the hollow of a large wave.
There is no wind. The waves roll gently.
   He ruffles his feathers.
His intelligent eyes
Shine.
A large swelling wave
Hides the duck.
I imagine his figure
In the invisible valley beyond,
Moving as he passes through the fearful, dark
Hills of waves.
Complete tranquillity.
The modesty of the purple markings on his head.

4

The duck, rolled by the waves,
Again appears. Yes. He is there, there.
He comes riding up on a large, magnificent wave.
"Hey, hey," I want to call out to him.
He floats in perfect form.
"Bravo! Banzai!"

5

The duck entrusts himself
To the will of the huge swells.
In the middle of the boundless Tartar Sea,
The small webbed feet of the duck,
His closely set breast down,
Blazing deep green.

6

Just one duck.
The rays of the sun grow more distant as we travel
   north.
The sky extends coldly.
The clouds are thick.
The waves do not glitter.

As far as the eye can see, lusterless waves,
Visible on all sides,
That truth,
Rolling in large umbrageous swells.

7

The duck floats quietly.
His beak is pure yellow.
Rocking, riding, sliding,
The small, harmonious,
Beautiful, precise
Shape of the duck.
One intelligence.
One perfect existence.
He disappears, falling away from me.
And appears again, again.
The shrill sound of
A finger whistle. Mine.

8

The duck entrusts himself to the waves,
Riding on the large swells,
Which rise up, rise up,
Rocked by their massive, deep strength.
The duck's quiet eyes are open.
The primordial sea, the cold Tartar sky
Of summer in the north.
In all directions
The waves,
Uninterrupted waves,
Dark, lusterless,
Fearful, yet gentle.
The succession of rolling, swelling waves.
Damn it all!
Ass of a duck!
Night is come. Night is come.[37]

Most of Hakushū's previous poetry had described certain motifs: ennui and melancholy in *Heretical Faith*, reminiscences of youth in *Memories*, sabi in *Sparrow's Eggs*, and his attraction to traditional approaches to art and poetry in *Poems in Monochrome*. The tanka and shi from this period, however, describe his subject matter directly, with no motifs or poses intervening between the poet and his material. Although this was in part a natural reaction against an approach to poetry for which he had not yet found any substitute—a breaking away from the constraints he had imposed upon himself while writing *Sparrow's Eggs*—more than anything else Hakushū's poetry at this time documents his facility with the forms of poetry, a facility so natural that he no longer had to depend upon theoretical underpinnings to justify his manner of composition. Viewing the relationship between the poet and his material in terms of poetic distance, Hakushū seems to be standing closer to his subject matter at this period than ever before. The speaker in his poems is not the melancholy young man of Meiji or a modern Bashō, but Hakushū himself.

This is particularly true of the tanka he wrote in Odawara. Hakushū no longer tried to fit his observations into the pattern dictated by his understanding of sabi. A certain artificiality that characterized even the best tanka in *Sparrow's Eggs* had vanished. His observations remained keen, but the range of his lens opened up, as he allowed himself to record his subject matter more naturally, free from the pressure of maintaining a pose. In addition, forced use of imagery of mingled sense perception was noticeably absent, and the tone of his tanka became warmer.

The character of the speaker that emerges in the shi has many similarities to the man who appeared in the conversational poems of *Poems in Monochrome*. Absorbed in the scene before him, he reacts excitedly to the movements of the duck, calling out and even whistling at him. The poem opens with an announcement of his sighting of a duck riding the large waves in the sea before him. On board ship, with nothing in the vast expanse of gray ocean and sky to occupy his attention, the speaker attaches particular significance to the duck. The repetition of the word "duck" three times in the first line of the poem suggests his excitement. After a detailed description of the duck, its yellow bill, and the way it rides the waves, in the third stanza the duck disappears behind a wave. Even as he imagines the duck's appearance now, the poet waits for him to reappear. In the next stanza, he exclaims to himself as the duck again comes into view (*miete kuru, a, deta, deta*), and finally, unable to contain his joy, shouts "Bravo! Banzai!"

In the fifth and sixth stanzas, the poem describes in fuller detail the duck and the dark ocean scenery, with its large clouds and dull gray swells, preparing the way for the explanation of the significance of the duck for the poet in the seventh stanza. A large number of exclamations, unavoidably lost in translation, indicate his excitement in finding here "one perfect existence," perfect in the harmony between the duck and the sea, in the way he entrusts himself to the waves, and in the intelligence and beauty with which nature has endowed him. The speaker again loses sight of the duck, and when it appears once more he whistles out in joy. The eighth stanza returns to description of the floating duck, the dark sea and cold sky, and the continuous succession of gray rolling waves. In the last three lines, meant to be humorous, the sky grows dark, all but hiding the duck, who has turned away from the poet.

The poem may also be interpreted on a more symbolic level. The poet obviously sees himself mirrored in the duck. By comparing his relationship to nature with that of the duck to the sea, the poem suggests that only when living close to nature—by allowing themselves to participate in its changes —do both the poet and the duck reveal their true characters. This approach was similar to that in the Introduction to *Sparrow's Eggs*, but Hakushū's understanding of the poet's relationship to nature had changed in one important way. No longer did he suggest that the poet should attempt actively to penetrate nature; instead, he entrusted himself to it in the same way that the duck allowed himself to be borne along by the waves.

"Wild Duck" was modern free verse in the sense that it was in the colloquial and its rhythms changed freely with each line and were not dependent upon five- and seven-syllable groupings. Hakushū used the colloquial naturally, at the same time skillfully grouping his words into phrases that suggested the rhythm of the rolling waves. Of the several examples of free verse in *Seals and Clouds*, "Wild Duck" was by far the most successful.

Hakushū's attitude toward free verse, however, remained remarkably conservative, his experiments with it for the most part too timid to attract much response from more innovative contemporaries. In his criticism of this time, he devoted many pages to justifying his own inclination, chastising other poets for neglecting rhythm in their free verse.

> The essence of free verse can be defined as expressing through the rhythms of one's language the internal rhythms of one's subject matter. Free verse, therefore, is never absolutely free. In poetic expression, poetic rhythms appear of their own accord, but the poet should not allow them to be unrestrained or vague. Poetic rhythm, furthermore, can never be even like the rhythms of prose.[38]

For Hakushū rhythm was basic to poetry, the main characteristic distinguishing it from prose. In writing free verse, the poet had to create new rhythm which would reflect the "internal rhythms" of his subject. This seemed a much more difficult task for him than writing in the traditional 5, 7 syllable rhythms.

The large number of poems in set forms or variations of the familiar 5, 7 syllable rhythm in *Seals and Clouds* is more evidence that Hakushū was in fact more comfortable writing traditional rather than free verse. Some of the best poems in the collection were only four lines, each line twelve syllables (seven plus five syllables). These poems represented, at least in form, a return to the imayō used in *Platinum Top*.[39] Those poems had often gone beyond the four lines of the pure imayō, but now in *Seals and Clouds*, Hakushū returned to the original four-line form, and used it to describe the transience of nature in an extremely lyrical manner. Nor did his lyricism depend on traditional diction, for there were examples in both the literary language and the colloquial.

Ate no Nai Shōsoku

Ate no nai shi demo kakō yo.
Wataridori kuru hiyori nara,
Mado ni oto suru shigure nara,
Take no jinenjō, tsuta no hana,
Toritome no nai aki naraba.

Message to Nobody in Particular

I want to write a poem for nobody in particular.
If fine weather brings migrant birds,
If cold rain strikes the window,
If autumn comes bursting on the scene
With the flowers on the wild potato vines that
    wind among the bamboo.[40]

Tsukiyo no Kaze

Aki wa honoka ni nezame shite,
Aware to omou ikuyo sa zo.
To sureba shirō fukitachite,
Tsukiyo no kaze mo kieyukeri.

Wind on Moonlit Nights

Autumn awakens softly.
How many nights have I sensed its poignancy?
In the wind stirring whitely in the moonlight,
Starting to blow and then dying out.[41]

Both poems treat the coming of autumn and, except for the addition of an introductory first line in "Message to Nobody in Particular," conform to the set rhythm of the imayō. The poetic conceptions, the language, and the imagery, however, are not characteristic of the *Ryōjin Hishō*, Hakushū's probable source for knowledge of the imayō, but of the tanka. This, together with the aural beauty of the poems, suggests that Hakushū's gift for composing in the traditional five- and seven-syllable rhythms and his training in the tanka was once again exacting a strong influence on his shi. (The use of an image of mingled sense in the second poem—the autumn "wind stirring whitely"—was, of course, unusual for him at this time.)[42]

Hakushū's sensitivity to the sound and rhythm of poetry, cultivated while he was working on *Sparrow's Eggs*, had become even keener by this period. Evidence can be found in all his poetry, but short verses like those above best document Hakushū's genius in this area.

In the Afterword to *Seals and Clouds*, written in 1929 just before the volume was published, he wrote:

> In poetic expression at its very best, the words appear to flow forth naturally like breathing. Form without form, colors somehow unreal, indescribable fragrances, voiceless voices, I make these the speech of my heart. I abhor the use of unusual or fabricated ideographs. After all, the importance of poetic expression is to be found not in the appearance of words but in their sounds, in the undulations of unheard sounds which are not lost even if the poem is read aloud. The best techniques are the purest. I dislike jarring noises—fine pebbles of sound which grate against the tongue—and I loathe carelessness and ostentation.[43]

Hakushū's absorption with sound was by no means typical at the time. Many of his contemporaries considered that the appeal of poetry was primarily to the eye, rather than to the ear. Such careful attention to sound and rhythm constituted the most obvious characteristic of *Seals and Clouds*, especially in the short poems.

Hakushū also divided the poems into three broad categories: poems adapting Shinto tenets to modern concerns, those in a "modern yūgen style," and others concerning his daily life.[44] The collection was more varied than this implies. It contained poems in many different forms and lengths, using both the classical language and the colloquial, on a wide range of subjects. Hakushū's classification, however, is of interest because it indicates the type of poetry he had consciously tried to compose.

In the most important of these categories, the poems Hakushū himself felt to be the most innovative, he attempted to express in modern terms the essence of ancient Japanese Shinto.

> I summoned up the *Kojiki*,[45] *Nihon Shoki*,[46] *Fudoki*,[47] and *norito*[48] from the distant and vast realms beyond the wind clouds, and prayed sincerely with the strength of my words for the revival of the ancient gods. I am fervently searching for illumination and symmetry in these modern times.[49]

Hakushū's personal rediscovery of the Japanese poetic tradition had begun with Bashō during the years writing *Sparrow's Eggs* and by the time *Poems in Monochrome* appeared, also included other poets and artists of Japan and China, particularly certain painters of ink landscape. Between 1923 and 1929, when he wrote the shi included in *Seals and Clouds*, Hakushū delved even deeper into his past, back to the most ancient sources of his tradition.

The *Kojiki, Nihon Shoki,* and *Fudoki* contained poetry recorded in the course of narrating various legends. This, together with the *norito*, especially attracted Hakushū, who made studied use of its parallelism, heightened diction, grandeur of tone, and declamatory style. Hakushū's approach was much the same as the one he had used for material associated with the early Tokugawa Christians while writing *Heretical Faith*. In both cases he was selective, borrowing from the earlier periods in order to produce modern poems whose mood suggested their predecessors.

"Minakami" (The Source of Water) opened *Seals and Clouds* and began the chapter "Kodai Shinshō" (New Eulogies to Ancient Times), in which the majority of the Shinto poems were found. The poet stands at a natural spring contemplating the primeval state of nature. In his imagination, the ancient gods once again assume form.

> We should give thought to the source of water.
>   Pure water flows from the moss.
>   The sun's rays pour down
>   Through the rhododendron and oak branches overhead.
>   The leaves of a holy camellia mirror-bright
>   sanctify the place.
> We should give thought to the source of water.
>
> We should give thought to the source of water.
>   The mysterious presence of the mountain
>   shines forth.
>   The rocks remain silent.

Crouching, bare-faced and rough in spirit,
The gods take form and gather here.
We should give thought to the source of water.[50]

Primitive Shinto was basically simple nature worship which attributed divinity to such awesome manifestations of nature as conspicuously large trees, unusual rocks, and mountains. It stressed ritual purity attained by ablution with water. The spring described here contains the elements of sanctity—pure water which gushes from deep beneath the earth, amidst a mountain scene of trees and rocks. In this setting the poet imagines an assembly of ancient gods.

Hakushū used many archaic words borrowed from his sources. The fifth line, for example, uses the prefix *ma-* (true) twice, a common feature of primitive song, and describes the camellia as *kagamiha no yuzu matsubaki* (the holy camellia with its mirrorlike leaves). The deliberately archaic diction, like *kototoi* (speak), *arasuhada* (barefaced), and *kami musubi, kami tsudoeru* (the gods take form and gather) found in the second stanza, has its source in ancient texts and gives a special dignity. The description of scenery in each stanza is set between the refrain *minakami o omoubeki kana* (we should give thought to the source of water). The characters for minakami 水 上 indicate that its meaning is the natural source of water, here a gushing spring which symbolizes the vitality of ancient times. A second meaning, usually written with different characters, is "god of water"; the refrain also contains this overtone.

"Kōtetsu Fūkei" (Landscape in Steel), was a completely modern poem in the colloquial language, deifying the steel which provided the structure for the large bridges, buildings, and machines of the modern age.

Landscape in Steel

A god exists in the insulators of steel towers.
A god exists in the oblique lines of a crane.

A god exists in the tops of steel poles.
A god exists in the arch of a steel bridge.

A god exists together with the clear sky.
A god exists in the glitter of steel.

A god exists in modern landscapes.
A god exists in the clangor of iron plate.

A god exists in mysterious steam boilers.
A god exists, turning with the motors.

A god exists, running with armored tanks.
A god exists, exploding with shells.

A god exists in sharp circular blades
Whose sawing sounds rend the sky.

A god exists in the holy noises of a dynamo.
A god exists, momentarily emitting electric sparks.

A god exists in the iron structure of theatres.
A god exists in the May Day celebrations of steel
    workers.

A god exists in the ruts made by wheels
Whose grating noises devour roadside vegetables.

A god exists in endless railroad tracks.
A god exists, reverberating in the thunderclouds.

A god exists in the solid forms of cubism.
The expressionists forge and bend the city.

A god exists, hauling with dignity.
A god exists, vigorously producing magnetism.

A god exists. His heavenly form is iron ore.
A god exists, burning hotly in flames.[51]

With three exceptions, each line of the poem begins with the phrase
kami wa aru (a god exists). The lines are grouped in pairs and exhibit
internal parallelism, often employing the same grammatical particles or verb
forms. As the poem progresses, this parallelism becomes more intricate,
breaking away from the simple two line parallelism of the first eight lines.
The rhythm of the poem is tight.

Early Shinto had sanctified manifestations of nature's power. Hakushū
similarly attributed divinity to the steel found in the dynamic structures and
machines of modern times, applying the animistic approach of Shinto to
modern material culture. His god, steel, was meant to be understood as a
modern Shinto god.

The novelty of this approach, the realism and modernity of imagery, the conciseness of language, and the rhythmic use of parallelism made this poem one of the best in the collection. Hakushū directly and effectively confronted contemporary subject matter. Unfortunately, this poem was unique in *Seals and Clouds*, a lonely monument to his positive attempt to write truly modern poetry.

The modern eulogies to Shintoism were the most innovative poems in *Seals and Clouds*. Hakushū distinguished two other categories: poems in a modern yūgen style, and poems whose subject matter was taken from his daily life. The latter, by far the largest group, contained short lyrics, colloquial verses about his family, and the majority of the poems written about his journey to Hokkaido and Sakhalin—in fact, all the poems that did not fit into the two more specific categories.

The poems in a modern yūgen style occurred in four of the thirteen sections of *Seals and Clouds*. They displayed a stronger affinity to the poems on moonlight and snow in *Poems in Monochrome*[52] than to the other poems in *Seals and Clouds*, both in their subject matter and in their predominantly lyrical tone, which owed much to Hakushū's experience writing tanka. Take the following, an ode to whiteness.

White

Things that strike my eye: mountain magnolia
    flowers,
The white breast down on a flock of plovers.

In summer, rocks and white peonies,
A pair of doves shining white.

In autumn, white birch trees on a moonlit night,
Deer standing in the white fog of a mountain forest.

Clouds that fly across the sky in winter,
A sorcerer taking form in a crane.

On a mountain peak, which bespeaks divinity,
The refinement of the snow echoes serenely.[53]

This is a list of things which attracted the poet's notice because of their whiteness. After the first two lines of introduction, they are arranged according to season. The images suggest not the sabi of his tanka in

Sparrow's Eggs but another aesthetic ideal, yūgen (mystery and depth), an ideal developed by Fujiwara Shunzei (1114-1204) and Fujiwara Teika (1162-1241) and characteristic of the style of the *Shinkokinshū*.[54] In his later tanka collections, yūgen would become a major poetic ideal for Hakushū; the first glimmerings can be seen in *Seals and Clouds*.

MODERN LANDSCAPES AND YUMEDONO

Hakushū spent eight years in Odawara, from 1918 to 1926, the only time in his life when he actually owned his own home. Had his house not been irreparably damaged during the earthquake, he would probably have remained in Odawara much longer. He moved back to Tokyo in May 1926, settling in a rented house across from the cemetery attached to the Tennōji Temple, near Ueno.

Throughout his life, changes in residence and travels provided important new inspiration for Hakushū's poetry. In the past, a major move such as that from Odawara to Tokyo had often signaled the beginning of a new style of poetry; his move to Tokyo at this time undoubtedly reflected a conscious decision to change the direction of his poetry. Hakushū immediately showed a renewed interest in the shi and in November 1926 founded a new magazine, *Kindai Fūkei* (Modern Landscapes), devoted exclusively to it.[55] Editing *Modern Landscapes* inspired new developments in his shi, and it was for this magazine that he wrote the most important poems later included in *Seals and Clouds*. "The Source of Water" appeared here in February 1928 and "Landscape in Steel" in July of the same year.[56]

Unlike *Poetry and Music* or *Sunlight*, magazines Hakushū had edited along with other writers, *Modern Landscapes* was his own magazine. Its purposes, stated in the first issue, were vague: in poetic language he called upon his contemporaries to join his enthusiastic attempt to portray modern landscapes in the shi form.[57] Hakushū did not need to define the magazine more specifically; his own conservative approach to poetry was well known. Furthermore, the contributors would no doubt be those poets who were already close to him, either as disciples or friends. Hakushū also had private reasons for wishing to publish a magazine of shi at this time:

> I have been hoping for a long, long time now to have a maga-
> zine of my own. This will give me the opportunity to concen-
> trate [on developing my shi]. To repeat myself, I will gladly
> work all night every night if it is for this magazine. It will be
> my pleasure. After all, this magazine is the forum for my
> work. I trust that my readers will not mistake my intentions
> and my enthusiasm for youthful ambition.[58]

Hakushū was forty-one years old when he began *Modern Landscapes. Poetry and Music*, it will be remembered, had folded in 1923, leaving him without a journal to edit. Other magazines accepted his work, but Hakushū wanted his own publication to assure him of a place to publish his shi and, as important, to force him to write the poetry and criticism he felt he was ready to compose. Hakushū did not write productively secluded in his study; he required the stimulus of association with other poets.

In less than a year, Hakushū moved again. At Tennōji, he had no study of his own to work in; furthermore, its convenient location encouraged visitors and Hakushū was not able to write without interruption. In March 1927, he found a house on the outskirts of Tokyo in Ōmori. The clean air and undefiled countryside no doubt also spurred the move. Although he was pleased with his new residence, he stayed in Ōmori barely a year before he moved once again in April 1928, this time to Wakabayashi in Setagaya Ward, in order to be closer to Seijō Gakuen, the school his children were attending. The house and garden were spacious and the rent extremely reasonable;[59] however, it was situated close to a main thoroughfare used by military vehicles. The constant noise of this traffic disturbed Hakushū, and after three years he moved once again, to Kinuta in Setagaya Ward in May 1931. The new house was within walking distance of his children's school.

During these five years, Hakushū continued to travel widely, as one can easily gather from the contents of his seventh collection of tanka, *Yumedono*,[60] which takes its title from the famous eighth-century octagonal chapel in the Hōryūji Temple complex at Nara. Hakushū had visited Nara with his wife and children in April 1929, directly after returning from a forty-day trip to Manchuria and Mongolia under the auspices of the South Manchurian Railway Company.[61] In a preface note to the section of poems "Nara no Haru" (Spring in Nara), he wrote that "my forty-day journey to the desolate areas of Mongolia and Manchuria seems to have been for the sake of making Hōryūji Temple seem more beautiful."[62] Not only was he happy to return to native soil; during his absence, spring had arrived in the warmer climate of Nara.

Sumire saku	Spring seems best at Yumedono
Haru wa Yumedono	Where violets bloom
Hi omote o	Under the strong sunshine
Ishikida no me ni	In the dry clay soil
Kawaku hanitsuchi.	Between the stone steps.[63]

It is doubtful that Hakushū would have written a poem if the violets had been blooming profusely in a flower bed nearby. What interested him in this scene was the unlikeliness of a flower growing in the dry clay between the steps leading up to Yumedono. The number of violets is not specified in the original, but probably there were no more than one or two scrawny plants growing in the scanty soil. The contrast between the ephemeral beauty of the violets and the imposing beauty of Yumedono, which had survived more than twelve centuries of vicissitudes, emphasized the mysterious beauty of the scene, an example of the yūgen which Hakushū would come to hold as his highest ideal.

One year earlier, Hakushū had participated in the first airplane flight by writers and artists in Japan. The *Osaka Asahi Shinbun* sponsored the flight, carrying exclusive coverage of the event as well as articles by the participants on their impressions while in the air. In order to involve as many artists as possible, the flight was divided into three legs: Hakushū and the poet and artist Onchi Kōshirō (1891-1955) flew from Tachiarai in north Kyushu to Osaka; the novelist and haiku poet Kume Masao (1891-1961) from Osaka to Tokyo; and the novelist Sasaki Mosaku (1898-1952) and his wife Sasaki Fusa (1897-1949), also a novelist, from Tokyo to Sendai.[64] Before his flight, Hakushū visited his birthplace Yanagawa, his first return visit since he had attended bankruptcy proceedings for the family business in 1909. The newspaper also arranged for Hakushū to fly once over Yanagawa before he left for Osaka. The tanka concerning these flights are found in the "Kyōdo Hishōgin" (Flying over my Birthplace) section of *Yumedono*.

Manashita no	The sun reflecting its shape
Fukada ni utsuru	On the wet rice paddies
Hi no arido	Directly below
Kagayaku shirushi	Forms a glittering mark
Tsuki no goto miyu.	Just like the moon.[65]

Hakushū's flight from Kyushu to Osaka on July 22, 1928, just one year after Charles Lindbergh's historic solo flight across the Atlantic, occasioned what were probably the first tanka to be written by someone in flight and as such attracted considerable notice. The note of exaggeration in this verse—the rather contrived comparison between the moon and the reflection of the sun on the water of the rice paddies—can be accounted for by Hakushū's excitement at being in the air. No doubt his readers welcomed the opportunity to participate vicariously through his poetry in the experience of flying.

Hakushū continued to write children's poetry and folk songs during this period, in addition to the shi later published in *Seals and Clouds*. He also wrote tanka inspired by the scenery surrounding each of his four successive residences. After the publication of *Seals and Clouds* in August 1929, he began to concentrate more seriously on these tanka in anticipation of publishing a new tanka collection.

WHITE BREEZES OF SUMMER

Shirahae (White Breezes of Summer), Hakushū's sixth volume of tanka, appeared in April 1934.[66] As we have seen, Hakushū had written a large number of tanka in Odawara. However, since they were not collected into the volumes *Out of the Wind* and *Edge of the Sea* until after his death, *White Breezes of Summer* was in fact only the fourth collection of Hakushū's tanka to appear in print—the first to be published after *Sparrow's Eggs*. This fact is particularly significant in terms of Hakushū's own attitude toward his tanka: he at last felt confident that he had some tanka worthy of publication. Most of his poetry hereafter would be in the tanka form.

The title of this volume referred to the south wind that blows just after the end of the rainy season, bringing with it the blue sky and warm weather of summer. In the Preface, Hakushū'explained that he had been inspired to write many tanka by the early summer weather, and that the collection contained comparatively few poems on spring and fall, the seasons most often treated by the Japanese. For these reasons, a title suggesting summer was particularly appropriate.[67]

Shirahae no	Gone are the wild roses;
Teriha no nobara	Only glittering leaves remain,
Suginikeri	Fluttering in a summer breeze.
Kawazu no koe mo	The croaking of frogs
Ta ni shimeritsutsu.	Soaks into the rice paddies.[68]

Hakushū had a specific time of year and scene in mind when he wrote this poem. In an essay on composing tanka published in 1936, he revealed that it was based on an actual experience.

It is the rainy season, but very little rain has fallen. The sky and clouds appear white and sultry. A south wind (*shirahae*) is blowing. South winds usually signal the end of the rainy season, but they also blow when it fails to rain. The glossy-leaved wild rose (*teriha no nobara*) in this poem is a type of wild rose; I did not invent this word. When most of the flowers have withered and fallen, its finely layered leaves begin to shine and glitter in the sunlight. Now and then a shower seems to threaten, and the croaking of frogs seems to soak into the rice paddies. I had a wild rose bush in my garden, and there were several more near the rice paddies and river.[69]

The interest of the poem rests on the unusual weather conditions described: the frogs are croaking in anticipation of rain which, despite the season, does not fall; instead, southerly winds have begun to blow, scattering the rose petals and causing the glossy leaves to flutter. These facts are not stated specifically; Hakushū intended to suggest them with the minimum of means and re-create for the reader the feeling of the wind, the sound of the frogs' calls, and the heavy humidity in the air. He later referred to this kind of suggestion as yūgen.

The majority of the tanka in this collection were seasonal poems. They were arranged chronologically, and divided into four sections according to the four different areas in Tokyo where Hakushū had lived: Tennōji, Ōmori, Wakabayashi, and Kinuta. Each time Hakushū moved he had found a new vantage point for observing the changes of season; had he stayed in one place during this period, he might have produced fewer tanka.

In the Afterword to *White Breezes of Summer*, Hakushū wrote careful descriptions of each house, its garden, and surroundings, supplementing the notes on the dates he had lived in each house that were given at the beginning of the section devoted to it. The fact that Hakushū felt obliged to supply detailed descriptions of the scenery around each house indicates how important place was to his tanka. For example, unless the reader knows that there were rice paddies across the road from his house in Kinuta (as explained in the Afterword[70]), the tanka above cannot be fully understood. As Hakushū sat in his house, gazing at the glossy leaves on his rose bush, he could hear the croaking of frogs in the paddies. Unlike the tanka in *Paulownia Flowers*, for the most part products of his imagination, the tanka in *White Breezes of Summer* were inspired by the small changes in nature that Hakushū actually observed.

Some people criticized Hakushū for having chosen such mundane subjects.[71] In reply he wrote "*Shirahae Zappitsu*" (Miscellaneous Comments on *White Breezes of Summer*), a relatively long discussion of why he had published this volume of poetry.[72] He reminded his readers that he had stated in the introduction, "I will not necessarily pursue my contemplation of nature at famous places, but will limit myself to the commonplace surroundings chosen along with my dwellings."[73] His reasons, that is, related first of all to his conception of *White Breezes of Summer*. From the start, it was to be about nature as observed in his daily life, and he therefore deliberately reserved the poetry inspired by his travels, which depicted grander subject matter, for a later collection, *Yumedono*. Furthermore, treating the changes in nature as observed in his own garden conformed more closely to his theory of poetry at this time.

> The real aspect of nature reveals itself even in a nearby thicket of small trees, or along the bank of an irrigation canal, or in the corner of a humble garden. You must pay attention, watching and listening, in order not to miss it. Most of these sights are neglected by the casual stroller. Even a single drop of dew or a stalk of wild grass inspires me with awe. Nature close at hand is encased with living jewels, and has a wealth to impart to those who choose to commune with it day and night in the quiet seclusion of their home. A mysterious life force can be felt beating within the most ordinary phenomena. At present I am living at the edge of Kinuta. My soul finds inspiration, indeed burns with happiness, at the daily happenings in my very ordinary garden. I sense deep significance in the small plot of nature which glitters before me. I am extremely thankful. Nature continually changes even in this minute scene. I could never possibly put all that I observe into verse. For me everything in nature is reality, is one aspect of truth.[74]

Nature changed with each season, revealing a mysterious vitality even in an ordinary garden. Any poet might be inspired to write tanka on such imposing subjects as Mt. Fuji; however, the true poet, Hakushū believed, needed to look no further than his own garden.

The true poet was distinguished from his peers by his attitude toward nature. "My contemplation of nature is based upon the following principle: I unite myself *(daiga)* with nature and understand myself and everything around me to constitute a perfect harmony *(enyū)*. In this state, my thoughts assume a transparency, moving like the wind, the sunlight, and the air."[75] *Daiga* and *enyū* are Buddhist terms. *Daiga* (larger self) refers to the ability of the true poet or the enlightened man to rise above personal concerns, which characterize man's *shōga* (smaller self), when he contemplates his surroundings. In this state, he understands that all phenomena, however distinct and separate they appear, partake of one perfect harmony *(enyū)*. Bashō's theory of poetry was itself strongly influenced by Buddhist concepts of this sort. Hakushū's understanding of the relation between the poet and nature, therefore, also reflected these same influences. However, it was not until "Halo of Art," the introduction to *Poems in Monochrome*, and "Comments" that Hakushū began to find Buddhist terminology useful in explaining his theories.

These ideas so closely resemble those in the Introduction to *Sparrow's Eggs* that the reader may be taken aback. This does not, however, mean that Hakushū's poetry itself had stagnated, but only that the theory of poetry he developed while working on *Sparrow's Eggs* continued to provide a viable foundation for his composition of tanka. This fact underlines the importance of the Introduction to *Sparrow's Eggs* as both the key to understanding Hakushū's later tanka and also a critical turning point for Hakushū's poetry, undoubtably the most important of his whole career.

Hakushū's attitude toward tanka composition remained conservative; this may be why he was unable to change his approach to the tanka more drastically. He made a careful distinction between his tanka and his shi, refusing to treat subjects in the tanka which he felt were inappropriate to the form. He may have had a narrow conception of the subject matter suited to the tanka, but he was sure that he brought to it a modern sensibility.

> I have restricted the subject matter for my tanka considerably. This was not a deliberate decision on my part, but happened quite naturally. Of late, my tanka have been either contemplations of nature or impressions of my occasional travels. I do not search widely for subject matter; the dimensions of my poems are narrow but deep. Although my tanka are not elaborate, I try to make them correct and original. My standard is the tanka tradition; yet I attempt to form my own style by always remaining true to myself and my perceptions, feelings, and thoughts as a modern man.[76]

Hakushū did not try to use strikingly modern subject matter or change the traditional form or language of the tanka. What he believed to be original and modern in his tanka was a unique point of view, expressed in imagery of sense perception.

The following poem is from "Tsuki no Gyogan" (A Moon Like A Fish's Eye), the last part of the final section of *White Breezes of Summer*. This section, containing the poems inspired by his life in Kinuta, is the latest in the collection. Hakushū obviously felt that this tanka, the only one in this part in which he used the image of a fish's eye, was one of the best in the collection, for he used the image as the name of the entire part.

Teriizuru	The moon comes out, shining
Tsuki wa gyogan no	Like a fish's eye.
Gotoku nari	The clouds blown in lines
Fukinagasu kumo	Across the sky
Yoroshiki miodachi.	Form channels.[77]

This tanka describes the full moon, as indicated by its heading "Jūrokuya" (Evening of the Sixteenth Day), which refers to the sixteenth day of a lunar month. In the moonlight, the clouds can be seen being blown across the dark sky. The interest of the poem rests upon the striking comparison Hakushū draws between the dark sky and the sea. If the sky is the ocean, then the clouds delineate channels for boats to pass through, and the moon glimmering in the darkness reminds him of a fish's eye peering out of the black sea. In seeing ordinary phenomena in this way, Hakushū imparted a peculiarly contemporary quality to his tanka.

The following tanka is from the earliest section of *White Breezes of Summer*. "Kōrogi no Sune" (Legs of a Cricket), the title of the part in which it is found, derived from the poem.

Sune tatete	His hind legs bent high,
Kōrogi ayumu	A cricket walks across
Tatami ni wa	The tatami floor
Sato no kona mo	On which crystals of sugar
Hi ni hikarishimu.	Sparkle in the lamplight.[78]

The heading, "Aki no Yo Shosai nite" (An Autumn Evening in My Study), clarifies the setting. Hakushū is in his study, a Japanese-style room with tatami (traditional straw matting) for the floor. Against the pale yellow mats a cricket is seen, the inverted V-shape of his hind legs conspicuous as he walks. Elsewhere on the tatami, sugar crystals are illuminated by the lamplight. These sharp details enabled Hakushū to capture the feeling of a cool autumn evening indoors.

Hakushū's ability to evoke mood in his tanka together with a sense of season and place made *White Breezes of Summer* noticeably different from his earlier tanka. As in *Sparrow's Eggs*, these poems are carefully conceived; after a short period of experimentation with spontaneous tanka in his Odawara compositions, he had returned to a more studied approach. *White Breezes of Summer* did not exhibit, however, the contrived effects found in *Sparrow's Eggs*, which had resulted from his conscious attempts to convey sabi. His observations were not only sensitive but genuine. In each poem he endeavored to evoke the feeling of the objects, places, and seasons he described. "Although I sometimes feel that I should be even more painstaking with my descriptions, if forced to choose, I remember the importance of yugen. I sense the importance of symbols. I value suggestion. I treasure refinement."[79]

It was the suggestive and evocative qualities of the tanka which absorbed him at this time. In "Comments" he termed the style of these tanka "kindai yūgentai" (modern yūgen style),[80] the first time that he had used that term to refer to a style of tanka. The shi in *Seals and Clouds*, which he had characterized as being in a "modern yūgen style," had relied for their effect on traditional imagery. However, in this volume, yūgen is discovered even in such everyday subjects as a fish's eye, crickets, and sugar. In *White Breezes of Summer*, Hakushū had once again established a new style of tanka.

THE TAMA TANKA ASSOCIATION AND *TAMA*

Hakushū did not fully appreciate the significance of *White Breezes of Summer* when he published it in April 1934, and did not characterize these poems as his "modern yūgen style" until he reconsidered the collection in January 1935. Then, when he organized the Tama Tankakai (Tama Tanka Association)[81] in June 1935 he formulated a new theory of tanka to explain this style.

Hakushū had not had a tanka group of his own since disbanding the Thatched House of Purple Smoke in 1917. At that time, it will be remembered, he had felt that taking responsibility for a group of disciples would hinder his own endeavors to create the new style of poetry which eventually resulted in *Sparrow's Eggs*. Young poets, nevertheless, had continued to gather around him. After he published *White Breezes of Summer*, he acquiesced to their requests and once again created a formal association under his leadership, with its own magazine. The principles of poetry that the group espoused were Hakushū's own, first put into practice in *White Breezes of Summer*, but as yet not formulated as a theory of poetry. The formation of the Tama Tanka Association and the publication of the first issue of its magazine, *Tama*, in June 1935, stimulated Hakushū to elucidate these theories.

In "Tama Sengen" (Tama Proclamation), published in the first issue of *Tama*, Hakushū reaffirmed his conservative approach to the tanka.

> In forming the Tama Tanka Association we establish our position in the mainstream of Japanese tanka. Not only do we inherit both the spirit and the tradition of the tanka as a set form of poetry; we also believe that the tanka as it stands has a glorious future and propose to participate in its development by bringing to it our modern perceptions and intellect as we act now and in the future.[82]

His group did not intend to change either the form or the language of the tanka; instead, they saw themselves as modern heirs to its long tradition. What they would bring to the tanka, as modern poets of the form, were the perception and intellect of the modern age. In this sense, Hakushū's understanding of the tanka had changed little from 1913 when in the introduction to *Paulownia Flowers* he had likened the tanka to an ancient emerald which would glitter anew in the hands of its modern owners.

The members of the Tama Tanka Association believed that they were initiating a literary movement.

> What do we at Tama hope for? A revival of romanticism. A rebirth of "poetry." The fourth symbolist movement in Japan. The establishment of a modern yūgen style. An earnest occupation with purity, born of the artistic conscience inherited from our tradition.[83]

The tanka they proposed to write would be modern because they would bring to their verse the viewpoint of modern Japanese; their ideals, however, were traditional. Hakushū believed that symbolism constituted the most important characteristic of traditional Japanese poetry. He traced the development of traditional symbolism through three periods: the late twelfth century when the *Shinkokinshū* was compiled, Bashō's haikai in the seventeenth century, and the tanka written for *Morning Star* in the early 1900s. The Tama poets proposed to write modern tanka in this tradition. Their compositions would, therefore, establish a fourth and completely modern period of symbolism.

After the Manchurian Incident of September 1931, poets, even such important members of the Araragi Group as Saitō Mokichi and Tsuchiya Bunmei, had begun to write realistic tanka touching on political conditions, the army, and war, often thereby destroying the traditional poetic effects of the tanka.[84] Such poets were convinced that they had to compose this sort of verse if they were not to appear behind the times. It was against this background that Hakushū and his group called for a "revival of romanticism" and a "rebirth of 'poetry'." "When I talk of the revival of romantic spirit," wrote Hakushū, "I do not speak of my own poetry. I speak instead to poets in the other half of the modern tanka world who have forgotten the original spirit of poetry. I urge them to reflect."[85] The Tama Tanka Association advocated romanticism not so much because their subject matter was romantic, in the manner of the tanka published in *Morning Star*, or because they felt that the poet's imagination allowed participation in mysteries not open to ordinary human beings, but because they wished to suggest an alternative to the realism in vogue at the time.

The appearance of the Tama Tanka Association was an early manifestation of the revival of interest in Japan's cultural tradition, fostered by militarism within the government and army. This does not mean that

Hakushū and his group were writing tanka in support of the army or militarism—Hakushū did not begin to write jingoist verse until several years later—but it does help to explain why Tama quickly became one of the two major forces in tanka, the other being the Araragi poets. At this juncture, its conservative approach to poetry had appeal. Its success also serves as proof of Hakushū's strong position of leadership in the world of poetry.

Hakushū traced the beginnings of symbolist poetry in Japanese literature back to the *Shinkokinshū*, a collection which exerted a strong influence on his own tanka at this time. During the period of the *Shinkokinshū*, the late twelfth century, which he labelled the "first symbolist movement," poets refined the tanka, employing overtones of language to suggest an atmosphere of mysterious beauty. Hakushū and his disciples, however, saw one major fault in this approach: an inability to penetrate deeply into subject matter, which often resulted in a preoccupation with the surface beauty of language.

This fault, they believed, was remedied by Bashō, whose poetry stemmed from the poet's profound contemplation of nature. His haikai represented the "second symbolist movement." The third period singled out was the "tanka revolution" that had occurred in the pages of *Morning Star* in the early 1900s. There poets had changed the nature of traditional tanka by bringing to it the new feelings and techniques of Western poetry under the influence of Ueda Bin's translations.

Hakushū's analysis, for all his theorizing about symbolism, seems in the end to have been an attempt to discover similarities between periods which had influenced his own verse. It was weakest when treating the tanka found in *Morning Star*. Full of the dreams and emotions of the romantic young poets of the time, these tanka were not in any sense "symbolic." It was the shi where symbolism had developed at that period, with Hakushū's own *Heretical Faith* an important milestone along the way. Hakushū's use of the word "symbolism" to refer to tanka poetry of the same period was obviously because he wished to include it in his analysis for personal reasons.

Yosano Tekkan's sudden death from pneumonia on March 26, 1935 strengthened Hakushū's resolve to make a stand with his disciples in favor of a more "romantic" approach to the tanka. In a long essay in remembrance of Tekkan, published in the May issue of *Tanka Kenkyū* (Tanka Research), he wrote:

Since the beginning of the Taishō era, the tanka world has been guilty of many wrongs against Yosano Tekkan and altogether disrespectful toward him; such an attitude cannot be forgiven without a written apology today. I stand ready to do battle to avenge his death; I feel myself trembling with belligerence merely at the thought of this injustice.[86]

Tekkan had died from natural causes, and Hakushū did not mean that he would assail those who had slighted Tekkan: his revenge took the form of advocating romanticism, the ideal Hakushū associated with Tekkan and *Morning Star*.

Despite the personal disagreements which had made Hakushū withdraw from Tekkan's New Poetry Society in 1907, he believed, at least in retrospect, that Tekkan's attitude toward the tanka had been correct in its day, particularly when compared with that of the Araragi Tanka Group, whose insistence upon shasei had led the tanka world to its present preoccupation with realism. For these reasons, Hakushū included the "period of *Morning Star*" as an epoch in Japanese symbolism. He did not intend to imitate the tanka published in *Morning Star*, which, as even he reluctantly admitted, did not follow an orthodox approach.

Hakushū believed that the Tama Tanka Association would give rise to a "fourth symbolist movement" following the path laid out by poets during the three preceding periods of symbolism. Kimata Osamu, Hakushū's major tanka disciple when he formed the Tama Tanka Association, explained its point of view in the June 1938 issue of *Tama*:

> The advocacy of shasei has constituted the mainstream of tanka poetry in the Taishō and Shōwa eras, flooding tanka journals with poems lacking poetic spirit. At this juncture, we at Tama have stood up, bearing the standard of symbolism. We believe that our tanka mark the fourth period of symbolism....We aspire after a new and original world of symbol, unlike anything thus far employed in the history of the tanka and best characterized as "modern yūgen," although we stand firmly on tradition.[87]

Kimata's essay, written three years after Tama was founded, illustrated how its poets saw themselves in the contemporary tanka world. By advocating symbolism, they established ties with tradition—the poems of the *Shinkokinshū*, Bashō's haikai, and the tanka in *Morning Star;* at the same time, they claimed uniqueness for their poetry by terming it "modern yūgen style."

MOUNTAIN STREAM AND *BEECH TREE*

Although Hakushū's interest in yūgen can be traced back to *Seals and Clouds*, he did not use the term to refer to a style of tanka until the essay "Comments," written but a few months prior to the establishment of the Tama Group. In January 1935, the month he completed the essay, he visited Izu Yūgashima Hot Springs for twenty days with his family. Thirty-seven tanka inspired by the scenery there were published in March (three months before the appearance of *Tama*) under the title *"Keiryūshō"* (Mountain Stream).[88] If in *White Breezes of Summer* we can trace the beginnings of his "new yūgen style," these tanka stand as his first conscious experiments in that style.

> This series of tanka, "Mountain Stream," heralded the begin-
> ning of a style developed later in *Tama*. It has a momentous
> significance for me.
>   In June of that same year, I had at last established the
> magazine *Tama* for my disciples. Fortune turned our way with
> the publication of "Mountain Stream."[89]

The appearance of this series marked the commencement of a new period in Hakushū's tanka. He later made it the first section of his eighth tanka collection, *Keiryūshō* (Mountain Stream).[90]

> Yuku mizu no   The blue froth
> Me ni todomaranu   On the surging water
> Aominawa   Quickly disappears from sight.
> Sekirei no o wa   For a moment, a wagtail's long
> Furenitarikeri.   feathers
>   Touched the foam.[91]

The Yūgashima Hot Springs are situated in the mountainous area at the center of the Izu Peninsula. The poet stands near a mountain stream flowing swiftly between the rocks. As he watches the rushing water, he notices the froth being churned up, only to be carried away at once by the stream. A wagtail by the edge of the stream jerks its tail and for a moment touches the foam. This was the scene that inspired this tanka.

Hakushū, however, did not try to capture the pictorial qualities of this mountain scene. Indeed, he failed to convey all but the barest outlines. His description focused instead on the foam, which formed only to disappear, and the tail of the bird as it briefly touched the water. In a speech given on

August 13, 1940, at the Third National Convention of Tama Poets, Hakushū offered this analysis:

> This poem from "Mountain Stream" is important because from it we at Tama trace the origins of our group today. The first three phrases, *yuku mizu no/ me ni todomaranu/ aominawa* (the blue froth on the surging water quickly disappears from sight), were intended to convey evanescence—the pathos of the transience of flowing water. A wagtail has alighted by the stream amidst the ephemerality of nature, and for one short second his tail touched the stream. At this moment, through the wagtail, we experience the significance of nature's transience. I believe that something vibrant and alive is revealing its significance here. Therefore, although this poem is descriptive (shasei), it is not description (shasei) in the normal sense of that term. The wagtail represents us, both in form and in spirit, neither more nor less. This is what I mean by a symbolist poem, and I would like you to give serious thought to the use of symbolism in your own tanka.[92]

As Hakushū explained it, the tanka was meant to symbolize the relationship between the poet, specifically the poets in his Tama Tanka Association, and nature. It was not the beauty of nature which interested him, but its transience. The foam made by the churning water and the swiftly flowing stream suggested nature's changeability. Like the wagtail whose tail feathers touched the water for an instant, the poet who cultivated his sensitivity and contemplated his surroundings could also experience the essence of nature. Capturing his observations in a tanka, not by describing what he saw but by suggesting its significance through the techniques of symbolism, was the task of the true poet.

Hakushū espoused the same approach that had characterized traditional Japanese poetry since the *Shinkokinshū*. Although his subject matter occasionally included lamps, movie cameras, and other objects that had not previously been considered refined enough to be mentioned in a tanka, he looked at even these objects from his own particular point of view, not ostentatiously modern, but definitely unique in its sensitivity to sounds, colors, smells, and light effects. Hakushū, in effect, made the traditional approach to the tanka valid for himself and his twentieth-century readers. If the tanka by Hakushū and his disciples at the Tama Tanka Association were not as innovative as they imagined in moments of enthusiasm, the group still provided an alternative to the Araragi style of poetry and helped to make the traditional approach to tanka relevant to the day—functions that gave it significance in the history of modern tanka.

Hakushū's enthusiasm infected a large number of young poets, with each monthly issue of *Tama* carrying over two hundred pages of tanka submitted by members from all areas of Japan. The Tama Tanka Association also stimulated Hakushū to carry to a final conclusion the approach to poetry which he had first begun while working on *Sparrow's Eggs*. *Mountain Stream* and its companion volume *Tsurubami* (Beech Tree)[93] represent a high point in the last year of Hakushū's poetry. They also contain the last tanka he wrote before his eyesight began to fail in the autumn of 1937.

Although the tanka in these collections, much to Hakushū's dismay, failed to impress all but his closest disciples, they were well-wrought gems, the most perfectly worked poems in fact of his career. Perhaps their content was too unpretentious for contemporary taste. Compared to Hakushū's early shi or the tanka in *Paulownia Flowers*, which spoke loudly and clearly of a young man's melancholy in language which startled readers with its musical refrains and mingled sense perceptions, Hakushū's later tanka may seem lusterless. However, if we accept the standards of poetry which Hakushū set while writing *Sparrow's Eggs* and redefined in *Tama*, it is difficult not to conclude that these poems are much more important than has hitherto been believed.

The following two tanka begin one of the seven major sections that make up *Beech Tree*.

Mono no ha ya	Leaves and stalks of grass.
Asobu shijimi wa	Flitting butterflies.
Suzushikute	Coolness.
Mina aware nari	I sense pathos in each element.
Kaze ni soreyuku.	The butterflies drift away on the wind.[94]

Honoakaku	Faintly red blossoms
Hana wa kemurishi	Had covered the mimosa tree
Niwa no nemu	in my garden
Kaze soyogu nari	Like smoke.
Utsushi mi no saya.	Yet how much more genuine seem the pods Which now sway in the wind.[95]

Both poems describe the first signs of autumn in Hakushū's garden at Kinuta.[96] The commencement of a new season or the last days of an old one, times of transition, were of particular interest to him because he believed that the evanescence of nature, revealed through its changes, constituted reality.

Hakushū explained the significance of both poems in a speech delivered at the August 1940 convention of Tama poets. In his remarks about the first, he gave a detailed description of the experience that inspired it.

> I am sitting in the detached house in my garden at Kinuta, gazing at a small pond in the foreground. Although I did not mention this in the poem, there is a small pond in my garden, surrounded by various grasses and plants—pampas grass, bell flowers, and purple asters. A cool breeze, the weak rays of the sun, Chinese grass, and the white heads on the pampas grass all suggest the commencement of autumn. A group of small butterflies, *shijimichō* of a light blue color tinged with purple, now flutter about. Their playing and flying conveys the coolness of autumn. One by one they attempt to alight on a blade of grass, only to be carried away ever so slightly by the wind. It is not a strong breeze, but the butterflies ride on it, one by one slowly drifting away. Neither staying nor going—this is what moves me. I do not intend this poem to be merely descriptive (shasei). As we observe each element, we sink into thought. Although we do not perhaps assign the scene deep significance, do we not sense something important in this scene of early autumn lying before us? Do we not feel something which cannot be captured by ordinary description (shasei)? I do not want to go into this in any further detail. I hope that you will ponder the significance of the poem, beginning with the last two phrases: *mina aware nari/kaze ni soreyuku* (I sense pathos in each element. The butterflies drift away on the wind).[97]

The way the butterflies flutter about among the grasses is described as "cool," mingling sense perceptions. There is also a sense of coolness in the colors of the scene: the withered beige grasses and the faded blue of the butterflies. Then, when we reach the end of the poem, we realize that the adjective "cool" refers even more directly to the wind. The butterflies gradually drift away, borne gently by a cool autumn breeze which interrupts their attempts to alight on the grass. Their movement, hardly distinct enough to be noticed except by a keen observer, suggests the pathos of the change in season which is just beginning, and also the evanescence of nature. This poem is an excellent example of what Hakushū meant when he referred to these tanka as his "modern yūgen style." Indeed, yūgen best describes the quality which evokes both the feeling of a season and place and the pathos of change.

Hakushū's poetry was personal in the sense that each tanka was based upon an actual experience. Without background information, such as provided in his speech, it is difficult for the reader to empathize with the poet to the degree necessary for full appreciation. This poem was probably dismissed by most of his contemporaries as being no more than a pretty description of butterflies. The difficulty of Hakushū's late tanka lies in the degree of commitment to Hakushū the poems demanded of the reader. Unlike the tanka in *Paulownia Flowers*, the meaning of which was apparent on first reading, to understand these tanka, the reader must first accept Hakushū's attitude toward nature; next, he or she must be willing to imagine with Hakushū the situation that gave rise to the poem. The fault and, at the same time, the merit of these poems is that so much is left to the reader's imagination.

In the same speech, Hakushū told how his poem on the butterflies had been ignored in a poetry competition, where various writers, amateurs and professionals, had submitted their works anonymously for evaluation:

> On one occasion the poem was published in a competition sponsored by a certain tanka magazine. However, nobody even noticed it, and the judges refused to comment on the poem, placing it in the lowest category along with a lot of poems by other people. Readers were asked to indicate their reactions to these tanka by postcard, but not even one reply was received for my poem....The only person to truly understand this tanka was Shaku Chōkū, who wrote of his amazement at finding that the Japanese tanka had developed to this extent. I could only bow my head in thanks.[98]

Hakushū's discouragement at the inability of most readers to appreciate his poetry was assuaged by the support of such disciples as Shaku Chōkū and Kimata Osamu.

Both tanka consist of two parts. In the first, the description of the autumn scene is juxtaposed to the poet's discovery that the butterflies are being slowly carried away by the wind. The second devolves around the contrast between the pale red flowers on the mimosa tree in summer and the pods that it bears in autumn. Once again here is Hakushū's own explanation of the poem.

After the pale red blossoms on the mimosa tree had passed, I saw real pods swaying in the wind. There are some mimosa in one part of my garden at Kinuta. This tree stands just at the point where the garden begins to slope, on the border of a path leading down to the house below. In season, it is covered with long, frail, light red flowers which do indeed resemble smoke. However, after the bright flowers pass, the tree also bears green pods, which are now swaying in the wind, making me feel that autumn has already begun. I am not expounding any theory. I intended to convey a certain coolness associated with early autumn—coolness not as something lifeless and empty, but as something that constitutes reality.[99]

The blossom of the *nemu* tree described here consists of long pink filaments, the stamens of the flower. The other parts of the flower are too small to be seen except under close inspection. From a distance the tree does indeed appear to be enveloped in pink smoke. Although Hakushū appreciated these unusual romantic blossoms, it was the green pods, which the tree bore later, that seemed remarkable—not only because they typified the commencement of autumn but because they seemed so very genuine. By juxtaposing the two aspects of the tree, the flowers and the pods, Hakushū evoked nature's evanescence as symbolized by the rapid changes in the tree. He also suggested that although the flowers were beautiful, the pods they produced —rather unusual subject matter for a tanka—attracted him more, because they represented the reality of nature, a definitely modern viewpoint.

The following poem treated even more unusual subject matter—a movie camera.

Chika chika to	Click, click.
Jūroku miri ga	The sound of a sixteen
Oto tatete	millimeter movie camera.
Natsu no hizashi no	Wavelike clusters of wisteria
Fusa no fujinami.	In the summer sunshine.[100]

This poem was written in 1936; in February of that year, Hakushū had moved from Kinuta to Seijō, in the same area of Tokyo. In another tanka of the four-poem group in which it is found, Hakushū described his brother taking photographs of the peonies in his garden. It is unclear whether the person operating the movie camera here is also his brother.

Although *fujinami* (waves of wisteria blossoms) had been frequently treated in the tanka ever since the *Man'yōshū*, this no doubt was the first time wisteria flowers had been mentioned in conjunction with a movie camera. Hakushū, however, was not interested in the movie camera as such; neither the camera nor the photographer appeared distinctly in the poem. From where Hakushū sat, perhaps in a room adjacent to the garden, he could hear the faint clicking of the camera. Before him the purple wisteria flowers hung in clusters on a trellis under the bright summer sun. The rhythmic clicking of the camera, the flowers, and the sunlight connected in his mind to suggest early summer.

Given Hakushū's approach to poetry at this period, we can conjecture that this tanka probably resulted from some such experience. Nevertheless, it is unlikely that it was dashed off extemporaneously. A closer study of imagery and sound patterns reveals a careful construction. There are two parts: the former treats an auditory image, the latter half a visual one, although *natsu no hizashi* (summer sunlight) also suggests the warmth of the sunshine. By joining these images of sensation, Hakushū evoked the fresh and bright clarity of a summer day. The division of the poem is also reflected in the sound patterns. In the first half of the poem, which cannot help but startle the reader with its unusual image of a movie camera, the crisp sound of the onomatopoeic expression *chika chika* (click, click) in the first phrase is echoed in the "t" sounds of the third, *oto tatete*. The partial stops at the end of the first three phrases intensify the choppy effect. The latter half of the poem is, by contrast, much softer, the predominance of "s" sounds suggesting perhaps a light wind rustling through the wisteria and the last two phrases connecting to form a single long clause modifying *fujinami*.

In *Beech Tree* Hakushū used sound, rhythm, and imagery of sense perception with more care and skill then in his Odawara tanka or even *White Breezes of Summer*. In every sense, *Beech Tree* was the final destination on the carefully traveled road that Hakushū had traced out for himself starting with *Sparrow's Eggs*. After some meandering along side paths in his Odawara period, he had returned to the main route with *White Breezes of Summer*, a road shaded along its last stage by the foliage provided with redefinition of his approach to tanka in *Tama*.

Both *Sparrow's Eggs* and *Beech Tree* represented Hakushū's practical application of a theory of poetry, and this fact seems to have made him a more meticulous poet. During the intervening period, when he ceased to develop his ideas about the tanka, his poetry became more private, extemporaneous, and less exacting in its techniques. Just as his Misaki poetry, which displayed many of the same qualities as his Odawara poetry but in a much stronger fashion, represented a transitional period leading up to *Sparrow's Eggs*, so do the poems from his Odawara days seem to prepare the way for *White Breezes of Summer* and *Beech Tree*. And yet, although Hakushū's Misaki period and his Odawara period were times of transition, they also represented a retreat from the strict standards he set for his poetry. Or again, perhaps it would be better to conclude that Hakushū's poetry, as one would expect, did not develop on a straight continuum, but rather shifted between two broad types, between the private, extemporaneous poems of his Misaki and Odawara collections, and the more studied and technically meticulous verse of *Sparrow's Eggs* and *Beech Tree*.

6

BLINDNESS AND DEATH
1937-1942

In March 1937, Hakushū was chosen, along with nine other noted tanka poets, to select the poems to be included in a mammoth anthology of modern tanka, the *Shinman'yōshū* (New Man'yōshū), being planned by Kaizōsha Publishing Company.[1] The collection was to contain poems by both famous and unknown poets, covering the Meiji, Taishō, and Shōwa periods, and Kaizōsha had gathered over 400,000 tanka through announcements in *Tanka Kenkyū* (Tanka Review).[2] Each judge had to review all the poems; those selected by two or more judges were included in the anthology.

Hakushū did not begin reviewing tanka for the collection until August; his late start meant that he had to devote all his time to the task. The publishing company had made carbon copies of the manuscript, which it distributed to the judges. Hakushū complained that his copy was so illegible that he had to use a magnifying glass. By October, he was experiencing marked difficulty with his eyesight, forcing him to consult a doctor. The preliminary diagnosis was that overwork and eyestrain had caused inflammation of the retina, a condition that often arose in conjunction with either diabetes or nephritis, a kidney disease. Hakushū had suffered from diabetes for several years, and other symptoms, particularly some swelling in his legs, made the doctor suspect that nephritis might also be a cause. He ordered Hakushū to rest quietly at home.[3]

On October 14, the day after his medical examination, Hakushū left for Nagaoka Hot Springs in Izu to work on the poems for the *New Man'yōshū* with one of the editors from the publishing firm, which was eager to have the completed manuscript. Hakushū's doctor firmly opposed the trip, but the publishing firm was insistent. Completing the manuscript was also topmost in Hakushū's mind, and he spent two weeks in Izu finishing his work on the collection.

Immediately after he returned to Tokyo, Hakushū visited the doctor. Notwithstanding promises to the contrary, he had worked late into the night at Izu, straining his eyes over barely legible manuscripts. His vision had deteriorated considerably, and his eyes pained him. An examination by an opthalmologist revealed a hemorrhage behind his right eye. Hakushū entered the hospital on the tenth of November.

BLACK CYPRESS

He did not believe that his condition was serious, and expected that a period of rest would restore his vision. Only when the doctor explained that he would never recover full use of his eyes did Hakushū confront the fact that he was going blind. For a poet who depended so much on visual imagery, this must have seemed a misfortune of overwhelming proportions.

> I have overworked my eyes since my youth in reading, contemplating nature, and composing poetry. I have used my eyes more than my other sense faculties and trained them to absorb light, color, and form. These eyes are my most valuable faculty; they have been the window to my heart.[4]

Hakushū's last five years were spent in partial blindness.

Hakushū's tenth tanka collection, *Kurohi* (Black Cypress),[5] opened with the following poem, written on a moonlit night at the hospital.

Teru tsuki no	I strain my eyes
Hie sadaka naru	Toward a glass door
Akarito ni	Bright with the decisive cold
Me wa korashitsutsu	Of moonlight.
Shiite yuku nari.	I am going blind.[6]

This tanka marked the beginning of the final period in Hakushū's poetry. In it he confronted the harsh reality of his failing eyesight. Now, no matter how hard he strains, all he can make out is the moonlight. Shining through a glass door that leads out to a garden, it lights up the grey and black shadows of his hospital room. A few months earlier, he had been able to observe nature in detail. The situation symbolized the limitations that his failing eyesight placed upon his contemplation of nature; the confines of his hospital room represented those imposed by his poor vision. No longer would he be able to gaze upon the moon; instead, he would be forced to imagine its existence when he saw the moonlight shining on the floor, his vision encompassing a much narrower perspective.

Hakushū's emotions as he faced the fact of his failing eyesight and contemplated its implications for his life and his poetry were indicated, first of all, by the stark colors of the poem and secondly, by his choice of words. The moonlight was cold *(hie);* the coldness, furthermore, had a foreboding certainty *(sadaka naru)* to it, suggesting the inescapable reality of his situation. The use of the verb *koru* (to strain the eyes) may contain overtones of an older meaning for that word, "to freeze into ice," carrying over the bleak, cold imagery used to describe the moonlight. For Hakushū, a world which he could only partially discern seemed bleak and cold. He strained his eyes as if he could not believe his fate. In the last phrase of the poem, however, he finally admits that he "is going blind." The long "i" vowel in *shiite* (to go blind) effectively slows down the rhythm of the poem, strengthening the effect of this exclamation of combined resignation and despair.

Hakushū left the hospital on January 7, 1938, fully rested if not completely recovered. During the next three years, his vision continued to deteriorate, and he was plagued again with internal hemorrhaging behind his eyes. Nevertheless, he was determined to continue writing. His tanka from this time spoke of the new experience of confronting a world that he could not clearly see. Words pertaining to sight appeared in almost every poem.

Shiryoku toboshi	My eyesight is weak.
Te ni sayaritsutsu	With my fingers
Shirokiku no	I examine a white chrysanthemum.
Otorofuru hana no	Its withering petals
Ben netsubaminu.	Are still warm.[7]

Hakushū instinctively began to develop his other senses in order to compensate for his failing vision. In this tanka, from which the title of the first section of *Black Cypress*, "Netsubamu Kiku" (Warm Chrysanthemum), was taken, Hakushū described using his hands to examine a chrysanthemum. Before his eyes began to fail, he would not have thought to feel a flower in this manner. Because he could no longer depend on his eyes as fully as before, however, he concentrated upon his other senses—smell, hearing, taste, and touch. Once he decided to do this, a new world opened up. He found that the petals of a flower, even one that was beginning to wither, radiated warmth.

This poem can also be interpreted as a comment on his commitment to poetry. The word *netsu* (warmth) has a secondary meaning, "enthusiasm." Hakushū used the nuances of this word to compare his physical decline to the withering chrysanthemum. Like the flower that still remained warm, he had not lost his enthusiasm for poetry. He remained interested in life because of his poetry, and his love for poetry encouraged him to overcome his partial blindness. Very few poems in *Black Cypress* were as despairing as that first one written in the hospital.

The introduction to *Black Cypress* was short and poignant. Hakushū made no plea for sympathy from his readers. Poetry was his life, the tranquility embodied in a black cypress his prime concern.

> The tranquility of a black cypress. Is it possible to comprehend this even after the flowers have withered and fallen?
> For two and a half years now, living in a state of twilight, I have thought over this question again and again. I never believed that I would overcome my affliction. I trust the darkness; I do not ask for pity. I merely continue to follow the path I love through the smoke and mists of suggestion, earnestly and, as always, reverently.[8]

Black Cypress occupies a unique position in the history of modern Japanese poetry. Not only is it probably the best, if not the most significant of Hakushū's contributions to the tanka, it stands as a monument to his courage in overcoming blindness.[9]

The title of *Black Cypress* derived from two poems which open a section of the same name.

Kuroki hi no	The stillness
Chinsei ni shite	Of the black cypress
Utsushikeki.	Is reality.
Hana osamarite	Even better appreciated
Nochi ni koso nagame.	After the flowers have passed.[10]

Kaguroba ni	A summer mist
Shizumite niou	Enveloping those dark leaves
Natsu kasumi	Perfumes the air.
Wakakaru ware wa	In my youth I saw
Mitsutsu mizariki.	And did not see.[11]

These poems illustrate the change that partial blindness made in Hakushū's response to nature. Before, one lone cypress tree would not have moved him. It would have taken a larger scene, of flowers, insects, and grasses, where he could see the passage of the seasons reflected in slight changes, to hold his attention. But the thoughts of transience so occasioned did not fit the crypress, an evergreen. Hakushū's attention had turned from the evanescence of nature to the stillness and tranquility embodied by the black cypress. Even the fact that some flowers were blooming nearby did not heighten his appreciation of the cypress but moved him to thoughts of how much stiller and more tranquil the scene would be when the flowers had passed.

In the second tanka, Hakushū described the odor of the cypress leaves—an odor made more pungent by a summer mist. Although he had been aware of this phenomenon in his youth, it was only after his eyes began to fail that he deliberately cultivated his sense of smell. The static quality of the imagery in both poems contrasted sharply with the movement, however subtle, found in his tanka a few years earlier. Hakushū continued to assign broad significance to nature and remained concerned with the atmosphere of his imagery; in this sense, the style of this period is an extension of his earlier "new yūgen style." By this time, however, it was not the ephemeral quality of nature that attracted him; instead, he chose imagery which, like the black cypress, suggested an authentic tranquility, found only after or, perhaps, because his eyesight had begun to fail.

Black Cypress contained six tanka inspired by the eighth-century lacquer statue of the blind Chinese monk known in Japan by the name Ganjin.[12] Scattered throughout the volume, they formed a major theme.[13] Hakushū had seen Ganjin's statue at the Tōshōdaiji Temple during a trip to Nara in August 1936, before his vision began to fail; a photo of it was one of six in the collection. As Hakushū learned to cope with his loss of sight, this statue both comforted and encouraged him.

Shiihatete	Completely blind
Naoshi yawara to	Yet ever gentle.
Masu mami ni	What secret did you cherish,
Hijiri nani o ka	Saintly monk,
Yadoshitamaishi.	Within those eyes?[14]

Hakushū's blindness was far from total, although his vision was gradually deteriorating. Hakushū found in Ganjin, whose blindness seemed to ennoble him, a model to emulate. A soft smile (no doubt originally meant to suggest religious fulfillment), relaxed posture, and gently closed eyes, which form the central point of focus for the statue, evoked strength of character and a sense of inner peace. Ganjin's contentment and tranquility especially attracted Hakushū. "Deep within those eyes, what gives you such repose?" he asked rhetorically. Moreover, he did not envy Ganjin's tranquility; it was enough merely to contemplate the statue, to feel with Ganjin the serenity of being blind.

Black Cypress was divided into two parts. The second, comprising barely one-fifth of the collection, contained tanka about Japan's military aggression in China, aggression which had reached the proportions of an undeclared war between Japan and Chiang Kai-shek's Nationalist Government after the China Incident of July 1937, when Japanese and Chinese troops clashed in Peking. Needless to say, these patriotic poems on swords, soldiers and their families, and news of military activities have lost their relevance for modern readers. Hakushū saw no need to question the direction in which his country was going. Like most contemporary poets, he wrote his share of jingoist verse; poems on patriotic themes for children in particular enjoyed widespread popularity.

NEW EULOGIES, "SHIBO" AND "KIKYORAI"

During the years from 1939 to 1941, Hakushū experienced a short respite from the illness which had caused his hospitalization in 1937. In remarks published monthly in *Tama*, he remained optimistic about his health, even predicting that his eyesight would eventually return to normal. However, his vision in fact continued to deteriorate, and he could no longer read fine print. Yabuta Yoshio became his secretary in 1939, and until his mentor's death performed chores not requiring Hakushū's direct inspection. Hakushū also often had his wife and daughter read to him and copy out sections from books he wished to peruse more closely. He had to dictate most of the poems he composed during this period.

Taking advantage of his improved health, Hakushū moved in April 1940 to Asagaya in Suginami Ward, Tokyo, less for reasons of convenience than for a change of environment. Just as other moves had stimulated Hakushū's writing, he hoped that this move, the last he would make, would at least provide new subject matter for his poetry. In August he published *Black Cypress* and in October *Shinshō* (New Eulogies), his last volume of shi.[15]

The year 1940 had been designated by the Japanese government for celebration of the 2600th anniversary of the mythological founding of the Japanese state in 660 B.C. Hakushū published *New Eulogies* in commemoration of these celebrations. Unfortunately this volume did not compare favorably with Hakushū's other collections of shi. Its failure was occasioned largely by the special character of the collection. Most of the poems described in archaic diction subject matter derived from ancient sources and read like exercises in patriotic versification. Moreover, Hakushū had not been writing shi seriously for many years. He had failed to maintain contacts with professional journals of shi and had been concentrating his efforts almost exclusively on the tanka, particularly after the appearance of *White Breezes of Summer* in 1934. He could find only thirty-one shi to include in the collection.

Hakushū would probably not have published a collection of shi at this time had he not been asked in the summer of 1939 by the Central Federation on Japanese Culture[16] to compose two poems to commemorate these festivities. By October he had completed "Kaidō Tōsei" (Expedition by Sea to the East), a long shi of over two hundred lines in eight parts, glorifying the ocean voyage by Emperor Jimmu who, according to legends in the *Kojiki* and *Nihon Shoki*, had traveled with a large force of warriors from southern Kyushu to Naniwa, near present-day Osaka, prior to founding the Japanese state in 660 B.C. in Yamato on the Nara Plain; and "Genkō" (Mongol Invasion), another long poem celebrating the successful Japanese repulsion of Mongolian forces sent by the Yuan emperor in 1281 to north Kyushu.[17] The desire to have these poems published during the festive year 1940 was undoubtedly the major reason for bringing out *New Eulogies* at this time. The arrangement of the volume, which begins with "Expedition by Sea to the East" and ends with "Mongol Invasion," supports this supposition.

As the title *New Eulogies* suggests, these poems continued the style found in the first section, "Kōdai Shinshō" (New Eulogies to Ancient Times), of *Seals and Clouds*.

> One unifying theme [of all these poems] is the Japanese spirit, and their rhythms derive from the ancient meters of pre-*Man'yōshū* poetry—for the most part combinations of four-, five-, and six-syllable phrases. This style, which I began in "New Eulogies to Ancient Times" of *Seals and Clouds*, characterizes my poetry at present.[18]

In "New Eulogies to Ancient Times" Hakushū had borrowed archaic diction and certain other features of poems from ancient texts such as the *Kojiki* and *Nihon Shoki* in order to create modern poems whose mood would suggest their sources. The three longest poems in *New Eulogies*, "Expedition by Sea to the East," "Mongol Invasion," and "Takehaya Susanō" (Swift Impetuous Susa-no-o),[19] used this same style; they were the longest poems in Hakushū's career and the only ones in which he attempted to write in a narrative mode. Compared with the earlier poems in *Seals and Clouds*, they showed more variety in rhythm, and used more four- and six- syllable phrases instead of five- and seven- syllable ones. Hakushū no doubt believed that this added to the archaic flavor.

Another important category in *New Eulogies* was lyrical poems on scenes from nature, and they too resembled poems of this kind in *Seals and Clouds*. Hakushū grouped them into two sections, "Seimei Kochō" (Clarity and Ancient Rhythms) and "Enka Yojō" (Mists and Suggestion), characterizing them as "lyrical verses resulting from a sincere communication with nature."[20] Their diction was simple because, as he related in the Afterword to the volume, many were composed for popular women's magazines.[21] He insisted, however, that the meters derived from ancient sources.[22] Had Hakushū not characterized the metric structure as "ancient," the reader would certainly not recognize any difference between them and the lyrics in *Seals and Clouds*, which they resemble so clearly in every other respect. Indeed, most of them were written before Hakushū's eyesight began to fail in 1937. Each poem was constructed using a metric pattern based on four-, five-, six-, and seven- syllable phrases. No doubt it was the numerous deviations from a five- and seven-syllable meter that Hakushū was referring to.

One characteristic of early Japanese poetry prior to the *Man'yōshū* is an irregularity in the length of syllabic phrases. However, use of phrases of four and six syllables is common in traditional folk song forms even of a more recent date. Hakushū's rhythms probably derived from this popular tradition, which he had incorporated into the shi of *Seals and Clouds*. A chance similarity between these rhythms and the rhythm of ancient Japanese poetry furnished him with a plausible reason for including these poems in the collection, even though they seem out of place in other respects.

"Mongol Invasion" and "Expedition by Sea to the East" were set to music and performed, the former at the Kabukiza Theatre in April 1940 and the latter at the Tokyo School of Music in November.[23] A recording of the latter work was made and sent along with English and German translations of the poem to four foreign composers who had written pieces to commemorate the celebrations of Japan's founding as a state.[24]

In March 1941, the *Fukuoka Nichinichi Shinbun* presented Hakushū with its Culture Award for "Expedition by Sea to the East." Hakushū had initially declined an invitation to attend the presentation ceremonies, but when the newspaper offered to postpone them in order for him to be able to attend, he changed his mind. Fukuoka is located in north Kyushu, and a desire to return once more to Yanagawa, which he had not visited since 1928, prompted his decision. In "Shibo" (Longing),[25] a series of eleven tanka published in the March issue of *Tama,* and the shi "Kikyorai" (Returning to my Birthplace),[26] Hakushū wrote of his eager anticipation of the trip and of his yearning to see Yanagawa one last time, while his health still permitted.

Returning to my Birthplace[27]

Yamato,[28] where I was born,
Is a fine place. The clouds soar on south winds.
I should fly there once more.

Tsukushi.[29] That name
Brings back memories of tidal changes,
Of the flush of sunset over the bay.

But my eyes are blind,
Too blind to discern the new shoots in the reeds,
Or the fish traps, the sun glimmering on the water.

Yes, I will return. For the magpies,
That sky, and the sumac grove
Await me. Once more.

Yanagawa. Your children
Have aged, left for distant places.
What draws this childlike heart of mine to you?[30]

This poem was written for *Fujin Kōron* (Women's Forum). Comparison with the tanka series, written a few days earlier, shows marked similarities in subject matter, diction, and treatment. Within the series, however, each tanka functions independently, with no attempt made to suggest the contradictory facets of Hakushū's nostalgia. In this sense, the shi is superior and is considered the best poem of his last years, as well as his last important work in the shi form.[31]

The first two stanzas of "Returning to my Birthplace" open with two place names, full of associations for Hakushū. He anticipates his plane flight to Kyushu, remembering the flight over Yanagawa in 1928 sponsored by the *Osaka Asahi Shinbun*. If the thought of being able to visit Yanagawa at first brings back nostalgic memories of the area, he soon is aware of how much he will miss because of his partial blindness. However, memories of Yanagawa—young reed shoots, fish traps, and the glitter of the sun on the bay—soon supplant these doubts and in the fourth stanza Hakushū resolves to go. Everything he associates with Yanagawa remains as it was, urging him to come.

Only the people will have changed. Those he knew as children are now old and many have left Yanagawa. Despite this, despite his partial blindness, he is drawn to the place. "Why?" he asks rhetorically in the last line of the poem. Of course, he himself has already provided the answer. His decision is not logical but emotional. The memories of Yanagawa he has cherished throughout his life lure him back. Like a child, he cannot deny them.

After Hakushū attended the presentation ceremonies in Fukuoka on March 16, he spent eight days in Yanagawa where he visited with obvious enjoyment all those places, including his mother's home in Nankan, which he had longed to see. On March 21, the Kyushu Convention of Tama Poets was held in Yanagawa. He left for Miyazaki Prefecture on the twenty-fifth and at the invitation of the prefectural government toured the historical sites associated with the Emperor Jimmu, which he had described in "Expedition by Sea to the East."

On May 20, one month after he returned to Tokyo, following a stop-over in Nara where another meeting of Tama poets was held, Hakushū was appointed a member of the Imperial Academy of Art,[32] together with Shimazaki Tōson (1872-1943), Masamune Hakuchō (1879-1962), Shiga Naoya (1883-1971), Yamamoto Yūzō (b. 1887), and Kubota Utsubo in the field of literature.

PEONY TREE LOGS

Hakushū's last collection of tanka, *Botan no Boku* (Peony Tree Logs),[33] contained the poems written between his move to Asagaya in April 1940 and his death in November 1942. During the summer of 1942, he had begun making plans to publish a new collection of tanka and even decided upon a publisher; however, he died without actually starting work on the manuscripts. The collection was published in April 1943 by Kimata Osamu, Hakushū's closest tanka disciple.

Peony Tree Logs was in many ways a continuation of *Black Cypress*. Hakushū's blindness imparted a special quality to both collections, but *Black Cypress* was definitely the superior. First of all, *Peony Tree Logs* lacked unity. The poems were arranged chronologically without any attempt to group series on similar subjects into sections. No doubt this was the only choice open to Kimata Osamu when he decided on the organization of the collection. Hakushū, who had always carefully revised his tanka before publishing a collection, often adding new poems to round out a series or section and deleting others which did not satisfy him, of course had no hand in the editing. But perhaps the most important reason for the relative inferiority of *Peony Tree Logs* was that Hakushū lacked the time to write tanka carefully during his last two years. His illness was too serious to allow him to write freely. What little time he had he devoted to preparing earlier works for publication, not composing new ones. Most of the tanka in *Peony Tree Logs* appear to have been dashed off in order to have something—however inferior—to publish for the monthly issues of *Tama*.

In *Black Cypress*, we confronted Hakushū at a critical period in his life—the time when he was first coping with the challenge of partial blind-ness, a crisis which threatened the premises upon which his approach to poetry had been based. By contrast, in his last years, Hakushū seems to have accepted his blindness and no longer felt compelled to treat it in every tanka he wrote. Nevertheless, the poems that spoke of his failing sight were among the best of *Peony Tree Logs*.

Haru fukaki	We are well into spring
Botan ni zo omou	And I have thought of peonies
Kaganabete	For several days now.
Me o yamashi yori	How many years have passed
Ikutoshi tataru.	Since my eyesight failed?[34]

This poem was written soon after Hakushū moved into his new home in late April 1940. Now that he is settled, his thoughts turn to the peonies that should be in full bloom before long. Several years earlier, he would not have been content merely to think of a flower; he would have wanted to go out and experience spring to the full. Illness, however, had forced him to become more contemplative. Realizing this, he wonders to himself: "How many years have passed since my eyesight failed?"

As shown by this poem, Hakushū became introspective in his last years. This tendency, also evident in *Black Cypress*, was so conspicuous in *Peony Tree Logs* that it seemed to hinder his contemplation of nature. In *Black Cypress*, Hakushū still found consolation in the tranquility of nature; however, there were very few poems in *Peony Tree Logs* that even described nature. He was no longer able to actively seek inspiration from it.

The title of the collection was taken from a series of poems inspired by a present of firewood from a friend in north Japan. Wood from peony trees grown in Nasugawa City in Fukushima Prefecture was prized by tea connoisseurs. Hakushū took much delight in this gift.

Cha no shiro to	The ingredients for tea
Fuyu wa botan no	And a burning fire of peony
Ki o takite	tree logs
Nani tomoshimamu	In winter.
Ware ya wabitsutsu.	What more could I want?
	I find comfort in my solitary life.[35]

Although Hakushū was still in his fifties, poor health kept him at home much of the time. In this tanka, he assumes the pose of an old poet who has renounced the world to live in poverty and solitude, a tradition represented by such famous works as Kamo no Chōmei's *Account of my Hut*[36] or Bashō's *Unreal Dwelling*.[37] Of course, Hakushū was far from indigent; overindulgence in food and drink is often cited as an important cause of his failing health. Nevertheless, his attitude toward life had become more passive. He no longer actively searched for subject matter, but instead treated events that happened to occur as part of his daily life. For example,

Waga shiuru	With the patience
Yasurakeki gotoshi	Learned from blindness
Usu usu ni	I await
Sarusuberi no	The first faint blossoms
Saku o machitsutsu.	On our myrtle tree.[38]

Accepting the fact that his eyesight would never return to normal, Hakushū patiently awaited total blindness, resigned to his fate. With much the same attitude, he contemplated his surroundings, in this example patiently anticipating the blooming of a tree in his garden despite the hot summer weather.

LAST DAYS

Hakushū's short respite from illness ended in the fall of 1941 when he began to experience difficulty in walking; complications had caused his legs to swell and pain him. By the end of that year, high blood pressure and respiratory difficulties kept him confined to bed where, of course, he could not write freely. Hakushū's doctor diagnosed his illness as advanced nephritis, the kidney disease for which he had been hospitalized in 1937. His brother Tetsuo had been urging him to consult a well-known physician at Keiō University Hospital for a second opinion. Hakushū at last acquiesced and on February 21, 1941, on this doctor's advice, entered Keiō University Hospital.

From the first Hakushū was not pleased with his room, the nurses, or the food at the hospital. Because of the negligence of the doctor on duty and an overdose of medicine carelessly administered by a nurse, he nearly died on the night of March 8. Seven tanka about this experience appeared in the April issue of *Tama* and were later published in *Peony Tree Logs*.[39] As Hakushū's condition grew worse, the tone of his tanka became sharper, no doubt reflecting irritation at the sickness he could no longer ignore.

After this experience, Hakushū immediately requested to be removed from Keiō Hospital, and ten days later he was brought to Kyōundō Hospital, where he had stayed in 1937. During his absence from home, his mother had suffered a stroke due to cerebral thrombosis; her prognosis was not good. On April 8, Hakushū received permission to return home where his mother was resting. Although his doctor ordered complete bedrest, Hakushū immediately started to work. His bedroom, which was set up in the front parlor, promptly became his study, office, and receiving room for the numerous guests, friends, and disciples who visited him.

Hakushū resumed a busy schedule. In the next four months, he wrote new poetry, particularly children's verse, and prepared several collections of earlier poetry for publication. He spent one night in early summer dictating thirty poems for children, to which he added eighty more in the next four days to complete *Manshū Chizu* (Map of Manchuria), a volume of patriotic poems for children, which appeared in September.[40] He was also publishing other verses of this type weekly in *Shūkan Shōkokumin* (Young Citizens' Weekly); Yabuta Yoshio, who copied Hakushū's manuscripts for the publisher Asahi Shinbun, later collected these poems into *Daitōa Sensō Shōkokumin Shū* (Greater East Asian War: Verses for Young Citizens).[41]

With a diligence inspired by intimations of death, Hakushū worked to the limits his sickness permitted. He wrote *Nioi no Shuryōsha* (Hunter of Fragrance), a piece of prose in thirty-two sections discussing the fragrances he had discovered since losing his sight.[42] He finished revising and editing the tanka for *Mountain Stream* and *Beech Tree;* a collection of his essays on the tanka, *Tanka no Sho* (A Book on the Tanka); and a selection of early children's verses, *Asa no Yōchien* (Kindergarten in the Morning).[43] At the same time, he also began planning *Nihon Denshō Dōyō Shūsei* (Compilation of Traditional Japanese Children's Songs).[44]

The tanka Hakushū wrote during this time appeared monthly in *Tama*. At the end of September, Kimata Osamu searched through the notes and papers at his bedside for some tanka to publish in the October issue. The two he found were Hakushū's last works in this form.

Aogaya ni	The morning sun
Asa no hi sashite	Shines on the green reeds
Tsuyayakeki	Giving luster
Niwa no ichibu o	To one corner of my garden
Suzushimi mamoru.	And keeping it cool.[45]

Aki no ka no	The autumn mosquitoes
Mimimoto chikaku	Buzz
Tsubuyaku ni	Close to my ear.
Mata toriidete	I will have the mosquito net
Kaya o tsurashimu.	Taken out once more and hung.[46]

Had these not been Hakushū's last tanka, neither would have been worthy of note. Yet though not outstanding, they demonstrate in different ways Hakushū's ability to arrange his thoughts quickly and precisely in the tanka form. The first describes one part of Hakushū's garden, which seemed particularly cool because of the long grasses protecting it from the sunshine. Compared to this quiet description of nature, the last poem is more matter-of-fact. The sick poet, plagued by mosquitoes, considers having a mosquito net, which had already been put away for the winter, hung again. The sharp tone of the poem suggests Hakushū's annoyance at being ill and his irritation at being unable to leave his bed.

Well-meaning friends continued to suggest various remedies which they hoped might aid Hakushū's recovery. *Peony Tree Logs* records several poems on acupuncture and moxa.[47] Hakushū began the most drastic of these cures in July 1942. Without consulting his doctor, he stopped taking medication and began to swallow large amounts of salt, a substance which is now known to exacerbate high blood pressure and promote kidney malfunctions, the very conditions from which Hakushū suffered. Nevertheless, for a short period after this, Hakushū's health improved remarkably. Even his eyesight seemed keener, and he predicted that before long he would be able to forgo the use of his magnifying glass.[48]

The repercussions of this self-cure would be fatal. By early fall, Hakushū was having regular attacks of nausea and respiratory failure so severe that his heartbeat weakened. An oxygen tank was placed in his bedroom, which had been moved from the parlor to the detached house in the garden. Close disciples began to take turns keeping watch during the night. Everyone realized that the end was near.

On November 1, 1942, Hakushū had several attacks of an unprecedented severity, the worst of which brought his family and several close disciples to his bedside at 4:00 A.M. on the morning of November 2. Cyanosis and orthopnea indicated congestive heart failure. The doctor gave Hakushū an injection of medication to stimulate his heart, but the attack continued with ominous intensity for quite some while until almost miraculously it suddenly subsided.

Hakushū immediately requested something to eat. His wife brought him fresh apple juice which he refused, insisting instead on an apple, which he ate with relish. His son opened a window and Hakushū said, "I feel refreshed. Ryūtarō, what day is it today? November the second? A new life awaits me. A new life. You must remember this day, a glorious memorial to the new start I will make. Please open the window more....It feels wonderful."[49]

Everyone withdrew from the room to allow Hakushū some rest. Tetsuo quietly asked the doctor's opinion, which confirmed his forebodings. Some minutes passed before another attack, the last, began. Hakushū no longer had the strength or the will power to fight off death. "After experiencing such relief once, I don't have the energy to overcome this again. It's hopeless. Hopeless," he whispered feebly between gasps for breath.[50]

Hakushū, fifty-seven years old, passed away fifteen minutes later at 7:50 A.M.

The funeral was held on November 5 at the Aoyama Funeral Hall in Tokyo, with over three thousand people attending the farewell ceremonies immediately afterward. Condolences were received from important figures and organizations in the literary world. Twelve days later the government ordered that Hakushū be retroactively awarded the Fourth Order of the Decoration of the Sacred Treasure.

PATTERNS OF WATER

Among various notes and letters found beside Hakushū's bed after his death were several patriotic children's poems[51] and the unfinished manuscripts for the Preface and Epilogue of *Mizu no Kōzu* (Patterns of Water), a collection of poems and photographs of Yanagawa on which Hakushū and the photographer Tanaka Zentoku were collaborating.[52]

Tanaka had visited Hakushū on October 6, 1942 to show him the proofs of the book and request the parts that Hakushū had promised to write. Hakushū worked through the night with Tanaka at his side, writing portions of the Preface and Epilogue. He died before he was able to complete these sections, and they appeared in unfinished form when the book was published in January 1943. In them, in a style reminiscent of "Growing Up," the famous preface to *Memories,* Hakushū wrote once again of Yanagawa, reaffirming his ties. The youthful days he spent there had greatly influenced the development of his character and the style of his poetry. As he explained in the Epilogue, "The sky, sunlight, and earth of Yanagawa, and the colors, fragrances, warmth, and glitter of Yanagawa's water lovingly nurtured me in my youth. Its land, patterned by canals, has made me what I am."[53]

Hakushū's poetic sensitivity was fostered by his upbringing in Yanagawa. His early impressions became the subject matter of some of his most important poems. Throughout his life, Hakushū cherished these memories. His attachment to his birthplace, perhaps unequaled among contemporary poets, formed an important theme in his poetry. Furthermore, the sensitivity to sense perceptions learned in his youth in Yanagawa remained the most important characteristic of his poetry throughout his life.

At the beginning of the Preface were two short lines of introduction: "Late at night, when people have settled down to sleep, I write this preface, this testament for posterity." Hakushū called it "a testament for posterity" not merely because it would be one of his last works. Writing about Yanagawa at this time poignantly and appropriately consummated his life's work.

Yanagawa, town of canals, my hometown, my birthplace. Yanagawa and its water, the mother of my verse. Without the patterns of your waterways, the features of your land, my body could not have existed, my style would not have been formed. I find that I remember the past more deeply now that I have lost my eyesight, and the poignance of my memories grows stronger as my perception of reality[54] weakens. I have heard that an exalted personage of the past once remarked: "The descendants of a man whose life has been full will adorn his head with reeds and the dark oak leaves from Mount Heguri." What then do I have to regret, what then should I desire? Yanagawa—your clouds, water and winds, your perch, your fish of southern breed.[55]

As Hakushū awaited his fate, he thought about his youth and his life. Although men would not crown his head with leaves and grasses as had been the custom in ancient times, he felt assured that his life had been full; he could face death calmly and without regret.

CONCLUSION

My discussion of Hakushū's poetry has concentrated on an examination of the development of Hakushū's style and his activities as a literary figure of his age. In conclusion, it seems appropriate to assess the significance of Hakushū's achievements on a broader scale. In January 1942, ten months before Hakushū's death, Hagiwara Sakutarō wrote what must be considered the first serious assessment of Hakushū's lifetime contribution to poetry. A poet and one-time disciple of Hakushū, Sakutarō was perhaps better qualified than most of his contemporaries to pinpoint the importance of Hakushū's achievements:

Japan has produced many excellent poets since the beginning of the Meiji period; however, Kitahara Hakushū stands in a unique position because of the wide range of his achievements, because of the new territory which he opened in every field of poetry, and because of certain latent talents which he converted into literary genius. Hakushū both startled and at the same time stimulated contemporary poets of shi with such famous collections as *Heretical Faith*, *Memories*, and *Scenes of Tokyo*, even as he was also publishing [the tanka collections] *Paulownia Flowers* and *Mica*. Many a young man was enchanted by the new melodies of his verse, melodies that were as fresh as they were distinguished. Hakushū attained unprecedented dominion over both the world of shi and the world of tanka. He then proceeded to extend his talents beyond this into the field of the popular ballad—namely the folk song, children's poetry, the ballad, and the short lyric—and in these forms once again developed heretofore untouched territories. Japan has many poets, but generally speaking they limit their talents to one form of poetry, be it the shi or the haiku or whatever. Kitahara Hakushū and Hakushū alone has made outstanding contributions to Japanese poetry in each and every of its separate forms.[56]

Indeed, as Sakutarō recognized so clearly, Hakushū's contribution to modern Japanese poetry was patently different from that of his contemporaries because of its breadth. Hakushū composed verse in every poetic form: shi, tanka, chōka, haiku, short lyric, folk song, children's verse, as well as the tanshō of his own invention. And in every form in which he chose to write, his contribution in that form alone was not less than major. He was also an important innovator in the use of sound and rhythm in poetry. His contribution to lyrical poetry, both as a separate verse form and as an element of poetry in general, was seminal.

Despite the insight of Sakutarō's analysis, he displayed the same bias and probably in fact in his own way contributed to give authority to the slanted approach that colors most interpretations of Hakushū's poetry. For he all but ignored Hakushū's contribution to the tanka in the latter half of his life, a contribution which tends to be overshadowed by the obvious and indeed enormous significance of Hakushū's early collections. It would be wrong to overlook the importance of *Heretical Faith* and *Memories*, yet when we consider Hakushū's work in its entirety, it is difficult to escape the impression that one facet of Hakushū's genius revealed itself best in the tanka. Sakutarō singled out *Paulownia Flowers* and *Mica* for special praise. Influential as these works were in their day, however, it is unfair to judge Hakushū's contribution to the tanka in terms of them alone, particularly so because Hakushū's conception of the tanka at the time he wrote them did not take account of its possibilities as a distinct poetic form: he viewed the tanka as an extension of his shi. It was not until Hakushū began to compose the tanka later included in *Sparrow's Eggs* that he attempted to master the form for its own sake. With a few exceptions, the best poems of the lattter half of his life were tanka, and it was for the tanka that he formulated his most important poetic theories. *Sparrow's Eggs*, *White Breezes of Summer*, *Beech Tree*, and *Black Cypress* without doubt constitute major contributions to the modern tanka and deserve to be included in any assessment of Hakushū's contribution to modern Japanese poetry.

APPENDIX: ORIGINAL TEXTS OF POEMS

The original texts of the poems translated in this study, when brief, have been included in the body of the text. This appendix contains the originals of the longer poems with the English title of each poem cited following the Japanese title.

身　　　熱
Fever

母なりき。
われかき抱き、
朱欒ちる薄き陰影より
のびあがり、泣きて透かしつ。
『見よ、乳母の棺は往く。』と。

時は白日、
大路青ずみ、
白き人列なし去んぬ。
刹那、また火なす身熱、
なべて世は日さへ爛れき。

病むごとに、
母は歎きぬ。
『身熱に汝は乳母焦がし、
また、吾子よ、母を。』と。 ── 今も
われ青む。懸かる恐怖に。

靑　き　甕
The Green Urn

『靑甕ぞ。』 ── 街衢に聲す。
大道に人かげ絶えて
早や七日、溝に血も饐え、
惡蟲の羽風の熱さ。
日も眞夏、火の天爛れ、

雲燥りめ。——大家の店に、
人々は蟇なる恐怖、
香くすべ、靑う寝そべり、
煙管とる肱もたゆげに、
蛇のごと眼のみ光りぬ。

『靑甕ぞ。』——今こそ家族、
『聲す。』『聽け。』「血糊の足音。』
『何もなし。』——やがて寂寞。——
秒ならず、荷擔夫一人、
次に甕（これこそ死骸、）
また男——がらす戸透かし、
つと映る刹那——眞靑に
甕なるが吾を睨みぬ。
父りなりき。——（父は座にあり。）——
ひとつ眼の詛呪の光。

『靑甕ぞ。』——日もこそ靑め、
言葉なし。——蛇のとぐろを、
香匂ひぬ、苦熱の息吹。
また過ぎぬ、ひひら笑ひぬ。
母なりき。——（母も座にあり。）
がらす戸の冷たき皺み。
やがてまた一列、——あなや、
我なりき。靑き小甕に、
歔欷りつつ黑き血吐くと、
刹那見ぬ、地獄の恐怖。

紅 き 實
Red Fruit

日もしらず、
ところもしらず。
美しう稚児めくひとと
匐ひ寄りて、
桃か、林檎か、
朱の盆に盛りつととまでを。

餘は知らず、
また名もしらず。
夢なりや——
さあれ、おぼろに
朱の盆に盛りつとまでを、
わが見しは
紅き實なりき。

日 ざ か り
High Noon

嗚呼、今し午砲のひびき
おほどかにとどろきわたり、
遠近の汽笛しばらく
餞うるごと呻きをはれば、
柳原熱き街衢は
また、もとの沈黙にかへる。

河岸なみは赤き煉瓦家。

牢獄めく工場の奥ゆ
印刷の響たまたま
薄鐵葉着る鋏の音と、
柩うつ槌と、鑢と、
懶うげにまじりきこえぬ。

片側の古衣屋つづき、
衣紋掛重き恐怖に
肺やみの咳洩れて、
饐えてゆく物のいきれに、
陰隰のにほひつめたく
照り白み、人は黙坐す。

ゆきかへり、やをら、電氣車
鉛だつ體をとどめて
ぐどぐどとかたみに語り、
鬱憂き唸重げに
また軋る、熱く垂れたる
ひた赤き滿員の札。

恐ろしき沈黙ふたたび
酷熱の日ざしにただれ、
ぺんき塗褪めし看板
毒滴らし、河岸のあちこち
ちぢれ毛の痩犬見えて
苦しげに肉を求食りぬ。

油うく線路の正面、

鐵重き橋の構に
雲ひとつまろがりいでて
くらくらとかがやく眞晝、
汗ながし、車曳きつつ
葡萄ふがごと撒水夫きたる。

解纜
Weighing Anchor

解纜す、大船あまた。——
ここ肥前長崎港のただなかは
長雨ぞらの幽闇に海づら鈍み、
悶々と檣けぶるたたずまひ、
鎖のむせび、帆のうなり、傳馬のさけび、
あるはまた阿蘭船なる黑奴が
氣も狂ほしき諸ごゑに、硝子切る音、
うち濕り——嗚呼午後七時——ひとしきり、落居ぬ騷擾。

解纜す、大船あまた。
あかあかと日暮の街に吐血して
落日喘ぐ寂寥に鐘鳴りわたり、
陰々と、灰色重き曇日を
死を告げ知らすせはしさに、響は絶えず
天主より。——暗澹として二列、
海波の嗚咽、赤の浮標、なかに黃ばめる
帆は瘧に——嗚呼午後七時——わわなとはためく恐怖。

解纜す、大船あまた。——

黄髪の伴天連信徒蹌踉と
闇穴道はを磔負ひ驅られゆくごと
生ぬるき悔の唸順々に、
流るる血しほ黑煙り動揺しつつ、
印度、はた、南蠻、羅馬、目的はあれ、
ただ生涯の船がかり、いづれは黄泉へ
消えゆくや、── 嗚呼午後七時 ──鬱憂の心の海に。

鵠
Swan

わかうどなゆめ近よりそ、
かのゆくは邪宗の鵠、
日のうちに七度八度
潮あび化粧すといふ
伴天連の秘の少女ぞ。
地になびく髪には蘆薈、
嘴にまた赤き實を塗る
淫らなる鳥にしあれば、
絶えず、その眞白羽ひろげ
乳香の水したらす。
されば、子なゆめ近よりそ。
視よ、持つは炎か、華か、
さならずば實の無花果か、
兎にもあれ、かれこそ邪法。
わかうどなゆめ近よりそ。

ただ秘めよ
Please Don't Tell

日ひけるは
あな、わが少女
天艸の蜜の少女よ。
汝が髪は烏のごとく、
汝が唇は木の實の紅に没薬の汁滴らす。
わが鴿よ、わだ友よ、いざともに擁かまし。
薫濃き葡萄の酒は
玻璃の壺に盛るべく、
もたらしし麝香の臍は
汝が肌の百合に染めてむ。
よし、さあれ、汝が父に、
よし、さあれ、汝が母に、
ただ秘めよ、ただ守れ、齋き死ぬまで、
虐の罪の鞭はさもあらばあれ、
ああただ秘めよ、御くるすの愛の徴を。

謀叛
Rebellion

ひと日、わが精舎の庭に、
晩秋の静かなる落日のなかに、
あはれ、また、薄黄なる噴水の吐息のなかに
いとほのにギオロンの、その絃の、
その夢の、哀愁の、いとほのにうれひ泣く。

蠟の火と懺悔のくゆり

ほのぼのと、廊いづる白き衣は
夕暮の言もなき修道女の長き一列。
さあれ、いま、ギオロンの、くるしみの、
刺すばごと火の酒の、その絃のいたみ泣く。

またあれば落日の色に、
夢燃ゆる噴水の吐息のなかに、
さらになほ歌もなき白鳥の愁のもとに、
いと強き硝薬の、黒き火の、
地の底の導火燃き、ギオロンぞ狂ひ泣く。

眺り來る車輛の響、
毒の弾丸、血の烟、閃めく刃、
あはれ、驚破、火とならむ、噴水も、精舎も、空も。
紅 の、戦慄の、その極の
瞬間の叫喚燃き、ギオロンぞ盲ひたる。

邪 宗 門 秘 曲
Secret Song of the Heretics

われは思ふ、末世の邪宗、切支丹でうすの魔法。
黒船の加比丹を、紅毛の不可思議國を、
色赤きびいどろを、匂鋭きあんじやべいいる、
南蠻の棧留縞を、はた、阿刺吉、珍酡の酒を。

目見靑きドミニカびとは陀羅尼誦し夢にも語る、
禁制の宗門神を、あるはまた、血に染む聖磔、
芥子粒を林檎のごとく見すといふ欺罔の器、

波羅葦僧の空をも覗く伸び縮む奇なる眼鏡を。

屋はまた石もて造り、大理石の白き血潮は、
ぎやまんの壺に盛られて夜となれば火點るといふ。
かの美しき越歴機の夢は天鵝絨の薫にまじり、
珍らなる月の世界の鳥獸映像すと聞きけり。

あるは聞く、化粧の料は毒草の花よりしぼり、
腐れたる石の油に畫くてふ麻利耶の像よ、
はた、羅甸、波爾杜瓦爾らの横つづり靑なる假名は
美しき、さいへ悲して歡楽の音にかも滿つる。

いごさらばわれらに賜へ、幻惑の伴天連尊者、
百年を刹那に縮め、地の磔背にし死すとも
惜しからじ、願ふは極秘、かの奇しき 紅 の夢、
善主麿、今日を祈に身も靈も薫りこがるる。

曇　　　日
A Cloudy Day

曇日の空氣のなかに、
狂ひいづる樟の芽の鬱憂よ……
そのもとに桐は咲く。
Whiskyの香のごときしぶき、かなしみ……

そこここにいぎたなき駱駝の寝息、
見よ、鈍き綿羊の色のよごれに
饐えて病む藁のくさみ、

その濡る泥濘（ぬかるみ）に花はこぼれて
紫の薄き色鋭（するど）になげく
はた、空のわか葉の威壓。

いづこにか、またもきけかし。
餌（え）に饑（う）ゑしペリカンのけうとき叫（さけび）、
山猫（やまねこ）のものさやぎ、なげく鶯（うぐひす）、
腐れゆく沼の水蒸（む）すがごとくに。

そのなかに桐は散る……Whiskyの強きかなしみ……

もの甘き風のまた生（なま）あたたかさ、
猥（みだ）らなる獣（けもの）らの園内（かこひ）のあゆみ、
のろのろと枝に下（さが）るなまけもの、あるは、貧しく
眼（め）を据（す）ゑて毛蟲喙（けむしっ）む嗟嘆（なげかひ）のほろほろ鳥よ。

そのもとに花はちる……桐のむらさき……

かくしてや日は暮れむ、ああひと日。
病院の逃（のが）れ來（こ）し患者の恐怖（おそれ）、
赤子（あかご）らの眼のなやみ、笑ふ黑奴（くろんぼ）、
酔ひ痴（し）れし遊蕩兒（たはれを）の縦覧（みまはり）のとりとめもなく。

その空に桐はちる……新しきしぶき、かなしみ……

はたや、また、園（その）の外（そと）ゆく……
軍樂（ぐんがく）の黑き不安の壊れ落（なだ）ち、夜に入る時よ。
やるせなく騒ぎいでぬる鳥獣（とりけもの）、

また、その中^{なか}に、
狂ひいづる北極熊^{ほくきよくぐま}の氷なす戦慄^{をののき}の聲。

その闇^{やみ}に花はちる……Whisky の香^かの頻吹^{しぶき}……桐の紫……

空 に 真 赤 な
In the Sky, Deep Red

空に眞赤^{まつか}な雲のいろ。
玻璃^{はり}に眞赤^{まつか}な酒のいろ。
なんでこの身^みが悲しかろ。
空に眞赤^{まつか}な雲のいろ。

お か る 勘 平
Okaru and Kanpei

おかるは泣いてゐる。
長い薄明^{うすあかり}のなかでびろうど葵^{あふひ}の顫^{ふる}へてゐるやうに、
やはらかなふらんねるの手ざはりのやうに、
きんぽうげ色の草生^{くさぶ}の晝の光が消えかかるやうに、
ふはふはと飛んでゆくたんぽぽの穂のやうに。

泣いても泣いても涙は盡きぬ、
勘平^{かんべい}さんが死んだ、勘平さんが死んだ、
わかい綺麗^{きれい}な勘平さんが腹切った……
おかるはうらわかい男のにほひを忍んで泣く、
麹室^{かうぢむろ}に玉葱^{たまねぎ}の咽^むせるやうな強い刺戟だったと思ふ。
やはらかな肌^{はだ}ざはりが五月ごろの外光^{ぐわいくわう}のやうだった、

紅茶のやうに熱つた男の息、
抱擁められた時、晝間の鹽田が靑く光り、
白い芹の花の神経が、鋭くなつて眞蒼に濁れた。
顫へてゐた男の内股と吸はせた唇と、
別れた日には男の白い手に煙硝のしめりが泌み込んでゐた、
駕にのる前まで私はしみじみと新しい野菜を切ってゐた……

その勘平は死んだ。
おかるは温室のなかの孤兒のやうに、
いろんな官能の記憶にそそのかされて、
樂しい自身の愉樂に耽つてゐる。

（人形芝居の硝子越しに、あかい柑子の實が秋の夕日にかがやき、
黄色く霞んだ市街の底から河蒸氣の笛がきこえる。）

おかるは泣いてゐる。
美しい身振の、身も世もないといふやうな、
迫った三味に連れられて、
チョボの佐和利に乗って、
泣いて泣いて、溺れ死でもするやうに
おかるは泣いてゐる。

（色と香ひと音樂と。
勘平なんかどうでもいい。）

かるい背廣を
Wearing a Light Jacket

かるい背廣を身につけて、
今宵またゆく都川、
戀か、ねたみか、吊橋の
瓦斯の薄黄が氣にかかる。

金 と 靑 と の
Gold and Green

金と靑との愁夜曲、
春と夏との二聲樂、
わかい東京に江戸の唄、
陰影と光のわがこころ。

物 理 學 校 裏
Behind the School of Physics

Borum. Bromun. Calcium.
Chromium. Manganum. Kalium. Phosphor.
Barium. Iodium. Hydrogenium.
Sulphur. Chlorum. Strontium......
(寂しい聲がきこえる、そして不可思議な……)

日が暮れた、淡い銀と紫――
蒸し熱い六月の空に
暮れのこる棕櫚の花の悩ましさ。
黄色い、新しい花穂の聚團が

暗い裂けた葉の陰影から噎せるやうに光る。
さうして深い吐息と腋臭とを放つ、
歯痛の色の黄、沃土ホルムの黄、粉つぽい興奮の黄。

$C_2H_2O_2N_2 + NaOH = CH_4 + Na_2CO_3$ ......
蒼白い白熱瓦斯の情調が曇硝子を透して流れる。
角窓のそのひとつの内部に
光のない青いメタンの焔が燃えてるらしい。
肺病院のやうな東京物理學校の淡い青灰色の壁に
いつしかあるかなきかの月光がしたたる。

Tin.....Tin.....Tin. n. n. n......Tin. n.....
　 tire.....tire....tin. n. n. n......shan.....
ti.....ti.....ti.....ti.....tote.....tsn. n......
　 shan. n. n. n. n......
静かな悩ましい晩、
何處かにお稽古の琴の音がきこえて、
崖下の小さい平屋の亜鉛屋根に
コルタアが青く光り、
柔らかい草いきれの底にLampの黄色い赤みが點る。
その上の、見よ、すこしばかりの空地には
濕つた胡瓜と茄子の鄙びた新しい臭が
惶ただしい市街生活の哀愁に纏れる……
汽笛が鳴る。四谷を出た汽車のCadenceが近づく……

暮れ悩む官能の棕櫚
そのわかわかしい花穂の臭が暗みながら噎ぶ、
歯痛の色の黄、沃土ホルムの黄、粉つぽい興奮の黄。

寂しい冷たい教師の聲がきこえる、そして不可思議な……
そこここの明るい角窓のなかから。

Sin.....Cosin.....Tan.....Cotan.....Sec.....Cosec.....

　　etc.....

Lon. Dynama. Roentgen. Boyle. Newton.

Lens. Siphon. Spectrum. Tesla の火花

攝氏、華氏、光、Bunsen. Potential. or,

　　Archimedes. etc. etc.....

棕櫚のかげには野菜の露にこほろぎが鳴き、

無意味な琴の音の稚びた Sentiment は

何時までも何時までもせうことなしに續いてゆく。

汽笛が鳴る……濠端の淡い銀と紫との空に

停車つた汽車が蒼みがかつた白い湯氣を吐いてゐる。

静かな三分間。

悩ましい棕櫚の花の官能に、今、

蒸し暑い魔睡がもつれ、

暗い裂けた葉の縁から銀の鬱憂がしたたる。

その陰影の捕捉へがたき Passion の色、

歯痛の色の黄、沃土ホルムの黄、粉つぽい興奮の黄。

Neon. Flourum. Magnesium.

Natrium. Silicium. Oxygenium.

Nitrogenium. Cadimium or, Stibium.

　　　　　　etc, etc.....

序　　詩
Preface Poem

思ひ出は首すぢの赤い螢の
午後のおぼつかない觸覺のやうに、
ふうはりと靑みを帯びた
光るとも見えぬ光？

あるひはほのかな穀物の花か、
落穂ひろひの小唄か、
暖かい酒倉の南で
ひき毟しる鳩の毛の白いほめき？

音色ならば笛の類、
蟇蛄の啼く
醫師の藥のなつかしい晩、
薄らあかりに吹いてるハーモニカ。

匂ならば天鵞絨、
骨牌の女王の眼、
道化たピエローの面の
なにかしらさみしい感じ。

放埒の日のやうにつらからず、
熱病のあかるい痛みもないやうで、
それでゐて暮春のやうにやはらかい
思ひ出か、ただし、わが秋の中古傳説？

夜
Night

夜は黒……銀箔の裏面の黒。
滑らかな潟海の黒、
さうして芝居の下幕の黒、
幽霊の髪の黒。

夜は黒……ぬるぬると蛇の目が光り、
おはぐろの臭のいやらしく、
千金丹の鞄がうろつき、
黒猫がふはりとあるく……夜は黒。

夜は黒……おそろしい、忍びやかな盗人の黒、
定九郎の蛇目傘、
誰が頸すぢに觸るやうな
力のない死螢の翅のやうな。

夜は黒……時計の數字の奇異な黒。
血汐のしたたる
生じろい鋏を持つて
生膽取のさしのぞく夜。

夜は黒……瞑つても瞑つても、
青い赤い無數の靈の落ちかかる夜、
耳鳴の底知れぬ夜、
暗い夜、
ひとりぼつちの夜。

夜……夜……夜……

公 園 の 薄 暮
Dusk in the Park

ほの青き銀色の空氣に、
そことなく噴水の水はしたたり、
薄明ややしばしさまかへぬほど、
ふくらなる羽毛頸巻のいろなやましく女ゆきかふ。

つつましき枯草の濕るにほひよ……
圓形に、あるは楕圓に、
劃られし園の配置の黄にほめき、靄に三つ四つ
色淡き紫の弧燈したしげに光るるほふ。

春はなほ見えねども、園のこころに
いと甘き沈丁の苦き莟の
刺すがごと泌みたりき、瓦斯の薄黄は
身を投げし靈のゆめごと水のほとりに。

暮れかぬる電車のきしり……
凋れたる調和にぞ修道女の一人消えさり、
裁判はてし控訴院に留守居らの點す燈は、
疲れたる硝子より弊私的里の瞳を放つ。

いづこにかすずろげる春の暗示よ……
陰影のそこここに、やや強く光劃りて
息ふかき弧燈枯くさの園に歎けば、
面黄なる病兒幽かに照らされて迷ひわづらふ。

朧げのつつましき匂のそらに、

なほ妙にしだれつつ噴水の吐息したたり、
新しき月光の沈丁に泌みも冷ゆれば
官能の薄らあかり銀笛の夜とぞなりぬる。

白 金 ノ 獨 樂
The Platinum Top

感涙ナガレ、身は佛、
獨樂ハ廻レリ、指尖ニ。

カガヤク指ハ天を指シ、
極マル獨樂ハ目ニ見エズ。

圓轉、無念無想界、
白金ノ獨樂音モ澄ミワタル。

薔 薇 二 曲
Two Poems on the Rose

一

薔薇ノ木ニ
薔薇ノ花サク。

ナニゴトノ不思議ナケレド。

二

薔薇の花。
ナニゴトノ不思議ナケレド。

照り極マレバ木ヨリコボルル。
光リコボルル。

城 ケ 島 の 雨
The Rain on Jōgashima Island

雨はふるふる、城ケ島の磯に、
利休鼠の雨がふる。
雨は眞珠か、夜明けの霧か、
それともわたしの忍び泣き。
舟はゆくゆく通り矢のはなを、
濡れて帆あげたぬしの舟。

ええ、舟は櫓でやる、櫓は唄でやる。
唄は船頭さんの心意氣。
雨はふるふる、日はうす曇る。
舟はゆくゆく、帆がかすむ。

りすりす小栗鼠
Squirrel, Squirrel, Little Squirrel

栗鼠、栗鼠、小栗鼠、
ちよろちよろ小栗鼠
杏の實が赤いぞ、
食べ食べ、小栗鼠。

栗鼠、栗鼠、小栗鼠、
ちよろちよろ小栗鼠、

山椒の露が青いぞ、
飲め飲め、小栗鼠。

栗鼠、栗鼠、小栗鼠、
ちょろちょろ小栗鼠、
葡萄の花が白いぞ、
揺れ揺れ、小栗鼠。

落　葉　松
Chinese Pines

一

からまつの林を過ぎて、
からまつをしみじみと見き。
からまつはさびしかりけり。
たびゆくはさびしかりけり。

二

からまつの林を出でて、
からまつの林に入りぬ。
からまつの林に入りて、
また細く道はつづけり。

三

からまつの林の奥も、
わが通る道はありけり。
霧雨のかかる道なり。
山風のかよふ道なり。

四

からまつの林の道は、
われのみか、ひともかよひぬ。
ほそぼそと通ふ道なり。
さびさびといそぐ道なり。

五

からまつの林を過ぎて、
ゆゑしらず歩みひそめつ。
からまつはさびしかりけり、
からまつとささやきにけり。

六

からまつの林を出でて、
浅間嶺にけぶり立つ見つ。
浅間嶺にけぶり立つ見つ。
からまつのまたそのうへに。

七

からまつの林の雨は、
さびしけどいよよしづけし。
かんこ鳥鳴けるのみなる。
からまつの濡るるのみなる。

八

世の中よ、あはれなりけり。
常なけどうれしかりけり。
山川に山がはの音、

からまつにからまつのかぜ。

雪　後　の　聲
Call after a Snowfall

蜩 が啼いてる、あ、月夜の
雪明りの中、
なんとしたことだ、あの
時ならぬ刻みは、聲音は。

あまりのこの閑けさ、
遠さ、幽けさ、
あ、また金の線が弾ける。

鴨
Wild Duck

鴨だ。鴨だ。鴨が
すべりあがる。おお、
大きいうねりの窪みから——
深い深い底の奥から、
もこりもこりと盛りあがる部厚な波、
そのうねりの阪へかかつた、搖り搖られて。

鴨の、なんと、
黄色い 嘴 だ、鮮かな、
横を向いて、
留る、と、高みきつたうねり波の峰が

飛沫ひとつ立てずに、廣くなだれる。
平かに
はるばるとした世界が見える。

鴨はすべる。
すうつと落ちてゆく、大きいうねりの窪みへ、
風も無い穏かなうねりだ、尾羽根を立てて、
なんとまた、光つた
叡智の瞳。
鴨が、あつ、かくれた、
大きいうねり波に、さうして、
見えない向うの渓間にゐる
あの姿勢。──
わたしは直感する、
おそろしく、冥い、冥い、動いてゐる
波の丘陵を透して、
全くの静謐、
虔ましい頬の紫。

鴨がまた、揺られて、
見えて來る、あ、出た、出た、
大きい、すばらしいうねりに乗って來る。
『おうおう。』とでも呼びかけたい。
いいかたちで、浮んで、浮んで。
ブラボウ、萬歳。

鴨はまかせる、
大きいうねりの意志に。

はてしもない韃靼海のただなかだ。
小さい鴨の水搔、
ぴつたりとつけた胸毛の
燃えるやうな濃い靑。

鴨は一羽だ。
北へゆくほど遠くなる日の光だ。
空の世界も寒いが、
雲は深いが、また、
波は光らぬ、
見わたすかぎり光らぬ波、
平かに平かに見えても、また、
そのじつ、
大きく大きくうねつてゐるのだ、暮って。

鴨は啼かない。
まつたく黄色い嘴だ、さうして、
おお、おお、搖れてる、乗つてる、辷つてゐる。
小さい、整った、
美しい、きつちりした
鴨の象、
個の叡智、
ああ、一つの正しい存在。
あ、かくれた、向こうへ落ちてゆく。
あ、出た出た。
ぴゆう――
指笛だ、俺のだ。

鴨はまかせる。

大きいうねりに坐(すわ)って

盛りあがる、盛りあがる、部厚な、

底ぢからに搖られる。

鴨は開(あ)けてる、閑(しず)かな眼(め)を。

劫初(ごふしよ)からの海、韃靼の寒空。

しかも、夏、夏、夏、

どちら向いても、

うねりの

絶間もないうねりの、

冥(くら)い、光らぬ、

おそろしく、また、穩やかな、

波濤(はたう)と波濤と波濤の連續。

ええ、ちきしょう。

鴨の尻(けつ)。

夜が來る。夜が來る。

水　　　　　上
The Source of Water

水上(みなかみ)は思ふべきかな。

苔清水湧(こけしみづわ)きしたたり、

日の光透(す)きしたたり、

橿(かし)、馬酔木(あしび)、枝さし蔽(おほ)ひ、

鏡葉(かがみは)の湯津眞椿(ゆづまつばき)の眞洞(まほら)なす

水上(みなかみ)は思ふべきかな。

水上(みなかみ)は思ふべきかな。

山の氣の神處の澄み、
岩が根の言問ひ止み、
かいかがむ荒素膚の
荒魂の神魂び、神つどへる
水上は思ふべきかな。

水上は思ふべきかな。
雲、狹霧、立ちはばかり、
丹の雉子立ちはばかり、
白き猪の横伏し喘ぎ、
毛の荒物のことごとに道塞ぎ寝る
水上は思ふべきかな。

水上は思ふべきかな。
清清に湧きしたたり、
いやさやに透きしたたり、
神ながら神寂び古る
うづの、をを、うづの幣帛の緒の鎮もる
水上は思ふべきかな。

水上は思ふべきかな。
青水沫とよみたぎち、
うろくづの堰かれたぎち、
たまきはる命の渦の
渦巻きの湯津石村をとどろき搖る
水上は思ふべきかな。

鋼　鐵　風　景
Landscape in Steel

神は在る、鐵塔の碍子に在る。
神は在る、起重機の斜線に在る。

神は在る、鐵柱の頂點に在る。
神は在る、鐵橋の弧線に在る。

神は在る、晴天と共に在る。
神は在る、鋼鐵の光に在る。

神は在る、近代の風景と在る。
神は在る、鐵板の響と在る。

神は在る、怪奇な機関に在る。
神は在る、モオタアと廻轉する。

神は在る、装甲車と駛る。
神は在る、砲弾と炸裂する。

神は在る、圓形の利刃に在る。
截音は空をも削る。

神は在る、ダイナモの靈音に在る。
神は在る、一瞬に電光を放つ。

神は在る、鐵筋の劇場に在る。
神は在る、鐵工のメーデーに在る。

神は在る、車輪のわだちに在る。
轢音（れきおん）は野菜を咳（くら）ふ。

神は在る、はてしなき軌道（きだう）に在る。
神は在る、雷雲に反響する。

神は在る、立體のキユビズムに在る。
表現派は都市を彎曲（わんきよく）する。

神は在る、颯爽と牽引（けんいん）する。
神は在る、鮮麗に磁氣を生む。

神は在る、天體は鐵鑛である。
神は在る、炎炎と熾（おこ）つてゐる。

白
White

目ざましきもの、花辛夷（はなこぶし）、
白き胸毛の百千鳥（ももちどり）。

夏は岩が根、白牡丹（しろぼたん）、
白光（びやくくわう）放つ番（つが）ひ鳩（ばと）。

秋は月夜の白かんば、
白き鹿（しか）立つ杣（そま）の霧。

へうと飛びゆく雲は冬、

鶴に身をかる幻術師。

何か坐します、山の秀に、
雪の氣韻は澄みのぼる。

歸　去　來
Returning to My Birthplace

> 飛行して郷土を訪問せるはすでに
> 十二年の昔となりぬ

山門は我が産土、
雲騰る南風のまほら、
飛ばまし今一度、

筑紫よかく呼ばへば
戀ほしよ潮の落差、
火照泌む夕日の潟。

盲ふるに、早やもこの眼、
見ざらむ、また葦かび、
籠飼や水かげろふ。

歸らなむ、いざ鵲、
かの空や櫨のたむろ、
待つらむぞ今一度。

故郷やそのかの子ら、

皆老いて遠きに、
何ぞ寄る童ごころ。

NOTES

PREFACE

[1]Tamagawa Daigaku Shuppanbu.

[2]*Hakushū Zenshū*, 18 vols. (Arusu, 1929-1934).

[3]Kimata Osamu—an important scholar of modern tanka as well as a noted tanka poet and Hakushū's closest tanka disciple—is the only scholar who has examined Hakushū's tanka in detail. Although most other studies of Hakushū's poetry concentrate on his early collections, the few that do treat his late tanka are based on Kimata's works, particularly *Hakushū Kenykū* (Yakumo Shorin, 1943), *Hakushū Kenkyū I: Tanka Hen* (Shinten Shobō, 1954), and *Hakushū Kenkyū II: Hakushū to Sono Shūhen* (Shinten Shobō, 1955).

CHAPTER 1

[1]Hakushū's birth date is mistakenly recorded on official documents in Yanagawa as February 25, 1885. As was local custom, his mother Shike had gone to her parents' home to give birth to Hakushū. She probably did not return to Yanagawa until late February which explains the delay in registering Hakushū's birth.

[2]His father Chōtarō had two children by a previous marriage: a son who died in infancy and a daughter Kayo (b. 1883). Shike bore her husband four more children after Hakushū: Tetsuo (1887-1957), Chike (1889-1901), Ie (1892-1959), and Yoshio (b. 1895). Ie married the painter Yamamoto Kanae (1882-1946); their son Yamamoto Tarō (b.1925) is an important modern poet.

[3]Kitahara Tetsuo founded Oranda Shobō with Hakushū in April 1915. He sold this firm two years later and in July 1917 set up a new publishing house, Arusu. Under Tetsuo's direction, Arusu became one of the most important publishers of modern Japanese poetry.

Kitahara Yoshio is president of Atorie Publishing Company.

[4]Yabuta Yoshio, *Hyōden Kitahara Hakushū* (Tamagawa Daigaku Shuppanbu, 1973), p. 16.

[5]As of 1853, the Yanagawa han, the fief of the Tachibana family, had an assessed revenue of 19,600 *koku* of rice, which placed it among the top 15 percent of all the han in terms of revenue. It was the sixth largest han in Kyushu. See "Table of Daimyo Han as of 1853" in Toshio G. Tsukahira, *Feudal Control in Tokugawa Japan: the Sankin Kōtai System* (Cambridge: Harvard University Press, 1966), pp. 140-173.

[6]Yabuta, p. 18. The sake they produced was known as "Ushio" (Tide).

[7]*Memories* (Tōundō, 1911). See Chapter 2 of this study for a more detailed discussion.

[8]*Memories*, pp. IX-XLVII.

[9]"Growing Up," *Memories*, pp. XII-XIII.

[10]Ibid., p. XIII.

[11]One would expect these characters to be read as Rokki; however, Rokkyu is the pronunciation indicated by Hakushū in "Growing Up." Ibid., p. XXI. Although there is no way to verify the authenticity of this legend, it is of interest because it reflects a tradition handed down through generations of inhabitants in the area.

[12]Ibid., p. XXI.

[13]Ibid., p. XXIII.

[14]Ibid., p. XXXVIII.

[15]Among other items that impressed Hakushū as being exotic were the oil painting in his room, cinnamon and peppermint, which he mixed with water and carried around with him in little bottles, and the geese and turkeys which his father raised in their garden. Ibid., pp. XXIII, XXXVIII, XXXIX.

[16]Ibid., p. XX.

[17]Note following the poem "Kokugura no Homeki" (Flush on the Granary), *Memories*, pp. 104-105.

[18]See Kamachi Yoshiyuki, "Hakushū to Yanagawa," *Tanka* (January 1963), pp. 61-67 and Noda Utarō's afterword, "*Omoide* ni tsuite," to the facsimile of the first edition of *Memories* published by Nihon Kyōdo Bungei Sōsho (Meizen Insatsu Kabushiki Kaisha, 1967), pp. 1-34. Both these scholars, who grew up in north Kyushu, agree concerning the derivation of "Tonka John." "Tonka" is a dialectic variation of *futoi* (large), or in a less standard form *futoka*, found elsewhere in the area as *futonka*. "Tinka" (the usual transcription would be *chinka*) derives from *chisai* (small) by similar logic. Noda notes that "John" or *jon* is widely used in the area as an appellation for a young boy child. One example he gives is *aa yoka jon* (good boy!). Noda, p. 26. Kamachi adds that this word may be a variation of *jin* used in a dialectic expression such as *anjin* (that man). Kamachi, p. 63. Another reliable scholar specializing on Hakushū, Kawamura Masatoshi, states that "John" is definitely of foreign origin although he does not attempt to suggest the derivation. See *Kitahara Hakushū Shū*, Nihon Kindai Bungaku Taikei, Vol. 28 (Kadokawa Shoten, 1970), p. 537, note 282.

[19]"Gonshan" probably derives from the standard Japanese *jōsan* (young lady). Noda, pp. 25-26. Kamachi suggests another derivation: the "n" sound which was

often added to words in the Kumamoto and Yanagawa area is affixed to the honorific *go* to which was appended *shan,* an obvious variation of *san* (Miss, Mr., or Mrs.). Kamachi, p. 63.

[20]Note following "Hako" (Box), *Memories,* p. 98.

[21]*Memories,* p. 269. Hakushū uses the English word "ball." It is unclear whether this word was also used in Yanagawa.

[22]"Growing Up," p. XVII. *Banko* (bench) is a word of foreign origin, derived from either the Spanish word "banco" or the Dutch "bank." This word, which entered Japan from Nagasaki, is still widely used in northwest Kyushu. Noda, p. 28. Kawamura, p. 240, note 6.

[23]"Growing Up" was written in Tokyo in 1911, seven years after Hakushū had left Yanagawa.

[24]"Growing Up," p. XXVIII. Cf. Kitahara Tetsuo, "Osanaki Koro," *Kaisō no Hakushū,* ed. Inoue Kōbun (Hobun Shorin, 1948), p. 21. Tetsuo does not recall actually ever having been locked in a warehouse; the threat alone seems to have proved sufficient.

[25]"Growing Up," p. XL. Hakushū refers to the garden as *chūmaenda.* This term, used within Hakushū's family, is not dialect, nor can it be found in any dictionary. See Noda, p. 25. According to Hakushū's brother Tetsuo, his father built a large chicken house where he kept several hundred chickens, continually adding new breeds to his flock. After they were eaten by wild dogs, he began to raise ducks. Tetsuo recalls that the large flock was quite noisy. When he tired of ducks, he turned to pigs, still considered unusual animals at that time. The pigs, which were not being bred to eat, multiplied fast until Hakushū's grandfather insisted that they be given away. Kitahara Tetsuo, "Osanaki Koro," pp. 16-17.

[26]See the sketch of this house found in Yabuta, p. 5.

[27]A map showing the layout of the gardens can be found in Yabuta, p. 3.

[28]"Growing Up," p. XXXIX.

[29]First stanza of "Minetsu" (Fever), *Memories,* pp. 126-127.

[30]See, for example, "Shimo" (Frost), ibid., pp. 117-119.

[31]See the translation of "Kumoribi" (Cloudy Day) in Chapter 2, particularly the eleventh line from the end, which reads, "The dread of the patient who escaped from his hospital."

[32]Last stanza of "Aoki Kame" (The Green Urn), *Memories,* pp. 152-153.

[33]"Growing Up," p. X.

[34]"Growing Up," p. XLI.

Kibyōshi (yellow-back books) belong to the genre *kusazōshi* (picture books), short illustrated tales written mainly in *hiragana* (phonetic script) and popular during the Tokugawa period. Like other books of this genre, their purpose was to entertain. The quality of the illustrations was, therefore, important in determining the popularity of a work. The literary value of the stories themselves varied. The subject matter was often topical and the style punctuated with witticisms, jokes, and puns, as well as detailed descriptions of the latest vogue in dress and manners.

Tales of Moonlight and Rain (Ugetsu Monogatari) by Ueda Akinari (1734-1809) appeared sometime after 1776, the date of the preface. This collection of nine stories of the supernatural, based on Chinese models, is remarkable for its style and skill at narration. There are two English translations of this work: *Tales of Moonlight and Rain*, trans. Kengi Hamada (University of Tokyo Press, 1971) and *Ugetsu Monogatari. Tales of Moonlight and Rain*, trans. Leon M. Zolbrod (London: George Allen and Unwin, 1975).

Novels on the French Revolution. Whether this reference *(Furansu kakumei shōsetsu)* is to one or a number of novels on the French Revolution is unclear from the text. However, Kawamura Masatoshi, p. 257, note 26, believes that this is a direct reference to Miyazaki Muryū, *Furansu Kakumei Ki Jiyū no Kachidori*, published in 1882-1883. Hakushū remarks in another place that stories of the French Revolution *(Furansu kakumei monogatari)* interested him in the summer of his eleventh year. See "Kitahara Hakushū Nenpu", *Shinchō* (December 1917), p. 119.

Inspiring Instances of Statesmanship (Keikoku Bidan, 1884) by Yano Ryūkei (1850-1931)) is a political novel, concerning the establishment of democratic government in ancient Greece. See Donald Keene, *Japanese Novels and the West* (Charlottesville: University of Virginia Press, 1961), pp. 12-13.

Romance of the Three Kingdoms (San-kuo-chih yen-i), compiled by Lo Kuanchung (ca. 1330-1400), chronicles the history of the three kingdoms of Go, Wei, and Shu. It has been translated by C.H. Brewitt-Taylor, 2 vols. (Shanghai: Kelly and Walsh, 1925). See also C.T. Hsia's chapter on this work in *The Classic Chinese Novel* (New York: Columbia University Press, 1968), pp. 34-74.

Journey to the West (Hsi yu chi) by Wu Ch'eng-en (ca.1506-1582) is best known in its partial translation by Arthur Waley entitled *Monkey* (New York: John Day, 1944). It is a fanciful adaptation of legends concerning the seventh-century pilgrimage of the Buddhist priest Hsuan-tsang to India, in which Monkey and Pigsy help the priest overcome supernatural obstacles to his goal. See chapter by Hsia, pp. 115-164.

[35]"Growing Up," p. XLI.

[36]Ibid., pp. XXXII-III.

[37]*Library of Literature*, which appeared from 1895 to 1910, published poetry —tanka, haiku, and shi—as well as stories and literary criticism for which it is less well-known. Unlike most other contemporary literary journals, which functioned to print the work of an established group of writers, this magazine published all contributions that met the standards of its editors. For this reason, *Library of Literature* became an important journal for the young writer who was just beginning a career. Besides Hakushū, many other poets of his generation including Shimaki Akahiko (1876-1926), Miki Rofū (1889-1964), and Maeda Yūgure (1883-1951) published some of their first poems here.

[38]*Morning Star*, a magazine devoted to poetry, was published monthly beginning in April 1900 and ending with its 100th issue in February 1908. As the journal for Yosano Tekkan's (1873-1935) Shinshisha (New Poetry Society), it published important poetry by this group, whose members included Yosano Akiko (1878-1942), Hirano Banri (1885-1947), Ishikawa Takuboku (1886-1912), Takamura Kōtarō (1883-1956), Kinoshita Mokutarō (1885-1945), Yoshii Osamu (1886-1960), and Hakushū. Supported by older poets such as Mori Ōgai (1862-1922), Ueda Bin (1874-1916), Susukida Kyūkin (1877-1945), and Kambara Ariake (1876-1952), *Morning Star* published a variety of important poems, later characterized by literary

scholars as "romantic." This term refers to the group's antipathy toward naturalism as well as to the highly individualistic style of their poetry, which tended to treat imaginative and emotional subject matter. Furthermore, Tekkan as theorist for the group made *Morning Star* an important organ in the movement to modernize the tanka.

[39]*Seedlings*, published in 1897, was the first collection of poetry by Shimazaki Tōson (1872-1943), an important poet and novelist of this period. While the fifteen years prior to the appearance of *Seedlings* had produced a number of translations and imitations of Western poetry, this collection was the first volume of shi to speak of the concerns of a young man, namely, his youthful loves. As such, it signaled the beginning of a new era in the development of modern Japanese poetry, as Tōson himself recognized. See Donald Keene, "The Creation of Modern Japanese Poetry," *Landscapes and Portraits* (Kodansha International Ltd., 1971), pp. 138-139.

[40]Hakushū used this name throughout his life with two minor exceptions. In 1904, the year he went to Tokyo, he referred to himself, notably in correspondence with the poet Kawai Suimei (1874-1965), at the time editor of the shi department of *Library of Literature,* and in shi published in this same journal, as 薄愁 . See Yabuta, pp. 42-43. Although the pronunciation Hakushū is the same, these characters mean "faint grief." In this same year, he became friends with Wakayama Bokusui (1885-1928), the tanka poet, also a student at Waseda. For a brief time, he used the pseudonym Sansui (Spraying Water), together with another friend who adopted a pen name which also contained the character 水 sui (water). These three were known as "Waseda no Sansui" (the three waters of Waseda). See the photograph taken on October 12, 1904 of these three young men in *Kitahara Hakushū*, Nihon Bungaku Arubamu, Vol. 2 (Chikuma Shoten, 1954), p. 18.

[41]Nishimoto Akio, *Kitahara Hakushū no Kenkyū* (Shinseisha, 1965), p. 289.

[42]Ibid., pp. 21-22 and 289-293. The tanka is

Kono mama ni	Reminding me of the transience
Sora ni kiemu no	Of my own existence,
Waga yo to mo	A beautiful rainbow
Kakute aware no	Graces the sky
Niji utsukushiki.	But to vanish intact.

[43]Hattori's criticism concerned one of the twenty-nine tanka by Hakushū published in this issue. Hakushū's original read as follows:

Kamisabi ni	In holy splendor
Kagume Miminashi	Mt. Kagu and Mt. Miminashi
Narabitachi	Stand together.
Yamato honobono	To Yamato comes
Yo wa akenikeri.	The faint glimmer of dawn.

Hattori corrected this poem in two places before publishing it. In his stinging criticism following the poem, he attacked Hakushū's interpretation of Mt. Kagu as female—expressed by the suffix "-me" in "Kagume." By citing several poems from the *Man'yōshū* and references in the *Nihon Shoki* and *Kojiki* concerning Mt. Kagu, Mt. Miminashi, and Mt. Unebi, known as the "three mountains of Nara," Hattori proved that it was Mt. Unebi, not Mt. Kagu, which should be considered feminine.

Hakushū, who had relied on an interpretation found in a standard text on the *Man'yōshū*, *Man'yōshū Ryakkai* (Short Critique of the *Man'yōshū*) by Tachibana Chikage, 6 vols. (Osaka: Toshō Shuppan, 1892-1893), was deeply offended at Hattori's strongly worded attack.

In 1934, Hakushū recalled this incident: "When I wrote this tanka, I only knew of the interpretation found in the *Short Critique*. Hattori, who approached me as an equal, attacked this poem quite severely on several points. Still a young boy in middle school, I was astounded at his criticism. Out of dissatisfaction, I stopped writing tanka and turned to shi." "Goki" (Afterword), *Hakushū Zenshū*, Vol. 6 (Arusa, 1934), p. 508. See also Nishimoto, pp. 294-5 and 309-10.

[44]"Growing Up," p. XLIV.

[45]Ibid.

[46]This history teacher, Makino Yoshinobu, had graduated from Waseda. See Yabuta, p. 33.

[47]Kitahara Tetsuo, "Osanaki Koro," p. 34. My description of Hakushū's withdrawal from middle school is also based on Tetsuo's account found here.

CHAPTER 2

[1]The Russo-Japanese War had begun in February of this year. Nakajima committed suicide soon after receiving notice at school that he was under suspicion of spying for the enemy. In "Hakushū Nenpu" Hakushū mistakenly records the date of his death as September 1904. See Yabuta, pp. 36-40.

[2]The subject matter of "Sylvan Meditations" does not concern Nakajima's death. Several years later, Hakushū did write a poem "Tanpopo" (Dandelions), in which he recalls bringing Nakajima's corpse on a stretcher to his home through a field of dandelions. *Memories*, pp. 288-292.

[3]"Goki" (Afterword), *Hakushū Zenshū*, Vol. 4 (Arusu, 1931), p. 569.

[4]For a discussion of these poems, found in *Shinshō* (New Eulogies; Yakumo Shorin, 1940), see Chapter 6.

[5]The New Poetry Society, also known as the Tōkyō Shinshisha (Tokyo New Poetry Society), was founded in 1899 by Yosano Tekkan. Its members published their poetry in *Morning Star*, the journal for the group begun one year later. See Chapter 1, note 38.

[6]Yabuta, p. 48. Yabuta, who became one of Hakushū's disciples in 1918, includes much new information in his biography such as this description of Tekkan and Hakushū's first meeting, which helps explain Hakushū's sudden appearance as a member of the New Poetry Society.

[7]"The Day the Blossoms Fell," *Morning Star* (April 1906), pp. 85-86. The announcement of this competition, which had appeared in *Morning Star* (March 1906), p. 103, did not list Hakushū's name among the participants. Therefore, it seems likely that he was invited to join the New Poetry Society sometime during March 1906.

[8]*Morning Star* (May 1906), pp. 5-11.

213

[9]Kawamura Masatoshi, "*Myōjō* Jidai no Kitahara Hakushū." *Kokubungaku* (December 1964), p. 66.

[10]Kawamura Masatoshi suggests that this was because Tekkan found it politically more expedient to receive Hakushū not as a new poet whom the group would introduce but as a poet whose affiliations were naturally attuned to theirs. Ibid., p. 66.

[11]"Ominous Sounds of National Ruin" was published serially in *Niroku Shinbun* from May to October 1894.

[12]*North, South, East, and West* (Meiji Shoin, 1896) contained 260 tanka and several *shintaishi*, written for the most part in Korea where Tekkan had been teaching Japanese prior to his return to Japan in March 1896.

[13]Quoted by Senuma Shigeki, "Shinshisha no Kindaisei," *Kindai Tanka*, Nihon Bungaku Shiryō Sōsho (Yūseidō, 1973), p. 77.

[14]Quoted in Sasabuchi Tomoichi, "Myōjō-ha no Bungaku Undō," *Kokubungaku* (December 1964), pp. 19-20.

[15]Janine Beichman, *Masaoka Shiki: His Life and Works* (Ph.D. dissertation, Columbia University, 1974), pp. 129-131.

[16]*Purple* (Tōkyō Shinshisha, 1901). *Tangled Hair* (Tōkyō Shinshisha, 1901). See *Tangled Hair*, trans. Sanford Goldstein and Seishi Shinoda (Lafayette, Indiana: Purdue University, 1971).

[17]Yasuda Morio, *Ueda Bin Kenkyū* (Yajima Shobō, 1958), pp. 29-30.

[18]Thirty of his translations appeared in *Morning Star* from January 1904 to October 1905. See the list of these poems, arranged chronologically to show date and place of first publication, in Yasuda, pp. 60-63.

Sound of the Tide (Hongo Shoin, 1905) was published in October 1905, the same month that Bin's last translation appeared in *Morning Star*. The collection contains fifty-seven translations by twenty-nine poets from their French, English, German, Italian, and Provencal originals.

[19]A poet of shi, born ten years earlier than Hakushū, Kanbara Ariake grew up during the period when English Romantic poetry was in vogue, and his early shi were strongly influenced by Shimazaki Tōson's *Seedlings*. Later, together with Ueda Bin, he became an important figure in the symbolist movement. His interest in symbolist poetry in fact predated Bin's translations.

[20]Susukida Kyūkin's early shi were patterned after Tōson's, and his first collection of poetry *Botekishū* (Evening Flute; Kaneo Bun'endō, 1889), along with Tōson's *Seedlings*, is a classic in the tradition of romantic poetry. Although Kyūkin also wrote symbolist poetry, he is better known for his lyrical poems in the literary language, written in set forms. Kyūkin was the first Japanese poet to write sonnets.

[21]Kawamura Masatoshi, "*Myōjō* Jidai no Kitahara Hakushū,"*Kokubungaku* (December 1964), pp. 65-67.

[22]Nine of these poems appeared in the section entitled "Omoide" (Memories) of *Memories*; they are the earliest poems in this work, the earliest of Hakushū's verses to actually be published in book form. "Akaki Mi" (Red Fruit), pp. 122-123; "Shajō" (In a Wagon), pp. 124-126; "Shinnetsu" (Fever), pp. 126-128; "Nashi" (Pear), pp. 128-129; "Keito" (Cockscomb), pp. 130-131; "Shii no Hana" (Oak Blossoms),

pp. 132-133; "Asa" (Morning), pp. 145-147; "Aoki Kame" (Green Urn), pp. 150-153; and "Kyōfu" (Fear), pp. 160-161.

[23]"Akaki Mi," *Morning Star* (May 1906), p. 5.

[24]"*Omoide* no Omoide" (Recalling *Memories*), afterword to the new revised edition of *Memories* (Arusu, 1925), found in *Bi o Yumemiru Shijintachi*, ed. Itō Shinkichi et al., Gendaishi Kansho Kōza, Vol. 3 (Kadokawa Shoten, 1968), p. 422.

[25]*Spring Birds* (Hongō Shoin, 1905).

[26]Tamaki Tōru, *Kitahara Hakushū: Shiteki Shuppatsu o Megutte* (Yomiuri Shinbunsha, 1974), p. 74. The French Impressionist movement in painting, which was introduced to Japan at about the same time as symbolism, also received wide acclaim in literary circles. Hakushū was not the only poet to attempt to write "impressionist poetry"—verses in which the poet painted through his words the colors, light effects, and atmosphere of a scene. "Gaikō to Inshō" (Plein Air and Impressions), the third section of *Heretical Faith*, contains thirty-one examples of this type of verse, written between April 1907 and December 1908. Hakushū's chronology here is somewhat misleading. He did not, as he seems to suggest, move from "impressionist poetry" to symbolist verse. The strong coloring and light effects learned from the Impressionists may be found in all the poems in *Heretical Faith*.

[27]"Jo" (Preface), *Spring Birds*, found in *Bi o Yumemiru Shijintachi*, pp. 386-7.

[28]*Poems by Ariake* (Ekifūsha, 1908).

[29]"Preface," *Spring Birds*, p. 387.

[30]The first two stanzas of "High Noon," *Heretical Faith*, pp. 285-286.

[31]Hakushū's poems inspired by this trip can be found in the "Aoki Hana" (Blue Flowers) section of *Heretical Faith*, pp. 243-266.

[32]Yoshii Osamu (1886-1960) was a prolific tanka poet who also wrote some plays and novels. One year younger than Hakushū, he participated in many of the same organizations and magazines.

[33]Hirano Banri (1885-1947) also wrote tanka. When Hakushū and the other young poets left the New Poetry Society in 1908 in their search for more independence, he chose to stay with Tekkan.

[34]Kinoshita Mokutarō (1885-1945) is known as a poet and playwright. An interest in the early Tokugawa Christians prompted him to join this trip to Kyushu, the result of which would be his first poetry of merit. Together with Hakushū, he was a leader in poetry circles of this time and is remembered for his involvement in the Pan Society. He became disillusioned with verse in 1916, and at the age of thirty-one abandoned literature for a career in medicine.

[35]Noda Utarō in *Nihon Tanbiha no Tanjō* (Kadokawa, 1951), pp. 17-68, describes this trip in great detail. My discussion is based on his research.

[36]Yasuda, p. 179-181. Bin published a poem "Fumie" (Treading on a Picture of the Virgin) on the Japanese Christians during this period in December 1906.

[37]All of these poets published poems inspired by their trip in the autumn issues of *Morning Star*. Mokutarō wrote a travel sketch and a number of verses for the October and November issues, and Hakushū's "Amakusatō" (Amakusa Islands) series appeared in the latter. Banri, Osamu, and Tekkan also wrote tanka. See Noda, pp. 55-67. The first volume to be classified as *namban bungaku* is Hakushū's *Heretical Faith*. Mokutarō later published stories and plays using this subject matter;

Nanbanjimon Mae (In Front of the Foreign Temple) and *Amakusa Shirō* (Shirō of Amakusa) are well-known examples.

[38]Last stanza of "Weighing Anchor," *Heretical Faith*, p. 284. This poem was first published in *Morning Star*. Most studies of Hakushū trace his symbolist style back to "High Noon." Kawamura Masatoshi was the first scholar to note that this verse, written two months prior to "High Noon," also displays characteristics associated with the style of *Heretical Faith*. See Kawamura Masatoshi, *Kitahara Hakushū Shū*, p. 534, note 253 and idem, "Kitahara Hakushū Ron," *Kindai Tanka*, p. 259.

[39]Entitled "Gosoku no Kutsu—Gonin tsure" (Five Pairs of Shoes—Five Men), this travelogue was published serially in the *Tōkyō Niroku Shinbun* from August 7 to September 3, 1907.

[40]Nagasaki had been an important port for foreign trade in the fifteenth and sixteenth centuries. In 1639 Portuguese and Spanish merchants and missionaries were expelled from Japan; the only Europeans allowed to trade were the Dutch, who were confined to Dejima in Nagasaki. The New Poetry Society members probably inspected the remains of the Dutch settlement but no record remains of their visit.

[41]Quoted in Noda, pp. 39-40.

[42]The one exception is "Kogane Himawari" (Golden Sunflower), which was first published in August 1908 in *Morning Star*.

[43]*Heretical Faith*, p. 219.

[44]See for example "Jashūmon Hikyoku" (Secret Song of the Heretics), *Heretical Faith*, pp. 1-3; "Akaki Sōjō" (Priest in Red Robes), pp. 10-12; or "Muhon" (Rebellion), pp. 65-67.

[45]First five lines of "Swan," *Heretical Faith*, p. 238.

[46]Last three lines of "Please Don't Tell," Ibid., p. 232.

[47]The first complete translation of the Old Testament in the literary language (bungo) was published in 1887.

[48]Compare line 5 of "Please Don't Tell" with Song of Solomon 5:13 in Japanese translation.

[49]Compare line 4 of "Please Don't Tell" with Song of Solomon 5:11.

[50]Nishimoto, p. 312. Nishimoto has collected all the tanka published in *Morning Star*. See pp. 316-321.

[51]Nishimoto, p. 320. This tanka appeared in the November 1907 issue of *Morning Star*.

[52]See p. 22 above.

[53]Kinoshita Mokutarō, Yoshii Osamu, Nagata Hideo (1885-1949), Nagata Mikihiko (1887-1964), and two other young poets withdrew from the New Poetry Society along with Hakushū.

[54]Hirano Banri, Chino Shōshō (1883-1946), Ishikawa Takuboku, and Yosano Akiko remained with Tekkan. Takuboku's reasons for not participating in this action were probably related to his somewhat ambivalent attitude toward Hakushū, whom he seems to have resented for his financial independence. In addition, Takuboku continued to depend upon Tekkan's encouragement, which often took a monetary form.

[55]Yoshii Osamu, *Asahi Shinbun* (September 11, 1960), quoted in Irie Harutsuru, "Shinshisha Dattai Jiken Oboegaki," *Kokubungaku* (December 1964), p. 118.

[56]Wada Shigejirō, "*Myōjō* kara *Subaru* e," *Kokubungaku* (December 1964), p. 92.

[57]From a letter addressed to Takada Kōun, a young poet who lived in Tōyama Prefecture. Quoted by Kimata Osamu, "Myōjō Dattai Hannenmae no Hakushū to Tekkan," *Hyōron · Meiji Taishō no Kajintachi* (Meiji Shoin, 1971), p. 190.

[58]*Morning Star* was revived twice after this: from November 1921 to April 1927 by Tekkan and from May 1947 to October 1949 by Yosano Hikaru, Tekkan's son. The later periods of the magazine had little significance in literary history.

[59]*New Trends*, a literary magazine published for short periods some sixteen times, has published the writings of many important literary figures. The first period of publication lasted from October 1907 to March 1908 and is remembered for numerous translations of foreign plays by Ibsen and others.

[60]*Heretical Faith*, pp. 65-67.

[61]A number of the images that Hakushū used in the early verses of *Heretical Faith* seem to derive from poems found in Ueda Bin's *Sound of the Tide*. The violin is perhaps the most obvious example. Paul Verlaine's "Chanson d'Automne," rendered as "Rakuyō" (Falling Leaves), is one of Bin's most celebrated translations. Violins appear in the first stanza:

Aki no hi no	Les sanglots longs
Bioron no	Des violons
Tameiki no	De l'automne
Mi ni shimite	Blessant mon coeur
Hitaburu ni	D'un langueur
Ura kanashi.	Monotone.

[62]The rhythmic scheme can be diagrammed as follows:

5, 7
5, 5, 7
5, 5, 5, 7
5, 5, 5, 5
5, 5, 5, 5

[63]Scholars often point out a resemblance between this poem and two others: Ueda Bin's translation "Kataku" (Burning Houses) of Emile Verhaeren's "Les Villes," found in *Sound of the Tide*, and Kanbara Ariake's "Chie no Sōja wa Ware o Mite" (The Soothsayer "Knowledge" Looked at Me) from *Poems by Ariake*. See for example notes 89 and 92 on the poem by Kawamura, *Kitahara Hakushū Shū*, pp. 518-519. However, these similarities are not marked and certainly do not negate the originality of Hakushū's poem. More important than these two poems is the somewhat broader influence of Ariake's poetry in general, seen in the construction of "Rebellion."

[64]A painter and poet, Ishii Hakutei had contributed illustrations and shi to *Morning Star*. In 1907 he helped found the magazine Hōsun (Square Inch). He was also a founding member of the Pan Society.

[65]Yamamoto Kanae was a painter who worked in both oils and wood block prints. Like Ishii Hakutei, he contributed illustrations to *Morning Star* and was a founder of *Square Inch* and the Pan Society. His marriage to Hakushū's sister Ie in 1917 cemented his close friendship with Hakushū.

[66]The appearance of *Heretical Faith* marked the beginning of a new era in the design of poetry collections. The example set by Hakushū and Ishii Hakutei, who worked with Hakushū on the cover and layout of *Heretical Faith*, turned the eyes of other poets to this aspect of their collections. The cover of the second edition of *Heretical Faith*, published in 1911 by Toūndō, was executed by Takamura Kōtarō. Hakushū himself drew the picture of the foreign priest which graced the cover of the third edition, published again by Tōundō in 1916.

Hakushū designed the covers and layout for most of his poetry collections, and they occupy a significant position in the history of Japanese book binding. Photographs of the first editions of Hakushū's collections can be seen in "Hakushū no Hon," *Ginka* (Summer 1972), pp. 77-84. Following this is an article on the bindings of the most important collections: Kimata Osamu, "Shiō Hakushū no Hon," pp. 85-91.

[67]Murō Saisei, *Waga Aisuru Shijin no Denki* (Chūō Kōronsha, 1958), p. 3.

[68]*Heretical Faith*, unnumbered introductory pages.

[69]Ibid.

[70]Hakushū's inscription is clearly inspired either by Bin's translation or by a translation of the same stanza by Mori Ōgai found in *Sokkyō Shijin* (The Improvisatore).

> Per me si va nella vitta dolent,
> Per me si va nell' eterna dolvre,
> Per me si va tra la perduta gente.
>> Dante Alighieri, "Inferno," *The Divine Comedy*,
>> Canto III, lines 1-3.

> Koko sugite kanashimi no minato e,
> Koko sugite tō no nayami ni,
> Koko sugite horobi no tami e hito wa yuku.
>> Ueda Bin, *Dante, the Saint of Poetry* (Kinkōdō, 1901).

> Koko sugite suree no ichi ni
> Koko sugite nageki no fuchi ni
> Koko sugite ukabu toki naki
>> Mori Ōgai, *The Improvisatore* (Shunyōdō, 1902).

> Koko sugite melodea no nayami no mure ni,
> Koko sugite kannō no yūraku no sono ni,
> Koko sugite shinkei no nigaki masui ni.
>> Kitahara Hakushū, *Heretical Faith*.

See Kawamura Masatoshi's remarks in note 4, p. 509 of *Kitahara Hakushū Shū*.

[71]*Heretical Faith*, unnumbered introductory pages.

[72]Donald Keene, in "Kitahara Hakushū" *Nami* (May, 1976), pp. 38-39, discusses the introductory sections of *Heretical Faith*. He is probably not the only modern reader who feels exasperated at the pretentious manner in which Hakushū expressed himself in passages like this.

[73]Ueda Bin, "Introduction," *Sound of the Tide*, translated by Donald Keene, "Modern Japanese Poetry," *Landscapes and Portraits*, p. 140.

[74]Yasuda, p. 51. A. Vigié-Lecocq, *La Poésie contemporaine 1884-1896* (Paris: Mercure de France, 1897).

[75]Kenneth Cornell, *The Symbolist Movement* (New Haven: Yale University Press, 1951), p. 85.

[76]Donald Keene, in "Modern Japanese Poetry," *Landscapes and Portraits*, pp. 140-141, has pointed out that the popularity enjoyed by symbolism in Japan was due in part to the affirmation in symbolist literature of suggestion and ambiguity, qualities which characterized the traditional Japanese tanka. When Hakushū chose to describe mood through the nuances and overtones of his language, he in fact was employing a standard technique of traditional tanka poetry.

[77]"Reigen" (Foreword), *Heretical Faith*, p. II.

[78]*Heretical Faith*, pp. 1-3, trans. Donald Keene, *Modern Japanese Literature*, ed. Donald Keene (New York: Grove Press, 1956), pp. 204-205.

[79]See p. 29 above.

[80]"A Cloudy Day," *Heretical Faith*, pp. 25-29.

[81]Yanō Hōjin, "Kaisetsu," *Nihon Gendaishi Taikei*, Vol. 4, quoted by Kawamura, *Kitahara Hakushū Shū*, p. 508, note 1.

[82]The Pan Society, which was named for the Greek god Pan, held its first meeting in December 1908 and lasted until February 1911. The group's purpose, discussion of literary matters of mutual concern in a congenial manner over food and drink, was vague. Nevertheless, the number of participants grew rapidly, and almost every important literary figure of the age participated in one meeting or another with the major exception of the naturalists. See Noda Utarō, *Nihon Tanbiha no Tanjō*, particularly pp. 79-289.

[83]Kinoshita Mokutarō, *Kindai Fūkei* (January 1927), quoted by Noda, p. 97.

[84]*Square Inch* was an art journal published from May 1907 to July 1911. Started by the painters Ishii Hakutei, Yamamoto Kanae, and Morita Tsunetomo, it printed woodblock prints, art cartoons, and art criticism by these young artists and their friends. Hakutei, who was a regular contributor to *Morning Star*, solicited verse from Mokutarō, Hakushū, and other poets of the New Poetry Society for this magazine.

[85]Morita Tsunetomo (1881-1933), a painter, worked mainly in oils, although he did experiment with woodblock prints and watercolor. His early works show strong Impressionist influence.

[86]Nōda, pp. 81-83.

[87]*Pleiades* was published monthly from January 1909 to December 1913 for a total of sixty issues. The founding poets—Kinoshita Mokutarō, Yoshii Osamu, and Hakushū among others—included the young men who had withdrawn from the New Poetry Society in January 1908 as well as Ishikawa Takuboku who served as general editor for the first year. The publication of *Pleiades* began one month after *Morning Star* folded. Mori Ōgai, who had supported *Morning Star*, also lent his help to *Pleiades*.

[88]*White Birches*, a literary and art journal dating from April 1910 to August 1923, was begun by a group of writers graduated from the Peers School. The

magazine placed special emphasis on encouraging the individuality of its contributors, who also included Arishima Takeo (1878-1923) and his younger brother Satomi Ton (b. 1888).

[89]*Literature from Mita* was published from May 1910 to March 1962 at the Mita campus of Keiō University. The first six years under the editorship of Nagai Kafū, who immediately after he returned from France in April 1910 had become a Keiō professor, saw the appearance of works by Mori Ōgai and Ueda Bin—advisors for the magazine—, poetry by Hakushū and other writers from *Pleiades*, and fiction by Izumi Kyōka (1973-1939), Tanizaki Jun'ichirō (1886-1965), among others.

[90]"Sora ni makka na," *Heretical Faith*, p. 32.

[91]*Roof Garden* was a journal of verse and art published by Hakushū, Mokutarō, and the other young artists of the Pan Society as its official organ. Although the government ban on the second issue of January 1910 brought the magazine to its close, it occupies a disproportionately important place in the history of Japanese literature both as a document of contemporary interest in exotic subject matter and as one of the most luxurious publications of its time.

[92]Hakushū's poem "Okaru Kanpei" (Okaru and Kanpei) was cited as the cause:

> Okaru is crying.
> Like velvet hollyhocks trembling in the long twilight,
> Like the touch of soft flannel,
> Like the noon sunlight disappearing from a field yellow as buttercups,
> Like lightly flying dandelion fuzz.
> She cries and cries, no end to her tears.
> Kanpei is dead. Kanpei is dead.
> Handsome young Kanpei has taken his life.
>
> Okaru cries for the smell of her young man,
> Remembering its strong stimulus, suffocating as onions in a yeast room.
> The soft feel of his skin was like the sunlight of May.
> His manly breath warm as black tea.
> When he held me, the salt ponds glowed blue,
> My nerves like white watercress blooms became keen, then dropped
>   palely.
> *The inside of his thighs quivered, my lips pressed to his.
> On the day we parted, his white hands were moist with niter.
> I picked fresh vegetables before I boarded my palaquin.
> > > —first three stanzas of "Okaru and Kanpei," *Tōkyō Keibutsu Shi Sono Ta* (Scenes of Tokyo and other Poems; Tōundō, 1913), pp. 149-151.

The poem continues in this manner to describe a young Edo farm girl's sorrow over the suicide of her husband. The censors singled out the third line from the end of the third stanza as objectionable (line indicated with *), and Hakushū was forced to delete it when he published the poem in *Scenes of Tokyo*. Although the poem is not one of Hakushū's best, it is interesting for several reasons. Most of the poems in this collection were set in present-day Tokyo, but "Okaru and Kanpei" is based on a

220

famous episode from *Kanadehon Chūshingura* (1748), the Tokugawa *jōruri* and Kabuki play by Takeda Izumo, Miyoshi Shōraku, and Namiki Sōsuki. In order to raise money for Kanpei, who wished to be included in the revenge of his lord Enya's death, Okaru, with her parents' consent, sold herself into service at a brothel. Kanpei, who earned his living by hunting after having failed his lord at a critical moment, mistakenly shot a man. Thinking that he had killed his father-in-law, he committed *seppuku*, only to discover just before he died that he had actually shot the villain Sadakurō. Thus, he was allowed to add his name to the list of retainers who eventually revenged Enya's death. See *Chūshingura (The Treasury of Loyal Retainers)*, trans. Donald Keene (New York: Columbia University Press, 1971), pp. 77-103. Hakushū's poem describes Okaru's feelings at learning of Kanpei's *seppuku*. Sadakurō appears in another early poem "Night," found in *Memories* and discussed below. These poems suggest that Hakushū knew *Chūshingura* well, particularly Acts Five and Six which concern Okaru and Kanpei. He probably saw the Kabuki version in his youth and may have read it again at this time. The poem is also a rare example among his verses of this period because it describes a dramatic situation.

[93]*Scenes of Tokyo and Other Poems* (Tōundō 1913). In 1916, when *Scenes of Tokyo* went into its third printing, Hakushū changed the title to *Yuki to Hanabi: Tōkyō Keibutsu Shi* (Snow and Fireworks: Scenes of Tokyo), adding one more chapter, of twelve poems.

[94]*Scenes of Tokyo*, p. 3.

[95]Yarui Sebiro o," ibid., p. 215. The Miyakogawa was a restaurant where the Pan Society often met.

[96]"Kin to Ao to no," ibid., p. 220.

[97]From "Butsuri Gakkō Ura," *Scenes of Tokyo*, pp. 67-74.

[98]No change has been made in these portions of the translation.

[99]*Paulownia Flowers* (Tōundō, 1913).

[100]"One-sided Love," *Scenes of Tokyo*, p. 21. Donald Keene has also translated this poem in "Modern Japanese Poetry," *Landscapes and Portraits*, p. 144.

[101]"*Yuki to Hanabi* Yogen" (Afterword to *Snow and Fireworks*), *Snow and Fireworks: Scenes of Tokyo* (Saitō Shoten, 1949), p. 381.

[102]Ibid., p. 382.

[103]See pp. 17-18 above.

[104]*Flowers of the Heart* was a tanka magazine begun in February 1898 by Sasaki Nobutsuna, the tanka poet and scholar who had discovered and published *Ryōjin Hishō* in 1912. Begun as a publication for members of his Chikuhakukai (Bamboo and Oak Society), at the time Hakushū published these poems it was also publishing tanka by other poets as well.

[105]Kawamura, *Kitahara Hakushū Shū*, p. 545, note 331.

[106]Here he compared his symbolist verse to the "strongly colored paintings of the Impressionist school" and "Fragments" to the drops of turpentine glistening beneath the surface. "Growing Up," *Memories*, p. XII.

[107]*Memories*, p. 48.

[108]Ibid., p. 59.

[109]Compare these verses with the following tanka from *Paulownia Flowers*:

Hagakure ni   I feel sad
Aoki mi o miru   To see green fruit
Kanashimi ka   Hidden under the leaves.
Hana chirishi hi no Memories of the day
Waga omoide ka.   When the blossoms fell.
Paulownia Flowers (Tōundō, 1913), p. 29.

Haru no tori   Birds of spring,
Na naki so naki so   Cease your calling.
Aka aka to   The grass outside
To no mo no kusa ni   Glows crimson
Hi no iru yūbe.   In the sunset this evening.
Paulownia Flowers, p. 27.

[110]Itō Shinkichi, *Jojō Shōkyoku Ron* (Seiga Shobō, 1969), p. 29. Although lyrical poems existed prior to *Memories*, Hakushū was the first modern Japanese poet to consciously compose lyrical songs as a particular form of verse. Itō's study is the only one to my knowledge that treats the development of this type of verse—a phenomenon which only lasted for some fourteen years following the appearance of *Memories*—and its relationship to the traditional tanka.

[111]Itō classifies twenty of the fifty-seven poems in *Sound of the Tide* as short lyrical works. Ibid., pp. 40-41.

[112]Murō Saisei, *Collection of Lyrical Songs* (Kanjōshisha, 1918).

[113]Ishikawa Takuboku, *Meiji Yonjūichinen Nisshi*, (September 1, 1908), found in *Takuboku Zenshū*, Vol. 5 (Chikuma Shobō, 1967), p. 320. Kineorama, a type of visual entertainment much in vogue at this time, employed different-colored lights to produce changes in a picture of a scene from nature.

[114]Itō discusses thirteen unpublished verses entitled "Ima Kikoyu" (Now I Hear), which are obviously patterned after "Fragments." Itō, pp. 80-85.

[115]Ishikawa Takuboku, *A Handful of Sand* (Tōundō, 1910). Two translations of this work exist: *A Handful of Sand*, trans. Sananishi Shio (Boston: Marshall Jones Company, 1934) and *Takuboku: Poems to Eat*, trans. Carl Sesar (Kodansha International Ltd., 1960), pp. 25-88.

[116]Itō, pp 117-121. The strong resemblance for example between number 7 of "Fragments" and a tanka by Takuboku from this collection, noted by Kawamura, Masatoshi, *Kitahara Hakushū Shū*, p. 547, note 338, suggests that this subject deserves further research.

7

Miru to naku namida nagarenu.
Ka no kotori
Areba mata kite,
Ibara no naka no akami o tsuibami saru o.
Aware mata,
Tsuibami saru o.

I did not mean to observe it; my tears fell.
The same small bird

Came again, once again,
To peck at the red rosehips midst the wild roses.
Alas, once again,
He pecks and leaves.

Memories, pp. 45-46.

Urei kite
Oka ni noboreba
Na no shirenu tori tsuibamimeri akaki bara no mi.

When grief came,
I climbed a hill.
An unknown bird picking at red rosehips.

A Handful of Sand, found in *Takuboku Zenshū*, Vol.
1 (Chikuma Shobō, 1967), p. 40.

[117]"Joshi," *Memories*, pp. 1-4.

[118]"Growing Up," *Memories*, p. XVI.

[119]Ibid., p. XXXII.

[120]"Yoru," *Memories*, pp. 254-256.

[121]"Growing Up," *Memories*, p. XXXIV.

[122]Ibid., p. XXIX.

[123]Kitahara Tetsuo, "Osanaki Koro," p. 19.

[124]See note 92 above.

[125]See Chapter 4.

[126]"Omoide no *Omoide*," quoted in *Bi o Yumemiru Shijintachi*, pp. 420-421.

[127]Takamura Kōtarō, "Ano Koro," quoted in Onda Itsuo, *Kitahara Hakushū*, Hito to Sakuhin, Vol. 22 (Shimizu Shoin, 1969), p. 50.

[128]"*Omoide* no Omoide," p. 419.

[129]The votes among the four top competitors in this category were distributed as follows:

Kitahara Hakushū	....	11046
Kanbara Ariake	....	3304
Yosano Tekkan	....	483
Miki Rofū	....	467

Suzuki Ichirō, "Kitahara Hakushū to Matsushita Toshiko." *Kindai Tanka*, Nihon Bungaku Kenkyū Shiryō Sōsho (Yūseidō, 1973), p. 278.

[130]*Shaddock* was published from November 1911 to June 1913. Hakushū took the name of the journal from a citrus tree in his garden in Yanagawa. Twenty-six years old, he had attained an important position in literary circles with the publication of *Memories*, and writers from *White Birch, Literature from Mita*, and the Pan Society, established figures such as Ueda Bin, Kanbara Ariake, and Susukida Kyūkin, and friends from Tekkan's New Poetry Society, all contributed to this journal. Hakushū also introduced four young poets, Murō Saisei, Yamamura Bochō (1884-1924), Hagiwara Sakutarō (1886-1942), and Ōte Takuji (1887-1934), in its pages. He published a number of important verses, later included in *Scenes of Tokyo* and *Paulownia Flowers*, his first collection of tanka. As editor, Hakushū received a

salary of forty yen, a more than reasonable sum for the times, from the publisher Tōundō.

CHAPTER 3

[1]"Growing Up," *Memories*, pp. XLV-XLVI.

[2]Ibid., pp. XLVI-XLVII.

[3]The text in Japanese read: "Shijin Hakushū kiso saru Bungei ojoku no ichipeiji." See Yabuta, pp. 114-115 for the full text of the article. The story was not carried in any of the other major newspapers. Although *Yomiuri Shinbun* prided itself on giving fullest coverage to events of literary interest, the fact that it alone carried this news suggests that Matsushita Chōhei, Toshiko's husband, may have been behind its publication, hoping the bad publicity would injure Hakushū's reputation. The lack of taste displayed in the article, which was full of the most damaging insinuations, supports this interpretation.

[4]Yabuta has discovered a short story "Kare to Sono Shūi" (He and His Surroundings), preserved in the Kitahara family library, which he believes most faithfully represents Hakushū's position. Although the names of the characters have been changed, the story tells of the love affair between a young man and a married woman, whose relationship is not consummated until the night before the woman returns to her family's home to complete divorce proceedings from her husband. Yabuta, pp. 109-113.

[5]Suzuki Ichirō in "Kitahara Hakushū to Matsushita Toshiko," *Kindai Tanka*, pp. 276-284, has clarified the legal background of this incident, showing that Hakushū's account of the proceedings, found in *Shaddock* (September 1912), was not altogether factual. Hakushū reported that he was tried in court three times and found innocent. It is not clear whether Hakushū purposely distorted his account of the legal proceedings, hoping that this would help restore his reputation, or whether he misunderstood or forgot what had actually happened.

[6]*Paulownia Flowers*, p. 368.

[7]"Fusagi no Mushi," (Worms of Discontent), *Paulownia Flowers*, pp. 459-461.

[8]Not long after Hakushū met Toshiko and before the relationship became serious, Matsushita had moved out of his house. Furthermore, Toshiko's request for a divorce seems to have been granted before she and Hakushū consummated their relationship. Nevertheless, Hakushū did not attempt to prove his innocence in court. Matsushita took full advantage of Hakushū's desire to protect his name. Needless to say, the matter would have been settled much differently, and probably out of court, had Hakushū been someone of less renown.

[9]"Shū no Owari ni," *Paulownia Flowers*, p. xi.

[10]*Paulownia Flowers*, p. 367.

[11]Ibid., p. 376.

[12]Ibid., p. 378. There was little Hakushū could do to console his mother, who had arrived in Tokyo only six months before his indictment. Her sorrow at the loss of the family business and her home in Yanagawa was compounded by distress over his imprisonment. The effect of the poem lies in its understated emotion.

224

[13]Ibid., p. 382. *Suimitsutō* was a type of peach, prized for its juiciness.

[14]Ibid., p. 393.

[15]"Atogaki," *Paulownia Flowers* (reprint ed.; Arusu, 1933), quoted by Kawamura, *Kitahara Hakushū Shū*, p. 573, note 554. *Mica* (Oranda Shobō, 1915) is Hakushū's second collection of tanka.

[16]"Worms of Discontent," *Paulownia Flowers*, p. 470.

[17]Ibid., p. 487.

[18]"Kōen no Hakubo," *Scenes of Tokyo*, p. 9.

[19]*Paulownia Flowers*, p. 261.

[20]Ishikawa Takuboku, *Meiji Yonjūichinen Nisshi* (July 4, 1908), *Takuboku Zenshū*, Vol. 5, p. 289.

The Kanchōrō Tanka Group met the first Monday evening of every month at Mori Ōgai's house, which he called "Kanchōrō" (Ocean Lookout) because of the view of the sea from the upstairs veranda. Ōgai had organized this group in March 1907 to bring together tanka poets from the New Poetry Society and the Araragi Group. Their meetings lasted for three years.

[21]*Paulownia Flowers*, p. 27.

[22]The number of birds and their place is not specified in the Japanese. In his comments on this poem, a contemporary tanka poet, Wakayama Bokusui, expressed the opinion that it is a caged bird inside the house. Most other critics have understood the birds to be wild, an interpretation which seems less forced. The poem could be understood either way. See Kimata Osamu, *Kindai Tanka no Kanshō to Hihyō* (Meiji Shoin, 1973), p. 214.

[23]See p. 43 above.

[24]"Paulownia Flowers and Sponge Cake," *Paulownia Flowers*, pp. 11-14.

[25]The *suma koto* dates back to at least the eighth century. Its single string is fastened to a wooden frame, before which the player sits.

[26]"Paulownia Flowers and Sponge Cake," p. 15.

[27]Ibid., pp. 18-19. The comparison Hakushū makes here was one he used earlier in "Growing Up," the preface to *Memories*, to characterize the difference between the lyrical songs in "Fragments" and his symbolist verse. This fact suggests that, although he considered the poems in "Fragments" to be shi, they were actually in his own mind closer to tanka. It is interesting to speculate on how literary history might have changed had he published some of the shorter verses in "Fragments" as tanka. The credit which went to Ishikawa Takuboku for revolutionizing the tanka in *Handful of Sand* would instead have gone to Hakushū. Actually, Hakushū's conception of the tanka, being tempered by his respect for the tanka tradition, barred him from designating a poem as a tanka unless it conformed in form and to a certain extent in diction to the specifications of a traditional tanka. Nevertheless, he would continue to write short shi, later referring to them as *tanshō* similar to the tanka except for their form. It was not until 1923 that he discarded these prejudices and became one of the first Japanese poets to write successful tanka completely in the colloquial.

[28]Ibid., p. 22.

[29]*Paulownia Flowers*, p. 37.

[30]Ibid., p. 38.

[31]"Goki" (Afterword), *Shaddock* (February 1913), quoted in Yabuta, p. 128.

[32]Kitahara Ryūtarō, "Kōda Rentarō Sensei to Chichi Hakushū," *Hakuchō* (December 1962), pp. 6-7. Kitahara Ryūtarō, Hakushū's son, has recently uncovered this information on Hakushū's meeting with Hirota by comparing Hakushū's scanty notes on the trip with Kōda's recollections. He traces Hakushū's sudden interest in Buddhism at this time back to Kōda. Two tanka in *Mica* (Oranda Shobō, 1915), pp. 23-24, found under the subtitle "Misaki Shinfukuji," resulted from this visit.

I am indebted to Yabuta Yoshio for bringing this article to my attention and for lending me his copy.

[33]"*Kirarashū* Yogen" (Afterword to *Mica*), *Mica*, pp. II-III.

[34]"Goki"(Postface), *Hakushū Zenshū*, Vol. 5 (Arusu, 1930), p. 505.

[35]*Mica* (Oranda Shobō, 1915) contains 450 tanka inspired by Hakushū's experiences living in Misaki. The majority of the poems were written after he returned to Tokyo in July 1914. Hakushū himself drew the design of blowfish and turnips for the cover and the four sketches found inside.

Pearls (Kaneo Bun'endō, 1914) and *Platinum Top* (Kaneo Bun'endō, 1914) appeared in print prior to *Mica*; nevertheless, these shi do not relate as directly to Hakushū's life in Misaki as his tanka do. He began writing the poems for *Pearls* in the latter part of 1913, while he was still in Misaki. The majority of the verses in *Platinum Top* were composed during three days in the fall of 1914.

Hakushū had planned to publish his verse from this period in a three-volume series, *Indo Sarasa* (Indian Cotton). Many of the poems first appeared under this title in contemporary magazines. *Pearls* was the first volume of the series; *Platinum Top* the third. The second volume, tentatively entitled *Shōgakubō Gyakusatsu* (Slaughter of the Sea Turtle) and meant to include the tanka from this period, was never completed.

[36]"Afterword, "*Mica*, p. XI.

[37]*Mica*, p. 3.

[38]Ibid., p. 5.

[39]Ibid., p. 153.

[40]Ibid., p. 157.

[41]Ibid., p. 54.

[42]"Okugaki," *Platinum Top* (Kaneo Bun'endō, 1914), p. 3.

[43]*Mica*, p. 239.

[44]Ibid., p. 240.

[45]Ibid., p. 264.

[46]Ibid., p. 271.

[47]A poet in his own right, Sasaki Nobutsuna (1872-1963) is also remembered as a scholar of the *Man'yōshū* and the tanka. His discovery and publication of many forgotten works and his labors revising and notating texts provided the foundation for modern scholarship on Japanese literature.

[48]This anthology originally contained twenty volumes of poems in the imayō style and was compiled by the Emperor Goshirakawa (1127-1192) in 1179. Only a small portion of the original survives; the remaining poems are of three kinds: Buddhist hymns, songs about Shinto shrines and festivals, and folk songs. An imayō (modern style) verse consisted of four lines, each containing twelve syllables (a

seven- and a five-syllable phrase). See Konishi Jun'ishi, "Kaisetsu," *"Ryōjin Hishō,* Nihon Koten Zenshū (Asahi Shinbunsha, 1969), pp. 3-41. A selection of folk songs from this collection may be found in *Anthology of Japanese Literature,* ed. Donald Keene (New York: Grove Press, 1960), pp. 167-169.

[49]Kanbara Ariake in "Tsuiokuki," *Tama* (June 1943) states that when he visited Hakushū in Azabu he found a book on the art of India on Hakushū's desk and a religious mirror with a metal image half of Buddhist and half of Shinto origin in the wall. Hakushū lived at Azabu from 1914 to 1916 during which time he published his Misaki period collections of verse. Although it is difficult to document the books he was reading at this time, he clearly was exploring Buddhism, perhaps much more deeply than we can find evidence for. See Yabuta, pp. 163-164.

[50]Kimata Osamu, *Hakushū Kenkyū* (Yakumo Shorin, 1943), pp. 126-127.

[51]*Mica,* p. 252.

[52]Translated by Arthur Waley in *Anthology of Japanese Literature,* ed. Keene, p. 168. The original reads as follows:

> Asobi o sen to ya umarekemu.
>
> Tawaburesen to ya mumarekemu.
>
> Asobu kodomo no koe kikeba,
>
> Waga mi sae koso yurugarure.

[53]"Hakkin no Koma," *Platinum Top,* pp. 3-4.

[54]"Bara Nikyoku," ibid., pp. 54-55.

[55]*"Shinjushō* Yogen" (Afterword to *Pearls). Pearls,* unpaged.

[56]"See pp. 42-44 above.

[57]*Pearls,* p. 3. In my transcriptions of these one-line verses, I have divided each poem into lines according to phrase groupings.

[58]Ibid., p. 3.

[59]Ibid., p. 4.

[60]Ibid., p. 6.

[61]*Festival in the Fields,* found in *Hakushū Shishū,* Vol. 1 (Arusu, 1920), pp. 288-368. Because this work was never published as a separate collection, it is not usually counted among Hakushū's major volumes of shi. The collection contains verses written from 1913 to 1915.

[62]"Daiikkan Kaidai" (Bibliographical Introduction), *Hakushū Shishū,* Vol. 1, p. 2.

[63]See the Bibliography for a comprehensive list of Hakushū's works in this form.

[64]"Jōgashima no Ame," *Hakushū Shishū,* Vol. 1, pp. 367-368.

[65]Yabuta, p. 140.

[66]Ibid., p. 144. Most chronologies give April 3, 1914 as the date of this move. Yabuta's research has revealed that Hakushū, in fact, left Misaki on March 3.

[67]*Suzume no Tamago* (Sparrow's Eggs; Arusu, 1921), p. 189.

[68]See Chapter 4 for a discussion of this volume.

[69]"Jo"(Introduction) to "Transmigration: Three Parts," *Sparrow's Eggs,* pp. 181-183.

[70]*Sparrow's Eggs,* p. 217.

227

[71]Ibid., p. 219.
[72]Ibid., p. 221.
[73]Ibid., p. 241.

CHAPTER 4

[1]"Suzume no Seikatsu" (Life of Sparrows), *Hakushū Zenshū*, Vol. 12 (Arusu, 1930), p. 307.

[2]Yabuta, p. 159.

[3]Like many of his contemporaries, Hagiwara Sakutarō (1886-1942) began writing poetry in the tanka form. However, under the influence of Hakushū's *Heretical Faith* and *Memories*, he soon turned to the shi. Hakushū encouraged him to publish his first efforts in this form; they appeared in *Shaddock* in 1913. For the next three years, Sakutarō was Hakushū's closest disciple; the numerous letters exchanged during these years document the depth of their relationship. By 1917, however, Sakutarō had developed a unique style of his own; *Tsuki ni Hoeru* (Howling at the Moon), which appeared in February of that year, the first successful collection of shi in the colloquial, changed the course of modern Japanese poetry. Hakushū and Murō Saisei wrote introductions for this volume. With the publication of *Aoneko* (Blue Cat) in 1924, few critics doubted Sakutarō's position as the foremost poet of his age. After 1916, Sakutarō and Hakushū's paths diverged; nevertheless, throughout his life, Sakutarō continued to acknowledge the importance of his early friendship with Hakushū. Iijima Kōichi, "Hakushū to Sakutarō," *Yuriika* (August 1969), pp. 122-123. *Face at the Bottom of the World*, trans. Graeme Wilson (Tokyo and Rutland, Vermont: Charles E. Tuttle Co., 1969) is a collection of Sakutarō's verses in English translation. Miyoshi Tatsuji (1900-1963), a noted poet in his own right, has written the most stimulating study of Sakutarō to date, *Hagiwara Sakutarō* (Chikuma Shobō, 1963). The work is excellent except for Miyoshi's efforts to discredit Hakushū's influence on Sakutarō's development.

[4]This group lasted for three years until March 1916 when Hakushū dissolved it to form the Shien Sōsha (Thatched House of Purple Smoke). See page 123 below. From July 1914 to March 1915, he published *Chijō Junrei* (Pilgrimage on Earth) as its official magazine.

[5]Ōte Takuji (1887-1934), a minor poet of shi, was influenced by Baudelaire in his youth, and his verse continued to show strong similarities to French symbolism throughout his career. See the biography by Ubukata Tatsue, *Metorazaru Shijin* (Tōkyō Bijutsu, 1973).

[6]See note 130, Chapter 2.

[7]Kōno Shingo (1893-1959), a minor tanka poet, joined Hakushū's Pilgrim Poetry Society as a student at Waseda University and published his first tanka in *Pilgrimage on Earth*.

[8]Murano Jirō (1894-1975) wrote tanka quite independently of his career at a large steel company. He was a founding member of the Pilgrim Poetry Society and participated in later tanka magazines edited by Hakushū.

[9]Yashiro Tōson (1889-1952) began writing tanka in the colloquial language soon after *Pilgrimage on Earth* folded, breaking up the one-line tanka into several lines. He was a prominent figure in the Proletarian Tanka Movement in the early 30s. His best-known tanka describe the life of workers.

[10]*Ars*, transcribed on the cover as ARS and pronounced "Arusu," was directed at a much larger audience than *Pilgrimage on Earth*, whose purpose— publishing the verses of the young poets who gathered around Hakushū—was naturally limited. Established writers and artists, particularly those who had contributed to *Morning Star*, *Pleiades*, and *Shaddock*, gladly brought their works to this ambitious new journal. After *Pilgrimage on Earth* ceased publication in March, Hakushū devoted one section of *Ars* to printing the work of these young poets.

[11]They were introduced by the wife of the poet Ikuta Shungetsu (1892-1930), who had met Ayako after she came to Tokyo from Oita Prefecture following the break-up of her first marriage.

[12]Yabuta, p. 173, records that, although the sound of the drums and gongs for services at the temple interrupted Hakushū's work, it was his abhorrence for the priest that made him leave the temple so abruptly. Hakushū came to detest this man, who, it seems, interpreted all matters religious and otherwise in pecuniary terms.

[13]"Introduction," *Sparrow's Eggs* (Arusu, 1921), pp. 4-5.

[14]Ibid., pp. 12-13.

[15]Although Hakushū could have offered the collection to another publishing house at this point, he wanted to wait until Arusu was firmly established and publish it with them. There is evidence that he felt that his inability to complete *Sparrow's Eggs* had made him responsible for the failure of Oranda Shobō in some degree.

[16]Ibid., p. 23.

[17]*Mandala* published only three issues before its title was changed to *Zanboa* (Shaddock)—to be distinguished from the earlier magazine of the same name edited by Hakushū. The editor, Kōno Shingo, brought out nine issues before the journal ceased publication in September 1918.

Poems was published from December 1917 to October 1921. Edited by Iwasa Tōichirō (b. 1905), it printed poems by Hakushū and his disciples—Murō Saisei, Hagiwara Sakutarō, and Ōte Takuji—as well as by such famous poets as Horiguchi Daigaku (b. 1892), Kinoshita Mokutarō, and Hinatsu Kōnosuke (b. 1890).

[18]*Mandala* (September 1917), quoted in Yabuta, pp. 182-183.

[19]"Introduction," *Sparrow's Eggs*, pp. 23-24.

[20]*Coral Reef* was a small tanka magazine published by two minor tanka poets, Tachibana Munetoshi (1892-1959) and Morizono Tenrui (1889-1957), both originally from Kyushu. Begun in March 1917, it lasted until June 1919.

[21]*Miscellaneous Remarks on Concentration* (Arusu, 1921) will hereafter be cited as *Concentration*.

[22]*Concentration*, found in *Hakushū Zenshū*, Vol. 12 (Arusu, 1930), pp. 237-238.

[23]Ibid., p. 252.

[24]Bashō, the early Tokugawa poet, created haikai poetics. He traveled widely in search of inspiration for his verse. The most famous of his travel diaries is *Oku no Hosomichi* (Narrow Road to the North).

[25]Yamamoto Eizō, known by his Buddhist name Ryōkan, was a Zen priest and tanka poet. His tanka speak directly of his feelings instead of being composed on set subjects as was the custom at his time. His admiration for the *Man'yōshū* also strongly influenced his verse.

[26]The extent of this influence is difficult to document, for the tanka in *Sparrow's Eggs* were revised a number of times afterwards. Ryōkan's poems on children are among his most famous. Although there are only a few tanka in *Sparrow's Eggs* concerning children, they do seem to echo Ryōkan's verses. For example, compare:

Kono sato ni	In my hometown
Temari tsukitsutsu	I bounce a ball
Kodomora to	With the children.
Asobu haruhi wa	If only these spring days
Kurezu to mo yoshi.	Would not end.

—Ryōkan, quoted by Usami Kisohachi, "Ryōkan," *Kinsei no Kajin Nihon Kajin Kōza*, Vol. 5 (Kōbundō,1960), p. 173.

Haru wa ika ni	How happy
Ureshikararamu	Spring must make them feel.
Kodomora ga	Children
Sakura no shita ni	Playing catch
Mari nageasobu.	Under the cherry blossoms.

—Hakushū, *Sparrow's Eggs*, p. 392.

[27]Saitō Mokichi, *Tanka Shishō* (Hakujitsusha, 1916) contained detailed commentaries on selected tanka by Ryōkan, Minamoto Sanetomo (1192-1219), and other poets influenced by the *Man'yōshū*. Hakushū was friendly with the poets of the Araragi Tanka Group, particularly Mokichi, during the years 1913-1916. He had even published some of the tanka later included in *Mica* in their magazine *Araragi*. Mokichi's book may have inspired Hakushū's interest in Ryōkan.

Saitō Mokichi was a practicing psychiatrist as well as the most noted modern poet of tanka. An influential member of the Araragi Tanka Group, Mokichi together with Shimaki Akahiko (1876-1926) formulated the Araragi position on tanka composition, making Masaoka Shiki's concept of shasei (sketch from life) a main tenet and advocating a style strongly influenced by the *Man'yōshū*. Mokichi's earliest collections, *Shakkō* (Red Glow; Tōundō, 1913) and *Aratama* (Uncut Gems; Shun'yōdō, 1921), show strong similarities to *Mica*. Like Hakushū, Mokichi also admired the *Ryōjin Hishō*.

See Chapter 5 for further discussion of Hakushū's relations with the Araragi Group. Kimata Osamu, "Mokichi to Hakushū," *Hyōron ·Meiji Taishō no Kajintachi*, pp. 322-334, discusses the friendship and later estrangement of Hakushū and Mokichi in detail.

[28]Attributed to Bashō's disciple Hattori Tohō (1657-1730), *Three Copy Books* is compiled of three sections in which the author attempted to report faithfully

Bashō's ideas about *haikai*, illustrating his text with poems together with Bashō's comments.

[29]"Red Copy Book," *Three Copy Books*, found in *Renga Ronshū6 Haironshū*, Nihon Koten Bungaku Taikei, Vol. 66 (Iwanami Shoten, 1968), p. 398.

[30]"Thoughts at Noon," *Paulownia Flowers*, p. 112.

[31]*Red Bird* was managed and edited by Suzuki Miekichi from July 1918 to November 1936. The magazine fostered the literary development of children, but Miekichi's main efforts were directed toward publishing works for children by major artists and writers. The children's poems found in *Red Bird*—many of them written by Hakushū—are considered classics of their genre.

[32]Suzuki Miekichi (1882-1936) was a novelist and important writer of short stories for children. He was a disciple of Natsume Sōseki, whose recommendation led to the appearance of his first stories in *Hototogisu* (Nightingale). At the age of thirty-six he founded *Red Bird*, and he published his own stories for children as well as translations of foreign fairy tales. As editor of this magazine, he became a major figure in the movement for children's education in the arts.

[33]"Squirrel, Squirrel, Little Squirrel," *Red Bird* (July 1918), pp. 2-3. This issue also carried the famous story "Kumo no Itō" (The Spider's Thread) by Akutagawa Ryūnosuke, pp. 8-13, and other works by Shimazaki Tōson, Izumi Kyōka, and Suzuki Miekichi.

[34]Hakushū, Yamamoto Kanae, the critic Katakami Noboru and Kishibe Fukuo, a scholar of children's literature, founded this journal. It lasted only until November 1921.

[35]He went, for example, to Karuizawa in Nagano Prefecture in August 1921, where he lectured at the Summer Institute on Free Education, and also to Niigata City in June 1922 to read his children's poetry. Yabuta, pp. 217 and 222.

[36]A list of Hakushū's collections of verses for children may be found in the Bibliography. Although Hakushū is one of the most celebrated of children's poets, this study forgoes examination of his children's verse except as it relates to his tanka and shi.

Hakushū was also the first modern poet to translate foreign nursery rhymes. His renditions of *Mother Goose* began to appear in *Red Bird* in 1920. In 1921 he published a volume of these translations, *Mazaaru Guusu* (Mother Goose; Arusu). Although never as popular as his original poems, they are fine translations, faithful both in meaning and spirit to the originals.

[37]In March 1919 he published a short story "Katsushika Bunsho" (About Katsushika) in the magazine *Chūō Kōrōn* (Central Review) and began to serialize a longer work "Kingyō Kyō" (Goldfish Sutras) in *Yūben* (Eloquence). "Shindō no Shi" (Death of a Prodigy) was printed in *Shinchō* (Tides) in July. During January and February of the following year, the *Osaka Asahi Shinbun* carried installments of his novel *Koro* (My Dog Koro).

[38]Hakushū, "Minyō Shiron" (My Views on the Folk Song), found in *Hakushū Shiika Ikkagen*, ed. by Yabuta Yoshio (Tamagawa Daigaku Shuppanbu, 1970), p. 92.

[39]*Kouta by Hakushū* (Arusu, 1919).

[40]*Riyō* is the term used to designate popular songs of the Tokugawa period—one type of the larger category *kayō* (songs and ballads). Although most songs in this period were long pieces, often composed by known writers for a complicated samisen accompaniment, the *riyō* were short—sometimes popular ditties adopted from longer works but most often extemporaneous verses of unknown authorship sung to set tunes. By Tokugawa times, the basic rhythmic unit had evolved into a twenty-six syllable unit which may be diagrammed as follows: 7,7,7, 5. Hakushū used the term *riyō* to refer to Tokugawa songs of this sort and kouta to designate his own verses in this form. See Hakushū, "My Views on the Folk Song," pp. 85-86.

[41]Yabuta, p. 215.

[42]*Japanese Flute* (Arusu, 1922).

[43]Scholars of Japanese songs often distinguish between *kayō* (songs and ballads) and *minyō* (folk songs), using the first term to refer to the large body of songs dating from pre-modern times (i.e., through the Tokugawa period) and the latter term to designate folk songs of the modern period still sung in the countryside at festivals and to accompany work. Hakushū seems to have adopted this distinction. However, at other times, he also used the term *minyō* as a generic term to refer to all his poetry in a folk song style. The kouta would then be a specific form within this category.

[44]There is a record of Hakushū's songs, *Kitahara Hakushū Meisaku Senshū* (King Records Co., Inc., 1974), sung by Daaku Dakkusu, a modern vocal group. Many have ceased to be considered merely folk songs or children's tunes and have been established as classical modern vocal music, included in concerts by Japanese singers together with lieder by Franz Schubert and other staples of the concert repertory.

[45]A list of Hakushū's collections of folk songs will be found in the Bibliography.

[46]Money to help build the houses was contributed by Hakushū's friends and admirers. Suzuki Miekichi, on his own initiative, sent out requests for donations; contributors received in return handwritten examples of Hakushū's poetry. The letter sent by Miekichi is reproduced in Yabuta, pp. 201-202.

[47]Yabuta, p. 205, quotes a carpenter who witnessed this scene.

[48]Hakushū in his final letter to Ayako, dated June 26, 1920, implied that Ayako and Ikeda may have spent the night together. The letter may be found in Nishimoto Akio, *Kitahara Hakushū no Kenkyū*, pp. 120-124. Rumors about an affair between the two did circulate widely at the time. However, Yabuta Yoshio and other modern scholars doubt that any indiscretion occurred. Yabuta argues that, had Ayako and Ikeda actually spent the night together, Ikeda would no doubt have lost his job with *Hochi Shinbun*. Yabuta, pp. 204-205. Sasamoto Masaki in a recent study of Hakushū agrees with Yabuta, and cites new evidence, published in Harada Taneo, *Sasurai no Uta* (Shinchōsha, 1972), in which Ikeda denied any indiscretion when questioned directly about this incident. According to Harada, Ikeda was not an ordinary reporter. A graduate of the Tokyo School of Foreign Languages, he was fluent in six languages. He later received a doctorate in mathematics from the University of Berlin and published some two hundred books. In recognition of his

scholarship, he received an award from the German government. See Sasamoto Masaki, *Kitahara Hakushū Ron* (Gogatsu Shobō, 1975), pp. 111-114. Hakushū's nephew, Yamamoto Taro, on the other hand, has declared that he is in possession of documentary evidence to the contrary: a letter from Ayako to his father Yamamoto Kanae. See Yoshimoto Takaaki et al., "Kitahara Hakushū no Fukken," Yuriika (December 1973), pp. 159-160. Until Yamamoto Taro agrees to make this letter public so that scholars may inspect it, it is difficult to be sure what if anything happened between Ayako and Ikeda. Nevertheless, doubts about Ayako's fidelity were certainly an important factor in Hakushū's decision to divorce her.

[49]Yabuta, p. 204. Yabuta's description of these events is the most complete to date, and my discussion is for the most part based on his research.

[50]Tanizaki Jun'ichirō, who was also living in Odawara, had become a close friend of Hakushū's. The rift between them that occurred at this time seems to have been occasioned by Tanizaki's attempt to mediate in the discussions immediately following Ayako's departure. Tanizaki urged Hakushū to divorce Ayako so strongly that he incurred Hakushū's anger. See Yabuta, pp. 206-209.

[51]Kōno Kirinoya, an art critic, and his wife, who were also living in Odawara, introduced the couple. Hakushū's new wife had graduated from the same school in Ōita City in Kyushu as Ayako. Her desire to succeed where Ayako had failed seems to have been one important reason why the marriage was happy. Yabuta, p. 211.

[52]"Introduction," *Sparrow's Eggs*, p. 27.

[53]*Life of the Sparrows* (Shinchōsha, 1920), found in *Hakushū Zenshū*, Vol. 12, pp. 299-499. This work is composed of eight essays on sparrows. The majority were published serially in the magazine *Taikan* (Panorama) during 1918.

[54]A discussion of *sabi* as an ideal in traditional Japanese aesthetics may be found in Donald Keene, "Japanese Aesthetics," *Landscapes and Portraits*, pp. 20-23.

[55]*Life of the Sparrows*, p. 417.

[56]Ibid., p. 316.

[57]Ibid., p. 421.

[58]"Introduction," *Sparrow's Eggs*, p. 7.

[59]*Sparrow's Eggs*, p. 166.

[60]Ibid., p. 246.

[61]For a discussion of these verses, see p. 94.

[62]"Introduction," *Sparrow's Eggs*, p. 50.

[63]Ibid., pp. 50-51.

[64]Quoted in Kimata Osamu, *Hakushū Kenkyū* (Yakumo Shorin, 1943), p. 141. Hakushū, it will be remembered, termed the shi in *Pearls tanshō*. Each poem was printed in one line which I have broken up according to phrase lengths in my transcription of the original here. The form of this example resembles that of the tanka, except for the first phrase with two extra syllables.

[65]Ibid.

[66]Hakushū's interest in *sabi* echoes in his use of the word *aosabi* (patina) in the last line of this tanka.

[67]"Introduction," *Sparrow's Eggs*, p. 38.

[68]Ibid., pp. 38-39.

[69]Ibid., pp. 36-37.

[70]Honnami Kōetsu (1558-1637) was born into a family of professional sword connoisseurs. An early Tokugawa artist, his versatility extended to painting, calligraphy, and pottery. See Robert Paine and Alexander Soper, *The Art and Architecture of Japan* (2nd revised edition; Middlesex: Penguin Books Ltd., 1974), pp. 112-114.

[71]Ikeno Taiga (1723-1776), also known as Taigadō, was one of the major literary painters *(bunjinga)* of his age. His scrolls show the strong individuality characteristic of this type of painting. Paine and Soaper, pp. 129-130.

[72]Sen no Rikyū (1520-1591) was the creator of the Senko School of tea ceremony. Under his influence, the pottery and architecture associated with the tea ceremony assumed a new simplicity and severity in design. Hideyoshi was his patron.

[73]Kobori Enshū (1579-1647) was a famous master of tea ceremony and founded the Enshū School of tea. He is also known for his gardens and flower arrangement, pottery, tanka, and painting.

[74]*Letters from my Backpack*, found in *Bashō Bunshū*, Nihon Koten Bungaku Taikei, Vol. 46 (Iwanami Shoten, 1968), p. 51.

Saigyō (1118-1190) was a priest and waka poet of the late Heian and early Kamakura periods. Ninety-four of his verses were included in the *Shinkokinshū*. See Robert H. Brower and Earl Miner, *Japanese Court Poetry* (Stanford: Stanford University Press, 1961), pp. 22, 239-240, and 300-301.

Sōgi (1421-1502) was a *renga* (linked verse) poet in the Muromachi period. "Three Poets at Minase," the famous series composed by Sōgi, Sōhaku (1443-1527), and Sōchō (1448-1532), may be found in *Japanese Literature*, ed. Donald Keene, pp. 314-321.

Sesshū (1420-1506) is Japan's most celebrated artist of ink paintings. Although he was strongly influenced by the northern school of the Sung period in China, through diversity in style and his wide range of subject matter, he developed ink paintings into a truly Japanese form. Paine and Soper, pp. 83-85.

[75]Hattori Tohō, *Three Copy Books*, p. 398.

[76]The Araragi Tanka Group was and still is the largest and most influential of hundreds of modern tanka groups. Its founder, Itō Sachio (1864-1913), had originally been a member of Masaoka Shiki's Negishi Tanka Group. In 1909 he took over management of the newly founded magazine *Araragi*, moved its headquarters to Tokyo from Chiba Prefecture, and organized a new group of poets, many of whom had been originally associated with the Negishi Group or related magazines. Saitō Mokichi, Koizumi Chikashi (1886-1927), Shimaki Akahiko (1876-1927), Tsuchiya Bunmei (b. 1890), and Shaku Chōkū (1887-1953) were important members. Following Masaoka Shiki's lead, the group advocated a style of poetry characterized as *shasei* (sketch from life) and modeled on tanka found in the *Man'yōshū*. After the death of Sachio in 1913, leadership passed to Mokichi and Akahiko, who developed the group's theories of tanka as well as adding many new members. At the time Hakushū published *Sparrow's Eggs*, Araragi held a dominant position in the tanka world.

[77]For Hakushū's relationship with Saitō Mokichi and other Araragi poets, see Chapter 4, note 27 above and Chapter 5.

[78]"Introduction," *Sparrow's Eggs*, pp. 41-42.

[79]Ibid., p. 43.

[80]A discussion of symbolism in the traditional tanka may be found in Brower and Miner, pp. 30-33 and 293-299.

[81]*Sparrow's Eggs*, p. 43.

[82]"Shinshū Kawa" (Early Autumn Talk on the Tanka), *Tanka no Sho* (Kawade Shobō, 1942), p. 239. This essay is a transcription of the last portion of the talk Hakushū gave at an All Japan Convention of Tama Poets on August 13, 1940.

[83]A note at the end of this part explains the title. A wooden toy pheasant with wheels *(kijiguruma)*, sold at the Kiyomizu Temple near Yanagawa, was associated with his love for his parents and Yanagawa. *Sparrow's Eggs*, p. 400.

[84]*Sparrow's Eggs*. p. 365.

[85]Ibid., p. 5.

[86]My analysis up to this point is based on Kimata Osamu's discussion of the tanka in *Hakushū Kenkyū*, pp. 208-211.

[87]*Sparrow's Eggs*, p. 175.

[88]*Nozarashi Kikō*, found in *Bashō Bunshū*, Nihon Koten Bungaku Taikei, Vol. 46 (Iwanami Shoten, 1968), p. 37. An alternate title for this work is *Kasshi Ginkō* (Journey of the Year 1684). See Donald Keene, "Bashō's Journey of 1684," *Portraits and Landscapes*, pp. 94-108 for Keene's comments and translation of this work. The poem is referred to on pp. 96 and 98.

[89]Kimata Osamu, *Hakushū Kenkyū*, pp. 271-276.

[90]*Sparrow's Eggs*, p. 8.

[91]The chōka is a long poem composed of alternating five- and seven-syllable lines concluding with an extra seven-syllable line and one or more envoys in the tanka form. A major verse form of the *Man'yōshū* poets, it all but died out with the development of the tanka. See Brower and Miner, pp. 77-156.

[92]"Chōka Sōsaku Nenpyō" (Chronological Table of Chōka), *Takamura* (Bamboo Grove; Azusa Shobō, 1929), pp. 165-168. Four earlier works, later included in *Sparrow's Eggs*, were first published in 1916 and 1917 according to this chronology. Hakushū, we can conclude, discovered the chōka at this time. However, it was not until 1920 that he began to compose chōka in earnest.

[93]Kubota Utsubo (1887-1967) published his earliest tanka in *Library of Literature* and was a member of Yosano Tekkan's New Poetry Society from 1900 to 1901. After writing fiction patterned on the Naturalists' works for some ten years, he returned to the tanka and in 1914 founded the magazine *Kokumin Bungaku* (People's Literature). He is also known as a scholar of classical Japanese poetry. *Gazing at the Ground* (Kokumin Bungakusha, 1918) contains poems concerning his life and children after the death of his wife in 1917. The eighteen chōka and 345 tanka found here were written in three months in 1918.

[94]Kimata Osamu, *Kindai Tanka no Shiteki Tenkai* (Meiji Shoin, 1969), pp. 177-178.

[95]"Jo," *Autumn of Contemplation* (Arusu, 1922), p. 4.

[96]Ibid., p. 3.

[97]*Suibokushū* (Poems in Monochrome; Arusu, 1923) p. 267. The translation is by Donald Keene, *Landscapes and Portraits*, p. 144. Keene has rendered *karamatsu*, literally "larch," as "Chinese pines"; I follow his example.

[98]*Autumn of Contemplation*, p. 52. The rustle and movement described here is made by bamboo, which with the moon and falling snow forms a scene characterized by sabi. For the sake of comparison, I have divided the chōka into lines of twelve syllables. The originals of Hakushū's chōka were printed in one long paragraph; punctuation and grammatical pauses indicate the phrase lengths.

[99]For a discussion of *Sunlight*, see pages 195-197.

[100]The revival of *Morning Star* lasted from November 1921 to April 1927. Under Tekkan's management, the magazine published tanka, shi, and criticism by former members of his New Poetry Society. However, it never regained the importance it enjoyed in the 1900s.

[101]This institute (Jiyū Kyōiku Kaki Kōshūkai) had been organized by Kishibe Fukuo, a scholar of children's literature, and Hirota Ryūtarō, a composer. Besides Hakushū, Suzuki Miekichi, Yamamoto Kanae, Shimazaki Tōson, the two organizers, and others involved in creative education for children lectured there. Yabuta, pp. 217-218.

[102]Ibid., p. 218.

[103]"*Suibokushū* Kaisetsu" (Comments on *Poems in Monochrome*), *Poems in Monochrome*, p. 2.

[104]*Poems in Monochrome* (Arusu, 1923), pp. 267-272. In my translation, I have expanded on Donald Keene's rendition of the first, second, and last stanzas of this poem, found in *Landscapes and Portraits*, pp. 144-145.

[105]Donald Keene, *Landscapes and Portraits*, pp. 144-146.

[106]Nakano Shigeharu (b. 1902), a novelist and poet, recalled his own rather ambivalent reaction to the appearance of "Chinese Pines." He also remembered a friend who judged the poem to be worthless because of its diction. See *Kōzakai: Taisho Bungakushi*, ed. Yanada Izumi, Katsumoto Seiichirō, and Ino Kenji (Iwanami Shoten, 1965), pp. 587-588.

[107]*Sparrow's Eggs*, p. 27. These lines also recall the famous ending of the Noh play *Matsukaze*:

> Murasame to kikishimo kesa mireba,
> Matsukaze bakari nokoran
> Matsukaze bakari nokoran.
> I thought I heard the rain last night,
> But this morning only the wind in the pines remains.
> Only the wind in the pines remains.

This passage contains a play on the names of the two women Murasame and Matsukaze, used here in their literal meanings of "passing shower" and "pine wind." *Yōkyokushū*, Nihon Koten Bungaku Taikei, Vol. 40 (Iwanami Shoten, 1968), p. 65.

[108]Hakushū and the composer Yamada Kōsaku began *Poetry and Music* to encourage communication between poets and musicians. The front page of each issue featured a song, the joint effort of a writer and composer. Hakushū published many of the shi later included in *Poems in Monochrome* in this journal. The magazine

ceased publication in October 1923, one month after the Kantō Earthquake devastated Arusu, the publisher.

[109]"Aru Sakkyokuka ni, *"Poetry and Music*, (October 1922), pp. 106-109.

[110]*Poems in Monochrome*, p. 266.

[111]Miki Rofū (1889-1964), who also wrote children's poetry, made his most important contribution during the four years from 1909 to 1913 when he published three collections of shi: *Haien* (Abandoned Garden, 1909), *Sabishiki Akebono* (Lonely Dawn, 1910), and *Shiroki Te no Karyūdo* (White-handed Hunter, 1913). *Abandoned Garden* appeared six months after *Heretical Faith*; both collections represented new approaches to symbolist poetry. Hakushū published his first four collections during the same period that Rofū was active, leading critics to christen those years "Hakuro Jidai" (the period of Hakushū and Rofū).

[112]"Jo," *Howling at the Moon* (Kanjōshisha, 1917), pp. 1-12.

[113]"Okugaki," *Poems in Monochrome*, pp. 4-5.

[114]Ibid., p. 2.

[115]The People's Poetry Group, led by Katō Kazuo (1887-1951), Shiratori Seigo (b. 1890), and Fukuda Masao (1893-1952), called for the composition of poems in the colloquial language on subject matter that concerned the common man. The publication of the magazine *Minshu* (The People) from 1918 to 1921 in Odawara marks the height of this movement. Their experiments in writing free verse in the colloquial—poems which often could not be distinguished from prose—gives the group its significance in literary history.

[116]The Group to Discuss Poetry included at its inception all the major and many of the minor poets of the Taishō period with two important exceptions, Hagiwara Sakutarō and Takamura Kōtarō. The diversity of opinion within the group made all but the most innocuous projects controversial. In 1921, they sponsored a large celebration honoring the fiftieth birthday of Shimazaki Tōson and published a selection of poetry *Gendai Shijin Senshū* (Anthology of Contemporary Poems) to commemorate the occasion. Hakushū, Miki Rofū, Horiguchi Daigaku (b. 1892), and three other poets withdrew from the group at this time because of a disagreement with members from the People's Poetry Group concerning the choice of poems for the collection.

[117]The dispute began in October 1922 when Shiratori published an unfavorable critique of Hakushū's folk songs in *Nihon Shijin* (Japanese Poets), the journal sponsored by the Group to Discuss Poetry. After Hakushū's withdrawal in 1917, the People's Poetry Group had taken over leadership of the society and controlled the magazine. That same month, Hakushū had attacked two poems by Shiratori and Fukuda for paucity of poetic sentiment and lack of rhythm. See "Kōsatsu no Aki" (An Autumn for Thought), *Poetry and Music* (October 1922), pp. 66-68. In the November and December issues of *Poetry and Music*, Hakushū responded to Shiratori's article and to another by Fukuda, who had argued that modern society did not need the kind of folk songs Hakushū wrote; poems by his group were more appropriate because they concerned contemporary life. Hakushū asserted that folk songs by definition could not be read; they had to be sung. Poems by Shiratori and Fukuda had no rhythm; therefore, they did not qualify as folk songs or even as shi. "An Autumn for Thought," *Poetry and Music* (November 1922), pp. 95-98 and

"Kōsatsu no Fuyu" (A Winter for Thought), ibid. (December 1922), pp. 45-50. Shiratori and Fukuda continued to write strongly worded attacks on Hakushū and his poetry. Hakushū finally lost his patience and in "Reimei no Kōsatsu" (Considerations at Dawn), *Poetry and Music* (January 1923), pp. 106-131, the last and longest of his essays on this subject, he vehemently denounced both men. He repeated his views on the folk song, but refused to discuss his shi or to respond to their attacks on "Chinese Pines" and his other poems. Shiratori and Fukuda's dislike for Hakushū's poetry, particularly its musicality and the traditional rather than contemporary nature of his subject matter, no doubt reflected the opinion of many young poets of the day.

[118]"Halo of Art" was first published in *Poetry and Music* (September 1922) and in the same form included in *Poems of Monochrome*. *Halo of Art* (Arusu, 1927), a book of the same title, contains this essay and two other sections on the folk song and children's poetry.

[119]"Halo of Art," found in *Hakushū Shiika Ikkagen*, ed. Yabuta, pp. 72-73.

[120]Ibid., p. 54.

[121]*Poems in Monochrome*, pp. 3-5.

[122]Tanomura Chikuden (1777-1835) was a Japanese literati painter known for his simplicity of style in India ink paintings. He was also an important interpreter of theories for this kind of painting.

[123]Lao Tzu or "Old Master" is a mythical sage to whom has been attributed the authorship of the *Lao Tzu* (or *Tao-te Ching*), a Chou period classic of Chinese Taoism. Hakushū's poems dealt not with this work but with legends concerning Lao Tzu's life.

[124]For a discussion of the tanshō in *Pearls*, see pages 110-112 above.

[125]*Poems in Monochrome*, p. 198.

[126]Ibid., p. 203.

[127]Ibid., p. 207.

[128]Ibid., p. 214.

[129]*Poems in Monochrome*, pp. 13-14.

[130]"Niwa no Ichibu" (In a Corner of My Garden), *Poems in Monochrome*, p. 156.

[131]"Natsuno" (Summer Fields), ibid., p. 188.

[132]"Takibi" (Bonfire), ibid., pp. 259-263.

[133]Ibid., pp. 368-376.

CHAPTER 5

[1]Shino Hiroshi, "Hakushū-Akahiko Mohō Ronsō I," *Tanka* (July 1961), pp. 151-152.

[2]Shimaki Akahiko, "Takujō Gūgo" (Conversations after Dinner), *Araragi* (January 1917), p. 86.

[3]Found in *Hakushū Mokichi Gosen Kashū* (reprint ed. combining both works; Shiratama Shobo, 1949), pp. 162-163. Kimata Osamu, who is a reliable scholar of modern tanka as well as a poet, believes that Hakushū did indeed influence Mokichi and Akahiko, finding evidence for this in Mokichi's tanka collections *Shakkō* (Red

Glow, 1913) and *Aratama* (Uncut Gems, 1921) and in Akahiko's *Kiribi* (Flint Sparks, 1915) and *Hio* (Whitebait, 1920). At the same time, Hakushū was also being influenced by the Araragi poets, particularly Mokichi, with whom he shared his admiration for the *Ryōjin Hishō* and for Ryōkan. See Kimata Osamu, *Kindai Tanka no Shiteki Tenkai*, pp. 161-162 and idem, "Mokichi to Hakushū," *Hyoron ·Meiji Taishō no Kajintachi*, pp. 322-334. Akahiko's denial of these influences only provides further evidence of his antagonistic attitude toward poets outside the Araragi Group.

[4]In a critique of Yūgure's tanka collection *Shinrin* (Deep Forests, 1916), found in the December 1916 issue of *Araragi*, Akahiko characterized his poems as "high-sounding nonsense." Yūgure's wounded pride and inability to strike back at Akahiko were major reasons for his temporary withdrawal from the tanka world in 1919.

[5]"An Autumn for Thought," *Poetry and Music* (October 1922), pp. 66-109. It was in the same discussion, the reader will recall, that Hakushū had attacked two poems by Shiratori and Fukuda as lacking the rhythm and poetic sentiment of true verse. See note 117 above. Akahiko seems to have agreed with Hakushū on this point and did not challenge Hakushū's opinion.

[6]See the discussion of this dispute found in Shino, "Hakushū Akahiko no Mohō Ronsō II," *Tanka* (August 1961), pp. 146-151.

[7]*Sunlight* was published from April 1924 to December 1927, supported by the Nikkō Tanka Kai (Sunlight Tanka Group), a loose association of some thirty tanka poets among whom Hakushū, Maeda Yūgure, Koizumi Chikashi (1886-1927), and Toki Zenmaro (b. 1885) held positions of leadership and selected the poems to be published in sections allotted to them. The appearance of this magazine had important symbolic significance. As its name *Sunlight* suggested, the magazine proposed to bring sunlight into the dark stifling atmosphere of the tanka world, where contention among tanka groups was threatening the development of the tanka. In its pages, members published verse as individuals, free from the constraint of adhering to a set theory of tanka. Experiments in altering the traditional rhythm, dividing the tanka into lines, and using the colloquial language provided important stimulus to the modern tanka movement. The Sunlight Group functioned not as a new faction but only to support the magazine, and disbanded when *Sunlight* ceased publication in December 1927.

[8]"Sōkan no Kotoba" (On the Establishment of *Sunlight*), *Sunlight* (April 1924), p. 133.

[9]"Kadan Ishiki ni tsuite" (On Factionalism in Tanka Circles), *Sunlight* (June 1924), found in *Hakushū Zenshū*, Vol. 17, p. 39.

[10]*Window to the Seasons* (Arusu, 1926).

[11]Although poets of shi had already begun to employ the colloquial, tanka continued to be written in the literary language. Attempts to write colloquial tanka were hindered by disputes over how to fit the modern language into the set form of the tanka. See the discussion below.

[12]Maeda Yūgure, *Hakushū Tsuioku* (Kenbunsha, 1948), pp. 63-68. In a postcard to Yūgure, dated July 2, 1923, Hakushū wrote: "I received your postcard and have been eagerly awaiting your visit. I was disappointed, therefore, to get your telegram this morning [saying that you could not come today]....How about tackling

239

some colloquial tanka? I have composed twenty. [Note by Yūgure. 'Nōmin Bijutsu no Uta' (Tanka on Peasant Art)?] The next time we get together, I'd like to hear your comments on these poems." Ibid., p. 239.

[13]*Poetry and Music* (August 1923), pp. 1-34.

[14]Ibid., pp. 35-41.

[15]Ibid., pp. 36-37.

[16]"Kōgoka ni tsuite" (Concerning Colloquial Tanka), *Window to the Seasons,* found in *Hakushū Zenshū,* Vol. 17, p. 26.

[17]The beginnings of modern colloquial tanka must be traced back to Toki Zenmaro and Ishikawa Takuboku whose works in effect revolutionized the tanka. In his first collection, *NAKIWARAI* (Tearful Smile, 1910), Zenmaro had used a roman- ized script and printed his tanka in three lines. Takuboku's *Handful of Sand* (1909) also employed Zenmaro's three-line form. Although neither poet completely aban- doned the literary language, their diction in these and later collections was re- markably close to colloquial expression. Hakushū's contribution—using a conversa- tional form of the colloquial language and dividing his lines not by a set form but according to the natural rhythms of his language—was a logical development of the trend to colloquial tanka begun by Zenmaro and Takuboku.

[18]"Concerning Colloquial Tanka," *Sunlight* (June 1924), pp. 72-73, later included in *Window to the Seasons,* pp. 25-26.

[19]*Out of the Wind,* ed. Kimata Osamu (Bokusui Shobō, 1944) contains 748 tanka and twenty-one chōka inspired by daily events in his life at Odawara from 1923 to 1925. A small portion was published in 1929 as *"Odawarashō"* (Odawara Poems) in the volume devoted to Hakushū, *Kitahara Hakushū Shū* (Kaizōsha, 1929), of *Gendai Tanka Zenshū* (Anthology of Modern Tanka). Although Hakushū planned to publish these tanka in a collection, he was unable to revise them to his satisfaction. In 1941, 229 tanka and 18 chōka finally did appear in *Hakushū Shiikashū,* Vol. 3 (Kawade Shobō, 1941). However, it was not until 1944, two years after his death, that Kimata Osamu published all the tanka concerning his daily life from this period as *Out of the Wind.*

[20]*Edge of the Sea,* ed. Kimata Osamu (Arusu, 1949), contains 1,207 tanka and four chōka inspired by his travels from 1923 to 1927. Together with most of the poems later included in *Out of the Wind,* these tanka remained unpublished until 1941 when 438 tanka and four chōka appeared in *Hakushū Shiikashū,* Vol. 3. After Hakushū's death, Kimata prepared the collection for publication, but his completed manuscript was destroyed in a bombing raid in 1944. After the war ended, Kimata once again compiled the tanka for *Edge of the Sea,* which finally appeared in 1949.

[21]"Kaisetsu" (Comments), *Hakushū Shiikashū,* Vol. 3 (Kawade Shobō, 1941), p. 433.

[22]*Out of the Wind* (Bokusui Shobō, 1944), p. 137.

[23]Ibid., p. 137.

[24]*Kitahara Hakushū Kashū,* ed. Kimata Osamu (Ōbunsha Bunko; Ōbunsha, 1970), p. 101.

[25]*Out of the Wind* p. 256.

[26]Ibid., p. 163.

[27]"Usuine" (Mount Usui), *Kumo to Tokei* (Clouds and Clocks; Kaiseisha, 1939), p. 163.

[28]*Edge of the Sea* (Arusu, 1949), p. 234.

[29]Hakushū had become friends with this poet through the Sunlight Tanka Group, to which they both belonged.

[30]*Seals and Clouds* (Arusu, 1929), Hakushū's seventh collection of shi, contains 146 poems written during the six years, 1923-1929, following the publication of *Poems in Monochrome.*

[31]*Raspberries and Blackberries* (Arusu, 1928). These essays on his trip to Hokkaido and Sakhalin were originally published as fifteen installments in the magazine *Josei* (Women) from December 1925 to February 1927. The title incorporates the foreign names of two berry bushes, native to Sakhalin, the fruit of which is used to produce local wines.

[32]*Raspberries and Blackberries*, found in *Hakushū Zenshū*, Vol. 15 (Arusu, 1930), pp. 3-4.

[33]"Taido" (Attitude), *Window to the Seasons*, p. 85.

[34]*Edge of the Sea*, p. 291.

[35]Ibid., p. 323. In the shi "Kamo" (Wild Duck) quoted directly below, Hakushū gives a detailed description of the fowl found in these tanka. This description seems to match that of the *suzugamo*, a type of wild duck native to the Gulf of Tartary. The male is grey, except for a shiny green breast.

[36]Ibid., p. 290.

[37]*Seals and Clouds* (Arusu, 1929), pp. 277-284.

[38]"Jiyūshi ni tsuite" (Concerning Free Verse), *Kindai Fūkei* (Modern Landscapes; January 1927), found in *Hakushū Zenshū*, Vol. 17, p. 313. This essay and others published at this time were later collected and included in *Hakushū Zenshū* under the title *Asa wa Yobu* (Morning Calls). *Morning Calls* was never published as a separate volume.

[39]For a discussion of the *imayō* and the use of this verse form in *Platinum Top*, see Chapter 3.

[40]*Seals and Clouds*, p. 325.

[41]Ibid., p. 331.

[42]Bashō used a similar image in his famous haiku:

> Ishiyama no   Whiter than the rocks
> Ishi yori shiroshi Of Ishiyama Mountain
> Aki no kaze.   Is the autumn wind.
>
> *Oku no Hosomichi* (Narrow Road to the North) found in *Bashō Bunshū*, p. 94.

Ishiyama (Rock Mountain), in present-day Ōtsu City in Shiga Prefecture, was famous as a place to view the moon in autumn.

[43]"Goki" (Afterword), *Seals and Clouds*, p. 384.

[44]Ibid., pp. 382.

[45]The *Kojiki* (Records of Ancient Matters) was compiled in 712. It contains mythical accounts of the founding of Japan; records of later periods have some

historical accuracy. See the translation by Donald L. Philippi, *Kojiki* (University of Tokyo Press, 1968).

[46]*The Nihon Shoki* (or *Nihongi*, History of Japan) was compiled in 720 and contains variants on the mythological legends recorded in the *Kojiki*. See *Nihongi*, trans. W.G. Aston (Published for the Japan Society; London: Kegan Paul, Trench, Tribner and Company, Ltd., 1896).

[47]*Fudoki* is a generic name for the records, some still extant, compiled of the geography, products, governmental institutions, and legends of each province by imperial order in the eighth century. See *Izumo Fudoki,* trans. Michiko Aoki (Sophia University, 1971).

[48]*Norito* (ritual Shinto prayers) were used to evoke the presence of gods at festivals. They were not recorded in written form until the ninth century.

[49]"Afterword," *Seals and Clouds*, p. 382.

[50]The first two stanzas of "The Source of Water," *Seals and Clouds*, pp. 5-6.

[51]"Landscape in Steel," *Seals and Clouds,* pp. 165-168.

[52]For a discussion of these poems, see Chapter 4.

[53]"Shiro," *Seals and Clouds*, pp. 48-49.

[54]For a discussion of *yūgen* in the *Shinkokinshū*, see Brower and Miner, pp. 236-271.

[55]Twenty-two issues of *Modern Landscapes* appeared between November 1926 and March 1928. Hakushū was both editor and manager. Although he called for modern poets to join his effort to revitalize modern poetry, which he thought was in a state of confusion, he was above all desirous of writing his own shi. Among the contributors were many poets he had worked with earlier: Hagiwara Sakutarō, Kinoshita Mokutarō, Miki Rofū, and Murō Saisei. The magazine also introduced some new poets such as Ōki Atsuo (b. 1895), Yoshida Issui (1898-1973), and Yabuta Yoshio (b. 1902), who later also served as Hakushū's secretary.

[56]"The Source of Water," *Modern Landscapes* (February 1928), pp. 2-4. "Landscape in Steel," ibid. (July 1928), pp. 4-6.

[57]*Modern Landscapes* (November 1926), pp. 2-3.

[58]Ibid., p. 125.

[59]Hakushū paid nominal rent to the family of Yoshihara Masataka, a recently deceased politician from Yanagawa, in return for watching over the property. Yabuta, p. 255.

[60]*Yumedono*, not published until November 1939, contains tanka inspired by Hakushū's travels during the years 1927-1935, approximately the same period covered by *Shirahae* (White Breezes of Summer), his sixth tanka collection, containing poems based on his daily life. *Yumedono* is in every sense a companion volume to *White Breezes*. My following comments on the style of poetry found in this volume also apply to *Yumedono*. The 982 tanka and 30 chōka included in Yumedono are divided into two parts. In the first part, which constitutes eighty percent of the collection, the poems are arranged chronologically, according to the places they treat. The second part contains miscellaneous tanka about the school his children attended, his children, and minor trips.

242

I have followed Hakushū's practice in numbering his tanka collections. Even though the Odawara collections, *Out of the Wind* and *Edge of the Sea*, were not published until after his death, Hakushū referred to them as his fourth and fifth tanka collections, according to the chronological dates when these tanka were composed.

[61]Japan had received the Russian-built South Manchurian Railroad Company under the terms of the Treaty of Portsmouth, September 5, 1905, which concluded the Russo-Japanese War. When Hakushū visited the area in 1929, it was still under nominal Chinese sovereignty. It was not until two years later that Japan seized control of Manchuria, following the Manchurian Incident of 1931. Hakushū's trip began at Dairen. He traveled north along the South Manchurian Railway through Mukden and Changchun to Harbin, where he changed to the Chinese Eastern Railway for Manchuli. He retraced his journey to Dairen, whence he returned to Japan. Besides the 211 tanka composed on this trip and included in *Yumedono*, he also wrote several children's songs, including two famous works "Machiboke" (Waiting in Vain) and "Pechika" (By the Fireside). *Pechika* is the Japanese approximation for the Russian word *Pechka*, the term for the stone or brick hearth, used for cooking and warmth, found in houses in Manchuria.

[62]*Yumedono* (Yakumo Shorin, 1939), p. 287.

[63]Ibid., p. 289.

[64]Yabuta, pp. 257-260.

[65]*Yumedono*, p. 110. The diction is archaic, in contrast to its highly contemporary content.

[66]Published by Arusu, his brother's publishing house, *White Breezes of Summer* has a white cloth cover and leather binding with the title inscribed in gold. This collection contained 1,319 tanka and 14 chōka inspired by nature in his garden from 1926 to 1933.

[67]"Jo" (Preface), *White Breezes of Summer* (Arusu, 1934), p. 2.

[68]*White Breezes of Summer*, p. 345.

[69]"Kisetsu no Uta no Tsukurikata" (How to Write Seasonal Tanka), *Tanka no Sho* (Kawade Shobō, 1942), p. 341. *Tanka no Sho* (Book on Tanka) contains the most important essays that Hakushū wrote on the tanka during the latter part of his life. Most of them appeared first in the magazine *Tama*. His statement that he did not invent the word *teriha no nobara* (glossy-leaved wild rose) reflects criticism of his neologisms. Hakushū did often create new words, most noticeably in his poetry criticism. He also employed unusual characters of the same pronunciation as the one commonly used, in order to emphasize a term or give it a slightly different nuance.

[70]"Kanmatsuki" (Afterword), *White Breezes of Summer*, p. 642.

[71]At the party commemorating the publication of *White Breezes of Summer*, Yamamoto Kuninobu, president of Kaizōsha Publishing Company, urged him not to treat such commonplace subjects. "*Shirahae* Zappitsu" (Miscellaneous Comments on *White Breezes of Summer*), *Tanka no Sho*, p. 142.

[72]"Miscellaneous Comments on *White Breezes of Summer*" (hereafter cited as "Comments") is divided into three parts, which discuss the meaning of the title *White Breezes of Summer*, the "Preface" to the collection, and Hakushū's approach to poetry. It was written during the four months from September 1934 to January

243

1935, approximately half a year after he published *White Breezes of Summer* in April 1934, and later included in *Tanka no Sho*. Although this piece has largely been ignored by scholars, whose treatment of Hakushū's later tanka is far from complete, it contains important information on Hakushū's approach to poetry, significant because the introduction to *White Breezes of Summer* is so cryptic.

[73]"Comments," *Tanka no Sho*, p. 142.

[74]Ibid., pp. 143-144.

[75]Ibid., p. 149.

[76]Ibid., p. 140.

[77]*White Breezes of Summer*, p. 570.

[78]Ibid., p. 75.

[79]"Comments," *Tanka no Sho*, p. 154.

[80]Ibid., p. 153.

[81]During the nineteen years after the dissolution of the Thatched House of Purple Smoke in September 1917, Hakushū did not have a tanka association of his own. His disciples had formed their own groups and magazines; most were publishing in *Kōran* (Fragrant Orchid), founded by Murano Jirō in March 1923 with Hakushū as honorary advisor. One year after Hakushū published *White Breezes of Summer* in April 1934, sixteen poets including Kimata Osamu (b. 1906), Shaku Chōkū, and Hozumi Kiyoshi (1901-1954) met with Hakushū and drew up principles governing membership in the new group. They discussed their approach to tanka and decided on editorial policies for their magazine *Tama*, the first issue of which appeared in June 1935. The name "Tama" was chosen primarily because Kinuta, where Hakushū lived at this time, was part of the area close to the Tama River in west Tokyo; a secondary meaning for *tama* (jewel), written with different characters, suggested the reverence in which they held the tanka. Hakushū functioned both as leader of this group and managing editor of their publication. After his death in 1942, Kimata Osamu assumed leadership until December 1952 when the organization was dissolved with the publication of the final issue of *Tama*.

[82]"Tama Proclamation", *Tanka no Sho*, p. 55.

[83]"Tama Kōryō" (Platform of the Tama Tanka Association), *Tanka no Sho*, p. 65.

[84]Kimata Osamu, *Kindai Tanka no Shiteki Tenkai*, p. 283.

[85]"Tanka Shin'en" (My Feelings about the Tanka), *Tanka no Sho*, p. 72. All of the essays I have quoted from *Tanka no Sho* concerning the Tama Tanka Association originally appeared in *Tama* during 1935.

[86]"Yosano Hiroshi Sensei," *Tanka Kenkyū* (May 1935), p. 85.

[87] Kimata Osamu, *"Tama* no Bungaku Seishin"* (The Spirit of Literature in *Tama*), *Hakushū Kenkyū*, p. 318.

[88]*Tanka Kenkyū* (March 1935), pp. 2-7.

[89]"Goki" (Afterword), *Hakushū Shiikashū*, Vol. 4 (Kawade Shobō, 1941), p. 438.

[90]*Mountain Stream* contains 482 tanka and 9 chōka inspired by Hakushū's travels from January 1935 to May 1937. Although Hakushū had planned to publish this collection earlier, failing eyesight prevented him from preparing the manuscript

as planned, and it was not completed until two months before his death. *Mountain Stream* was finally published in November 1943 with a commentary by Kimizu Yasaburō, an editor with Seibunsha Publishing Company, which brought out the volume.

[91]*Mountain Stream* (Seibunsha, 1943), p. 10.

[92]Shinshū Kawa" (Early Autumn Talks on Poetry), *Tanka no Sho*, p. 240. The latter half of Hakushū's speech at the convention was later included under this title in *Tanka no Sho*.

[93]*Tsurubami* is the ancient name for the *kunugi* tree, a type of beech tree that grows in abundance in the area of western Tokyo where Hakushū lived. Hakushū took the title from a tanka about the tree, found in the collection. *Beech Tree*, which contains 531 tanka and 8 chōka written from 1935 to 1937, is a companion volume to *Mountain Stream;* the former contains travel poems and the latter, tanka written about his daily life. It was published in December 1943, one month after *Mountain Stream*, by the same publisher Seibunsha, with a commentary by Kimizu Yasaburō.

[94]*Beech Tree* (Seibunsha, 1943), p. 203.

[95]Ibid., p. 204.

[96]The subtitle of this series, which includes one more tanka, is "Kisshū" (The Beginning of Autumn).

[97]"Early Autumn Talks on Poetry," *Tanka no Sho*, p. 246.

[98]Ibid., pp. 246-247. Shaku Chōkū (Origuchi Shinobu) made this statement in the November 1936 monthly supplement to the *Tanka Bungaku Zenshū: Hakushū Hen* (Daiichi Shobō, 1936), adding that Hakushū's tanka "not only have the strongest affinity to the techniques of expression basic to the tanka as developed since the *Man'yōshū* but also display sentiments that are totally modern." Kimata Osamu, *Kindai Tanka no Kanshō to Hihyō*, p. 238.

[99]"Early Autumn Talks on Poetry," p. 247.

[100]*Beech Tree*, p. 141.

CHAPTER 6

[1]This collection was published from December 1937 to September 1938 in eleven volumes, including an index and a separate volume of poems by the imperial family. The other nine judges were Maeda Yūgure, Saitō Mokichi, Kubota Utsubo, Toki Zenmaro, Onoe Saishū (1876-1957), Ōta Mizuho (1876-1955), Yosano Akiko, Shaku Chōkū, and Sasaki Nobutsuna. The *New Man'yōshū* contained 26,783 tanka by 6,675 poets. Contemporary critics praised it highly because of the large number of poems by amateurs it recorded for posterity. As a scholarly reference, however, it has limited value, since the poems are not arranged chronologically but according to author and no dates of composition are given. It is also virtually inaccessible at the present date—not to be found in any of the major public or university libraries in Tokyo. I am indebted to Kimata Osamu for lending me his copy. Fifty tanka by Hakushū, the maximum number that could be included by one poet, may be found in Vol. 3, pp. 79-84. Thirty poems by Kimata, who was thirty-three years old at the

time, were included in the same volume, pp. 21-24. See Kimata Osamu, *"Shinman'yōshū* no Kansei," *Shōwa Tanka Shi* (Meiji Shoin, 1964), pp. 412-415.

[2]Yabuta, p. 340. Kimata, *"Shinman'yōshū* no Kansei," p. 412.

[3]The full text of the opinion of this doctor, Masaki Yoshifumi, and four others may be found in *Tama* (December 1937), pp. 167-174.

[4]"Hakumei ni Zasu" (In a World of Twilight), *Tanka no Sho*, p. 96. Hakushū dictated this essay in February 1938, one month after he left the hospital; it appeared first in *Tama*.

[5]*Black Cypress*, the last volume of tanka to be published during Hakushū's lifetime, contains 654 tanka and 5 chōka, written between 1937 and 1940, and records the dimly lit world of Hakushū's last years. The first edition was published by Yakumo Shorin on reclaimed paper, attesting to the dearth of paper caused by Japan's war effort. The collection contains six photographs, four of which were of Buddhist statues found in Nara. After the convention of Tama poets held at Mt. Shigi near Nara in August 1936, Hakushū had visited various temples in the Nara area. These statues remained an important memory after his eyesight began to fail.

[6]*Black Cypress* (Yakumo Shorin, 1940), p. 6.

[7]*Black Cypress*, p. 10.

[8]"Jo"(Introduction), *Black Cypress*, p. 2.

[9]Most Japanese scholars have ignored *Black Cypress*, along with Hakushū's other late collections of tanka. The magazine *Yuriika*, for example, devoted its December 1973 issue to articles concerning Hakushū; most of them dealt with his three earliest poetry collections—the most significant contribution by this poet in terms of their impact upon the world of poetry. Recent selections of Hakushū's poetry also tend to emphasize his early poetry. The reasons for this slanted approach are complex. First of all, there is no truly complete collection of Hakushū's poetry and criticism. Plans to publish a new edition of his complete works are continually discussed but have as yet not been realized. Secondly, Hakushū's tanka became increasingly difficult; many critics believe that *Black Cypress* can only be appreciated by sophisticated tanka poets. The reader of Japanese is advised to see the interesting discussion on "Kitahara Hakushū no Fukken" (Reinstatement of Kitahara Hakushū), *Yuriika* (December, 1973), pp. 140-164, in which five modern poets and critics discuss the importance of reevaluating Hakushū's poetry. I agree with the opinion of several of these men that Hakushū's importance as a tanka poet should be more carefully examined.

See also my discussion of *Black Cypress*, "Hakumei no Kakyō," *Eigo Bungaku Sekai* (June 1976), pp. 14-17.

[10]Ibid., p. 214.

[11]Ibid.

[12]This Chinese priest, Chien-chen, was an important founder of the Ritsu sect of Japanese Buddhism. He left China in 742 and after five unsuccessful attempts to reach Japan, during which he lost his eyesight, at last arrived in 754.

[13]*Black Cypress*, pp. 13-14, 70, 192, and 202.

[14]Ibid., p. 14.

[15]*New Eulogies* (Yakumo Shorin, 1940) contains thirty-one poems written during the ten years, 1930-1940, following the publication of *Seals and Clouds* in 1929. The three long poems, which make up the body of the collection, are unsuccessful attempts at writing narrative verse. The special nature of this volume, written in commemoration of the 2600th anniversary

of the founding of Japan as a state, and Hakushū's loss of interest in the shi at this time of his life make this collection a minor work which justly has not received much notice.

[16]The Central Federation on Japanese Culture (Nihon Bunka Chūō Renmei) was organized by Matsumoto Gaku to solicit poetry, folk songs, fiction, and music to celebrate the 2600th anniversary of the mythological founding of the Japanese state. Hakushū and other artists received monetary compensation for their works from the federation, which also arranged concerts and exhibitions, and published records and books for the works it commissioned. The organization was dissolved in 1942 with the completion of its tasks. Yabuta Yoshio, interview held in Tokyo, August 1976.

[17]"Expedition by Sea to the East," *New Eulogies* (Yakumo Shorin, 1940), pp. 4-51. "Mongol Invasion," pp. 199-222.

[18]"Kanmakki" (Afterword), *New Eulogies*, p. 228.

[19]According to legends in the *Kojiki* and *Nihon Shoki*, Susa-no-o was born to Izanami and Izanagi, mythological deities who gave birth to the islands of Japan, Amaterasu, and a number of other lower deities. An unruly god, Susa-no-o was banished to earth. Hakushū's poem, over two hundred lines in length, describes Susa-no-o's sorrow at being expelled. He originally intended to write three more parts, which would incorporate other legends about Susa-no-o, but the poem was never finished. See *New Eulogies*, pp. 54-82.

[20]"Afterword," *New Eulogies*, p. 233.

[21]Ibid.

[22]Ibid.

[23]Ibid., p. 234.

[24]Yabuta, p. 401.

[25]*Tama* (March 1941), pp. 6-7.

[26]The title is taken from the famous *fu* by T'ao Ch'ien (365-427) on this same subject, translated as "The Return" in Robert Payne, *The White Pony* (Mentor Books; New York: New American Library, 1943), pp. 144-145.

[27]In the original the title is followed by an explanatory note: "Twelve years have passed since I flew by plane to visit my hometown."

[28]Yamato is the county (*gun*) in which Yanagawa is located.

[29] An ancient name for Kyushu.

[30]*Fujin Kōron* (Women's Forum; April 1941), pp. 58-59.

[31]Hakushū wrote only one more shi, "Udo Jingu" (Udo Shrine), based on his visit to this shrine in Nichinan City, Miyazaki Prefecture, after he left Yanagawa.

[32]The Imperial Academy of Art (Teikoku Geijutsu In) had been established by the Japanese Diet in June 1937. It was reorganized after the war under a new name, the Japanese Academy of Art (Nihon Geijutsu In). Its functions are primarily honorary.

[33]*Peony Tree Logs* (Kawade Shobō, 1943), Hakushū's eleventh and last collection of tanka, contains 414 tanka and 4 chōka. The collection was published by Kimata Osamu, who gathered the tanka that had appeared previously (for the most part in *Tama*), arranged them chronologically, and chose the title from a series of poems on this subject. The three sections of the volume correspond to the years from 1940 to 1942 when these poems originally appeared.

[34]*Peony Tree Logs*, p. 4.

[35]Ibid., p. 7.

[36]*Anthology of Japanese Literature*, ed. Donald Keene (New York: Grove Press, 1960), pp. 197-212.

[37]Ibid., pp. 374-376.

[38]*Peony Tree Logs*, p. 11. The *sarusuberi* tree is related to the myrtle but much taller. It blossoms at the end of summer.

[39]Ibid., pp. 171-174.

[40]*Map of Manchuria* (Futaba Shoin, 1942).

[41]*Greater East Asian War: Verses for Young Citizens*, ed. Yabuta Yoshio (Asahi Shinbunsha, 1943). Several of these poems, the last works before his death, were found by Hakushū's bedside after he died. Yabuta placed them in a separate chapter at the end of this collection.

[42]*Hunter of Fragrance* (Kawade Shobō, 1942).

[43]*Kindergarten in the Morning* (Teikoku Kyōikukai Shuppanbu, 1942).

[44]Before his death, Hakushū requested Yabuta Yoshio to take responsibility for collecting and arranging the poems for this collection of traditional children's songs. Using the Tama Tanka Association, which had members living in all parts of Japan, Yabuta gathered a large number of poems and after the war published three volumes of the collection as *Compilation of Traditional Japanese Children's Songs*, Vol. 1, 2, and 6 (Kokumin Kankyōkai, 1947-1950). The collection remained incomplete until 1976 when Yabuta at last finished the other three volumes and published *Compilation of Traditional Japanese Children's Songs*, 6 vol. (Sanseidō, 1976). He received a special award from Nihon Dōyō Kyōkai (Association for Japanese Children's Songs) for his work.

[45]*Peony Tree Logs*, p. 224.

[46]Ibid.

[47]Ibid., pp. 79-83.

[48]See "Zassan" (Miscellaneous Remarks), *Tama* (August 1942), pp. 141-142 for Hakushū's enthusiastic description of his improvement.

[49]Quoted by Yonegawa Minoru, "Jūichigatsu Futsuka no Asa to Sono Zengo," *Tama* (December 1942), p. 30. This issue of *Tama* contains several accounts of Hakushū's last hours. Yonegawa was a doctor as well as a tanka poet, and his account seems the most accurate. I have based my description on his.

[50]Yonegawa, p. 31.

[51]These verses, Hakushū's last works, were written for *Young Citizens' Weekly*. See page 276, note 41.

[52]*Patterns of Water* (Arusu,1943) contains 98 poems by Hakushū about Yanagawa, taken from *Memories, Seals and Clouds, Yumedono*, and *New Eulogies*, and 108 photographs by Tanaka, which picture the subject matter of the poetry.

[53]"Goki" (Epilogue), *Patterns of Water*, unpaged.

[54]Hakushū used the Buddhist term *goun*, which refers to the five forms assumed by phenomena in the real world: color, sensation, ideation, will, and consciousness.

[55]"Hashigaki" (Preface), *Patterns of Water*, unpaged. This is the full text of the Preface. The piece ends with an incomplete sentence.

[56]Hagiwara Sakutarō, "Kitahara Hakushū no Shi: Shishū *Omoide* yori," *Nihon* (January 1942), found in *Hagiwara Sakutarō Zenshū*, Vol. 7 (Sōgensha, 1951), p. 199.

BIBLIOGRAPHY

Almost all the books consulted in connection with this study were published in Tokyo. The place of publication, therefore, has been omitted except in the few cases when it was not Tokyo. This applies to the footnote citations as well.

I. WORKS BY HAKUSHŪ

There exists no complete collection of Hakushū's writings, and I have consulted first editions of his poetry collections for this study. The first section of this part of the bibliography contains a list of selections of Hakushū's poetry, annotated with brief descriptions to indicate the contents. The next five sections list first editions of his poetry collections arranged according to verse form (shi, tanka, chōka, folk songs, and children's poems), and the last section contains collections of Hakushū's essays and criticism cited in the paper. All the works are arranged chronologically, according to the date of publication.

The reader wishing further information on Hakushū's writings should consult the bibliography found in Yabuta Yoshio, *Hyōden Kitahara Hakushū* (Tamagawa Daigaku Shuppanbu, 1973), pp. 466-481.

A. Selections of Hakushū's Poetry and Criticism

Hakushū Zenshū. 18 vols. Arusu, 1929-1934.
This is the only comprehensive collection of Hakushū's works, but it does not include any poetry or criticism after 1934. Hakushū's postfaces to each volume contain important comments on his poetry.

Kitahara Hakushū Shū. Gendai Tanka Zenshū. Kaizōsha, 1929.
An early selection of Hakushū's tanka. A small portion of his Odawara period tanka appeared here as "Odawarashō" (Odawara Poems).

Zenbō. 8 vols. Arusu, 1933-1940.
Zenbō was published to supplement the material found in *Hakushū Zenshū*. Each volume contains works published by Hakushū in one year. The years cover 1932 to 1939. Very few copies of this collection are still extant.

Hakushū Shiika Shū. 8 vols. Kawade Shobō, 1941.
Selections of Hakushū's poetry based on *Hakushū Zenshū*.

Mizu no Kōzu (Patterns of Water). Photographs by Tanaka Zentoku. Arusu, 1943.
Selection of Hakushū's poems concerning Yanagawa with photographs.

Hakushū. Edited by Yabuta Yoshio and Kimata Osamu. Bokusui Shobō, 1943.
Intended to supplement *Zenbō* by publishing the works for Hakushū's last three years in three separate volumes, only the first volume, for 1940, was completed.

Hakushū Shishū. 5 vols. Edited by Yabuta Yoshio. Kawade Shobō, 1947.
Selections of Hakushū's shi.

Hakushū Kashū. Edited by Kimata Osamu. Kawade Shobō, 1947.
Selections of Hakushū's tanka. Intended as a companion set to *Hakushū Shishū*, both are paper bound.

Kitahara Hakushū Sakuhin Shū. 3 vols. Edited by Yabuta Yoshio and
Kimata Osamu. Kawade Shobō, 1952.
Published to commemorate the tenth anniversary of Hakushū's
death. The editors planned ten volumes, but only three were
completed.

All the works cited above are out of print and not readily available even in
Tokyo. There are a number of recent selections of Hakushū's poetry that
contain standard samplings of his best tanka and shi. The most important are
listed below.

Kitahara Hakushū Kashū. Edited by Kitahara Ryūtarō and Kimata Osamu.
Shinchō Bunko. Shinchōsha, 1952.
One of the first paperback selections of Hakushū's tanka.

Kitahara Hakushū Bungaku Dokuhon. Edited by Yabuta Yoshio. Kawade
Shobō, 1956.
A selection of tanka, shi, folk songs, and children's poetry
arranged according to subject matter.

Hakushū Shishū. Edited by Kitahara Ryūtarō. Kadokawa Bunko. Kadokawa
Shoten, 1962.
A selection of Hakushū's shi arranged chronologically by col-
lection. The editor is Hakushū's son.

Kitahara Hakushū. Edited by Itō Shinkichi, Inoue Sei, and Yamamoto
Kenkichi. Nihon no Shiika, vol. 9. Chūō Kōron, 1968.
A representative selection of Hakushū's shi and tanka with
notes by Murano Shirō.

Kitahara Hakushū Shishū. Edited by Kimata Osamu. Sekai no Meishi, vol.
3. Kodansha, 1969.
Although this selection includes barely a hundred tanka and
shi, the accompanying commentary by Kimata Osamu makes
it a valuable introduction to Hakushū's poetry.

Kitahara Hakushū Kashū. Edited by Kimata Osamu. Ōbunsha Bunko.
Ōbunsha, 1970.
The most complete selection of Hakushū's tanka, arranged
chronologically with brief notes on a number of the poems by
Kimata Osamu, Hakushū's closest tanka disciple.

Kitahara Hakushū Shū. Nihon Kindai Bungaku Taikei, vol. 28. Kadokawa
Shoten, 1970.
Contains the complete text of *Heretical Faith, Paulownia
Flowers*, and two-thirds of *Memories* with extensive notes, an
index to the poems, introduction by Murano Shirō, chronology
of Hakushū's life, and complete bibliography of secondary
sources by Kawamura Masatoshi. The only variorum edition
of Hakushū's poetry to date.

Kitahara Hakushū Meisaku Senshū. Sung by Daaku Dakkusu. King Record
Co., 1974.
Two long-playing records containing twenty-two of the most
celebrated arrangements of Hakushū's songs sung by a modern
vocal group. The texts of the poems are included.

B. Collections of Shi

Jashūmon (Heretical Faith). Ekifūsha, 1909.

Omoide (Memories). Toūndō, 1911.

Tōkyō Keibutsu Shi Sono Ta (Scenes of Tokyo and Other Poems). Tōundō,
1913.

Shinjushō (Pearls). Kaneo Bun'endō, 1914.

Hakkin no Koma (Platinum Top). Kaneo Bun'endō, 1914.

Suibokushū (Poems in Monochrome). Arusu, 1923.

Azarashi to Kumo (Seals and Clouds). Arusu, 1929.

Shinshō (New Eulogies). Yakumo Shorin, 1940.

C. Collections of Tanka

Kiri no Hana (Paulownia Flowers). Tōundō, 1913.

Kirarashū (Mica). Oranda Shobō, 1915.

Suzume no Tamago (Sparrow's Eggs). Arusu, 1921.

Fūinshū (Out of the Wind). Edited by Kimata Osamu. Bokusui Shobō, 1944.[1]

Unazaka (Edge of the Sea). Edited by Kimata Osamu. Arusu, 1949.[1]

Shirahae (White Breezes of Summer). Arusu, 1934.

Yumedono. Yakumo Shorin, 1939.

Keiryūshō (Mountain Stream). Seibunsha, 1943.[2]

Tsurubami (Beech Tree). Seibunsha, 1943.[2]

Kurohi (Black Cypress). Yakumo Shorin, 1940.

Botan no Boku (Peony Tree Logs). Edited by Kimata Osamu. Kawade Shobō, 1943.

D. Collections of Chōka

Kansō no Aki (Autumn of Contemplation). Arusu, 1922.

Takamura (Bamboo Grove). Azusa Shobō, 1929.

E. Folk songs

Hakushū Kouta Shū (Kouta by Hakushū). Arusu, 1919.

Nihon no Fue (Japanese Flute). Arusu, 1922.

---

[1]*Out of the Wind* and *Edge of the Sea* were not published until after Hakushū's death. The tanka in the former were written, however, from 1925 to 1927 and those in the latter from 1923 to 1927. Hakushū considered them his fourth and fifth tanka collections, and this is the order they have been dealt with in this study.

[2]Once again the composition dates of the poems rather than the publication date of the collection dictates the position in the bibliography.

Ashi no Ha (Blades of Rush). Arusu, 1923.

Kitahara Hakushū Chihō Minyō Shū (Regional Folk Songs by Kitahara Hakushū). Hakubunkan, 1931.

Seinen Nippon no Uta (Songs for Japanese Youth). Ritsumeikan, 1932.

Yakushin Nippon no Uta (Songs for Our Progressing Nation). Arusu, 1936.

F. Children's Poetry

Tonbō no Megane (Dragonfly's Spectacles). Arusu, 1919.

Usagi no Denpō (Rabbit's Telegram). Arusu, 1921.

Masaaru Guusu (Mother Goose). Arusu, 1921.

Matsuri no Fue (Festival Flute). Arusu, 1922.

Hanasaki Jiisan (Old Man Who Made the Flowers Bloom). Arusu, 1923.

Kodomo no Mura (Town of Children). Arusu, 1925.

Nijū Niji (Double Rainbow). Arusu, 1926.

Karatachi no Hana (Orange Blossoms). Shinchōsha, 1926.

Zō no Ko (Elephant Child). Arusu, 1926.

Tsuki to Kurumi (Moon and Walnuts). Azusa Shobō, 1929.

Machibōke (Waiting in Vain). Shun'yōdō, 1933.

Minato no Hata (Harbor Flags). Arusu, 1942.

Asa no Yōchien (Kindergarten in the Morning). Teikoku Kyoikukai Shuppanbu, 1942.

Manshū Chizu (Map of Manchuria). Futaba Shoin, 1942.

G. Collections of Essays and Poetry Criticism

Suzume no Seikatsu (Life of the Sparrows). Shinchōsha, 1920.

Senshin Zatsuwa (Miscellaneous Remarks on Concentration). Arusu, 1921.

Kisetsu no Mado (Window to the Seasons). Arusu, 1926.

Geijutsu no Enkō (Halo of Art). Arusu, 1927.

Fureppu Torippu (Raspberries and Blackberries). Arusu, 1928.

Kumo to Tokei (Clouds and Clocks). Kaiseisha, 1939.

Tanka no Sho (Book on Tanka). Kawade Shobō, 1942.

Nioi no Shuryōsha (Hunter of Fragrance). Kawade Shobō, 1942.

Hakushū Shiika Ikkagen (Hakushū's Poetry Criticism). Edited by Yabuta Yoshio. Tamagawa Daigaku Shuppanbu, 1969.

II. POETRY JOURNALS EDITED BY HAKUSHŪ

Okujō Teien (Roof Garden). October 1909-January 1910.

Zanboa (Shaddock). November 1911-June 1913.

Chijō Junrei (Pilgrimage on Earth). July 1914-March 1915.

ARS (Ars). April-October 1915.

Tabako no Hana (Tobacco Flowers). November-December 1916.

Geijutsu Jiyū Kyōiku (Free Education in the Arts). January-November 1921.

Shi to Ongaku (Poetry and Music). October 1922-October 1923.

Nikkō (Sunlight). April 1924-December 1927.

Kindai Fūkei (Modern Landscapes). November 1926-March 1928.

Tama. June 1935-December 1952.

III. WORKS IN JAPANESE

For a complete list of secondary sources pertaining to Hakushū's life and poetry, the reader should consult the bibliography found in *Kitahara Hakushū Shū*, Nihon Kindai Bungaku Taikei, vol. 28 (Kadokawa Shoten, 1970), pp. 584-595.

Akai Tori. July 1918-November 1936.

Araragi. October 1908-November 1942.

Bi o Yumemiru Shijintachi. Gendaishi Kanshō Kōza, vol. 3. Edited by Itō Shinkichi, Inoue Yasushi, Noda Utarō, Murano Shirō, and Yoshida Seiichi. Kadokawa Shoten, 1968.

Bungei Nenkan 1976. Edited by Nippon Bungei Kyōkai. Shinchōsha, 1976.

Bunko. September 1895-August 1910.

Chosakuken Daichō: Bunka Jinmeiroku. Vol. 2. 16th edition. Nihon Chosakuken Kyōgikai, 1974.

Fukasawa, Margaret. "Hakumei no Kakyō." *Eigo Bungaku Sekai,* June 1976, pp. 14-17.

Gendai Meishi Sen. Edited by Itō Shinkichi. 3 vols. Shinchō Bunko. Shinchōsha, 1969.

Gendai Nihon Bungaku Daijiten. Edited by Hisamatsu Sen'ichi, Kimata Osamu, Naruse Masakatsu, Kawazoe Kunimoto, and Hasegawa Izumi. Meiji Shoin, 1971.

Gendai Nihon Bungaku Dainenpyō. Edited by Hisamatsu Sen'ichi, Kimata Osamu, Naruse Masakatsu, Kawazoe Kunimoto, and Hasegawa Izumi. 4 vols. Meiji Shoin, 1971.

Gendai Tanka Hyōshaku. Edited by Yoshida Seiichi. Gakutōsha, 1967.

257

Hagiwara Sakutarō. *Aoneko*. Shinchōsha, 1923.

_____. "Kitahara Hakushū no Shi: Shishū *Omoide* yori." *Nihon*, January 1942. Found in *Hagiwara Sakutarō Zenshū*. Vol. 1. Sōgensha, 1951.

_____. *Tsuki ni Hoeru*. "Jo" by Kitahara Hakushū. Kanjōshisha, 1923.

Hakushū no Hon." *Ginka*, Summer 1972, pp. 77-84.

Harada Taneo. *Sasurai no Uta*. Shinchōsha, 1972.

Hattori Tohō. *Sanzōshi*. Found in *Renga Ronshū Haironshū*. Nihon Koten Bungaku Taikei, vol. 66. Iwanami Shoten, 1968.

Iijima Kōichi. "Hakushū to Sakutarō." *Yuriika*, August 1969, pp. 112-123.

Imai Fukujirō. *Katairon*. Yūseidō, 1948.

Irie Harutsuru. "Shinshisha Dattai Jiken Oboegaki." *Kokubungaku*, December 1964, pp. 116-120.

Ishikawa Takuboku. *Ichihaku no Suna*. Tōundō, 1910.

_____. *Meiji Yonjūichinen Nisshi*. Found in *Takuboku Zenshū*. Vol. 5. Chikuma Shobō, 1967.

Itō Shinkichi. *Jojō Shōkyoku Ron*. Seiga Shobō, 1969.

Kaisō no Hakushū. Edited by Inoue Kōbun. Hobun Shorin, 1948.

Kamachi Yoshiyuki. "Kitahara Hakushū to Yanagawa." *Tanka*, January 1963, pp. 61-67.

Kan Takamichi. *Nihon no Jidō Bungaku*. Vol. 1: Sōron. Ōtsuki Shobō, 1972.

Kanbara Ariake. *Ariake Shishū*. Ekifūsha, 1908.

_____. *Shunchōshū*. Hongo Shoin, 1905.

Kawamura Masatoshi. "Kitahara Hakushū." *Kindai Kajin II*. Nihon Kajin Kōza, vol. 7. Compiled by Hisamatsu Sen'ichi and Sanekata Kiyoshi. Kōbundō, 1961. Pp. 55-126.

_____. "Kitahara Hakushū." *Kindai no Kajin II.* Waka Bungaku Kōza, vol. 9. Edited by Waka Bungakkai. Ōfūsha, 1970. Pp. 129-157.

_____. "Kitahara Hakushū Ron." *Kindai Tanka.* Nihon Bungaku Kenkyū Shiryō Sōsho. Yūseidō, 1973. Pp. 257-263.

_____. "Kitahara Hakushū Shiron: Sono Kankaku Hyōgen to Shiteki Ninshiki o megutte." *Nihon Kindai Bungaku,* May 1968, pp. 106-114.

_____. "*Myōjō* Jidai no Kitahara Hakushū." *Kokubungaku,* December 1964, pp. 65-72.

Keene, Donald. "Kitahara Hakushū." *Nami,* May 1976, pp. 38-39.

Kimata Osamu. *Hakushū Kenkyū.* Yakumo Shorin, 1943.

_____. *Hakushū Kenkyū I: Tankahen.* Shinten Shobō, 1954.

_____. *Hakushū Kenkyū II: Hakushū to Sono Shūhen.* Shinten Shobō, 1955.

_____. *Hyōron-Meiji Taishō no Kajintachi.* Meiji Shoin, 1971.

_____. *Kindai Tanka no Kanshō to Hihyō.* Meiji Shoin, 1973.

_____. *Kindai Tanka no Shiteki Tenkai.* Meiji Shoin, 1969.

_____. "Mokichi to Hakushū: Sono Shoki ni okeru Kōryū to Kairi no Jittai." *Kindai Tanka.* Nihon Bungaku Kenkyū Shiryō Sōsho. Yūseidō, 1973. Pp. 250-264.

_____. "Shiō Hakushū no Hon." *Ginka,* Summer 1972, pp. 85-91.

_____. *Shōwa Tanka Shi.* Meiji Shoin, 1964.

Kinoshita Mokutarō. "Shishū *Jashūmon* o Hyōsu." *Subaru,* May 1909. Found in *Bi o Yumemiru Shijintachi.* Edited by Itō et al. Kadokawa Shoten, 1968. Pp. 400-404.

Kitahara Hakushū. Nihon Bungaku Arubamu, vol. 2. Edited by Noda Utarō. Chikuma Shoten, 1954.

"Kitahara Hakushū Nenpu." *Shinchō*, December 1917, pp. 118-121.

Kitahara Hakushū. "Yosano Hiroshi Sensei." *Tanka Kenkyū*, May 1935, pp. 84-90.

Kitahara Ryūtarō. "Chichi Kitahara Hakushū no Omoide." *Toshō*, December 1964, pp. 31-35.

_____. "Kōda Rentarō Sensei to Chichi Hakushū." *Hakuchō*, December 1962, pp. 5-7.

Konishi Jin'ichi. "Kaisetsu." *Ryōjin Hishō*. Nihon Koten Zenshū. Asahi Shinbunsha, 1969. Pp. 3-41.

Kubo Tadao. "Hakushū no 'Haru no Tori' no Tanka." *Kindai Tanka*. Nihon Bungaku Kenkyū Shiryō Sōsho. Yūseidō, 1973. Pp. 265-275.

Kubota Utsubo. *Tsuchi o Nagamete*. Kokumin Bungakusha, 1918.

Maeda Yūgure. *Hakushū Tsuioku*. Kenbunsha, 1948.

Mandara. September 1917-September 1918.

Masaki Yoshifumi, Yamazaki Eiji, Sasa Kōhei, Mori Kenkichi, and Yasu Junko. "Hakushū Sensei no Gobyōjō." *Tama*, December 1937, pp. 169-174.

Matsuo Bashō. *Nozarashi Kikō*. Found in *Bashō Bunshū*. Nihon Koten Bungaku Taikei, vol. 46. Iwanami Shoten, 1968.

_____. *Oi no Kobumi*. Found in *Bashō Bunshū*. Nihon Koten Bungaku Taikei, vol. 46. Iwanami Shoten, 1968.

Meiji Taishō Yakushi Shū. Edited by Yoshida Seiichi. Nihon Kindai Bungaku Taikei, vol. 52. Kadokawa Shoten, 1971.

Miyoshi Tatsuji. *Hagiwara Sakutarō*. Chikuma Shobō, 1963.

Miyoshi Yukio. *Nihon no Kindai Bungaku*. Hanawa Bunko. Hanawa Shobō, 1972.

Mori Ōgai. *Sokkyō Shijin*. Shun'yōdō, 1902.

Murano Shirō, Miya Shōji, Takada Mizuho, Naka Tarō, Nishigaki Osamu, and Kawamura Masatoshi. "Zadankai: Kitahara Hakushū no Zaihyōka." *Tanka*, July 1968, pp. 92-111.

Murō Saisei. *Jojō Shōkyoku Shū*. "Jo" by Kitahara Hakushū. Kanjōshisha, 1918.

_____. *Waga Aisuru Shijin no Denki*. Chūō Kōron, 1958.

Myōjō. April 1900-February 1908.

Nakamura Hajime. *Bukkyōgo Daijiten*. 2 vols. Tōkyō Shoseki, 1975.

Nihon Bungaku Daijiten. 8 vols. Edited by Fujimura Tsukuru. Shinchōsha, 1952-1954.

Nihon Denshō Dōyō. 3 vols. Compiled by Yabuta Yoshio. Kokumin Kankyōkai, 1947-1950.

Nihon Denshō Dōyō. 6 vols. Compiled by Yabuta Yoshio. Sanseidō, 1976.

Nishimoto Akio. *Hakushū Ron Shiryō Kō*. Shinseisha, 1974.

_____. *Kitahara Hakushū Kenkyū*. Shinseisha, 1965.

Noda Utarō. *Nihon Tanbiha no Tanjō*. Kadokawa Shoten, 1951.

_____. *"Omoide* ni tsuite," afterword to *Omoide*, by Kitahara Hakushū. Facsimile of first edition. Nihon Kyōdo Bungei Sōsho, 1967.

Onda Itsuo. *Kitahara Hakushū*. Hito to Sakuhin, vol. 22. Shimizu Shoin, 1969.

Saitō Mokichi and Kitahara Hakushū. *Hakushū Mokichi Gosen Kashū*. Shiratama Shobō, 1949.

Saitō Mokichi. *Aratama*. Shun'yōdō, 1921.

_____. *Shakkō*. Tōundō, 1913.

_____. *Tanka Shishō*. Hakujitsusha, 1916.

Sakai Tadaichi. *Shi to Kokyō*. Ōfūsha, 1971.

Sasabushi Tomoichi. "Myōjō-ha no Bungaku Undō." *Kokubungaku*, December 1964, pp. 19-24.

Sasamoto Masaki. *Kitahara Hakushū Ron*. Gogatsu Shobō, 1975.

Senuma Shigeki, "Kitahara Hakushū: Sono Shi to Uta to no Kōryū. "*Kindai Tanka*. Nihon Bungaku Kenkyū Shiryō Soshō. Yūseidō, 1973. Pp. 232-243.

————. "Shinshisha no Kindaisei." *Kindai Tanka*. Nihon Bungaku Kenkyū Shiryō Sōsho. Yūseidō, 1973. Pp. 76-82.

Shihen. December 1917-October 1921.

Shimaki Akahiko. *Hio*. Iwanami Shoten, 1920.

————. *Kiribi*. Araragi, 1915.

Shimazaki Tōson. *Wakanashū*. Shun'yōdō, 1897.

Shinman'yōshū. 11 vols. Kaizōsha, 1937-1938.

Shinma Shin'ichi. *Kindai Kadan Shi*. Hanawa Bunko. Hanawa Shobō, 1968.

————. "Koten to Kindai: Gendai Shiika no Genryū to shite no Ryōjin Hisho." *Kokubungaku Kaishaku to Kanshō*, November 1946, pp. 21-32.

Shino Hiroshi. "Hakushū-Akahito Mohō Ronsō I." *Tanka*, July 1961, pp. 148-153.

————. "Hakushū-Akahito Mohō Ronsō II." *Tanka*, August 1961, pp. 146-151.

Subaru. January 1909-December 1913.

Susukida Kyūkin. *Botekishū*. Kaneo Bun'endō, 1889.

Suzuki Ichirō. "Kitahara Hakushū to Matsushita Toshiko." *Kindai Tanka*. Nihon Bungaku Kenkyū Shiryō Sōsho. Yūseidō, 1973. Pp. 276-284.

262

Tachibana Chikage. *Man'yōshū Ryakkai*. 6 vol. Osaka: Toshō Shuppan, 1892-1893.

Taishō no Bungaku. Edited by Kōno Toshirō, Miyoshi Yukio, Takemori Tenryū, and Hirada Toshio. Kindai Bungaku Shi, vol. 2. Yūseikaku, 1972.

Takada Mizuho. "Tanbiha." *Kokubungaku Kaishaku to Kanshō*, August 1969, pp. 64-68.

Tamaki Tōru. "Hakushū-teki oyobi Mokichi-teki." *Tanka*, May 1968, pp. 6-21.

_____. *Kitahara Hakushū: Shiteki Shuppatsu o megutte*. Yomiuri Shinbunsha, 1974.

Toki Zenmaro. *NAKIWARAI*. Rōmaji Hiromekai, 1910.

Ubutaka Tatsue. *Metorazaru Shijin*. Tōkyō Bijutsu, 1973.

Ueda Bin. *Kaichōon*. Hongo Shoin, 1905.

_____. *Shisei Dante*. Kinkōdō, 1901.

Usami Kisohachi. "Ryōkan." *Kinsei no Kajin*. Nihon Kajin Kōza, vol. 5. Kōbundō, 1960. Pp. 145-200.

Wada Shigejirō. "*Myōjō* kara *Subaru e*." *Kokubungaku*, December 1964, pp. 90-93.

Yabuta Yoshio. *Hyōden Kitahara Hakushū*. Tamagawa Daigaku Shuppanbu, 1973.

_____. Interview held in Tokyo, August 1976.

Yasuda Morio. *Ueda Bin Kenkyū*. Yajima Shobō, 1958.

Yonegawa Minoru. "Jūichigatsu Futsuka no Asa to Sono Zengo." *Tama*, December 1942, pp. 26-32.

Yosano Akiko. *Midaregami*. Tōkyō Shinshisha, 1901.

Yosano Tekkan, Kinoshita Mokutarō, Hirano Banri, Kitahara Hakushū, and Yoshii Osamu. "Gosoku no Kutsu—Gonin Tsure." *Tokyo Niroku Shinbun.* August 7-September 3, 1907.

Yosano Tekkan. "Bokoku no Oto." *Niroku Shinbun.* May-October 1894.

————. *Murasaki.* Tōkyō Shinshisha, 1901.

————. *Tozainanboku.* Meiji Shoin, 1896.

Yoshida Seiichi. "Kitahara Hakushū Ron." *Kindai Tanka.* Nihon Bungaku Kenkyū Shiryō Sōsho. Yūseidō, 1973. Pp. 244-249.

————. *Nihon Kindai Shi Kanshō.* 3 vols. Shinchō Bunko. Shinchōsha, 1953.

————. "Tanka ni okeru Kindaisei: Hakushū to Mokichi o Chūshin ni."*Tanka Kenkyū,* June 1948, pp. 1-7.

Yoshimoto Takaaki, Ayukawa Nobuo, Ōoka Makoto, Yamamoto Tarō, and Irizawa Yasuo. "Kitahara Hakushū no Fukken." *Yuriika,* December 1973.

Zadankai: Meiji Bungaku Shi. Edited by Yanada Izumi, Katsumoto Seiichirō, and Ino Kenji. Iwanami Shoten, 1961.

Zadankai: Taishō Bungaku Shi. Edited by Yanagida Izumi, Katsumoto Seiichirō, and Ino Kenji. Iwanami Shoten, 1965.

IV. WORKS IN WESTERN LANGUAGES

Anthology of Japanese Literature. Compiled and edited by Donald Keene. New York: Grove Press, 1960.

Anthology of Modern Japanese Poetry. Edited and translated by Ichiro Kōno and Rikutarō Fukuda. Kenkyūsha, 1957.

Anthology of Modern Japanese Poetry. Translated and compiled by Edith Marcombe Shiffert and Yūki Sawa. Rutland, Vermont, and Tokyo: Charles E. Tuttle Company, 1972.

Beichman, Janine. *Masaoka Shiki: His Life and Works.* Ph.D. dissertation, Columbia University, 1974.

Boxer, C.R. *The Christian Century in Japan, 1549-1650.* Berkeley: University of California Press, 1951.

Brower, Robert H., and Miner, Earl. *Japanese Court Poetry.* Stanford: Stanford University Press, 1961.

Chūshingura (The Treasury of Loyal Retainers). Translated by Donald Keene. New York: Columbia University Press, 1971.

Cornell, Kenneth. *The Symbolist Movement.* New Haven: Yale University Press, 1951.

Fairbanks, John K., Reischauer, Edwin O., and Craig, Albert M. *East Asia: The Modern Transformation.* Boston: Houghton Mifflin Company, 1965.

Hagiwara Sakutarō. *Face at the Bottom of the World.* Translated by Graeme Wilson. Rutland, Vermont, and Tokyo: Charles E. Tuttle Company, 1969.

Hsia, C.T. *The Classic Chinese Novel.* New York: Columbia University Press, 1968.

Ishikawa Takuboku. *A Handful of Sand.* Translated by Sananishi Shio. Boston: Marshall Jones Company, 1934.

_____. *Takuboku: Poems to Eat.* Translated by Carl Sesar. Kodansha International Ltd., 1960.

Izumo Fudoki. Translated by Michiko Aoki. Sophia University, 1971.

Keene, Donald. *Japanese Literature: an Introduction for Western Readers.* New York: Grove Press, 1955.

_____. *Japanese Novels and the West.* Charlottesville: University of Virginia Press, 1961.

_____. *Landscapes and Portraits: Appreciations of Japanese Culture.* Kodansha International Ltd., 1971.

265

_____. *Modern Japanese Poetry: An Essay*. Ann Arbor: University of Michigan Press, 1964.

Kojiki. Translated by Donald L. Philippi. University of Tokyo Press, 1968.

Modern Japanese Literature. Compiled and edited by Donald Keene. New York: Grove Press, 1956.

Monkey. Translated by Arthur Waley. New York: John Day, 1944.

Nihongi. Translated by W. G. Aston. Published for the Japan Society. London: Kegan Paul, Trench, Tribner and Company Ltd., 1896.

Paine, Robert, and Soper, Alexander. *The Art and Architecture of Japan*. Second revised edition. Middlesex: Penguin Books Ltd., 1974.

Payne, Robert. *White Pony*. Mentor Books. New York: New American Library, 1943.

The Penguin Book of Japanese Verse. Translated by Geoffrey Bownas and Anthony Thwaite. Middlesex: Penguin Books, 1964.

Romance of the Three Kingdoms. Translated by C. H. Brewitt-Taylor. 2 vols. Shanghai: Kelly and Walsh, 1925.

Sansom, George. *A History of Japan*. 3 vols. Rutland, Vermont, and Tokyo: Charles E. Tuttle Company, 1974.

_____. *Japan: A Short Cultural History*. Revised edition. Rutland, Vermont, and Tokyo: Charles E. Tuttle Company, 1973.

Storry, Richard. *A History of Modern Japan*. Middlesex: Penguin Books, 1960.

Symons, Arthur. *The Symbolist Movement in Literature*. Revised edition. New York: E. P. Dutton and Co., Inc., 1958.

Tsukahira, Toshio G. *Feudal Control in Tokugawa Japan: the Sankin Kōtai System*. Cambridge: Harvard University Press, 1966.

Tsunoda, Ryusaku, de Bary, William Theodore, and Keene, Donald. *Sources of Japanese Tradition*. 2 vols. New York: Columbia University Press, 1964.

Ueda Akinari. *Tales of Moonlight and Rain*. Translated by Kengi Hamada. University of Tokyo Press, 1971.

_____. *Ugetsu Monogatari: Tales of Moonlight and Rain*. Translated by Leon M. Zolbrod. London: George Allen and Unwin, 1975.

Ueda, Makoto. *Literary and Art Theories in Japan*. Cleveland: Western Reserve University Press, 1967.

Wilson, Edmund. *Axel's Castle*. New York: Charles Scribner's Sons, 1931.

Vigié-Lecocq, A. *La Poésie contemporaine*. Paris: Mecure de France, 1897.

Yosano, Akiko. *Tangled Hair*. Translated by Sanford Goldstein and Seishi Shinoda. Lafayette: Purdue University, 1971.

CORNELL EAST ASIA SERIES

For ordering information, please contact:
Cornell East Asia Series
East Asia Program
Cornell University
140 Uris Hall
Ithaca, NY 14853-7601
USA
(607) 255-6222.

5-93/.6M/BB

Ingram Content Group UK Ltd.
Milton Keynes UK
UKHW010649070723
424714UK00002B/111